REVISED
Separated
Brethren

REVISED
Separated Brethren

A Review of Protestant, Anglican, Eastern Orthodox & Other Religions in the United States

William J. Whalen

Our Sunday Visitor Publishing Division
Our Sunday Visitor, Inc.
Huntington, Indiana 46750

ISBN: 1-931709-05-X (Inventory No. T9)
LCCCN: 79-83874

Cover design by Rebecca Heaston
Interior design by Sherri L. Hoffman
Genealogy graphic design by Kevin Davidson

PRINTED IN THE UNITED STATES OF AMERICA

SEPARATED BRETHREN

We must get to know the outlook of our separated brethren. To achieve this purpose, study is of necessity required, and this must be pursued with a sense of realism and good will. Catholics, who already have a proper grounding, need to acquire a more adequate understanding of the respective doctrines of our separated brethren, their history, their spiritual and liturgical life, their religious psychology and general background.

The Decree on Ecumenism
of the Second Vatican Council, No. 9

CONTENTS

PREFACE

THIS VOLUME IS INTENDED TO OFFER AMERICAN CATHOLIC READERS A survey of Protestant, Anglican, and Eastern Orthodox churches and sects in the United States.

Strictly speaking, the term "separated brethren" refers to Christians united by baptism and commitment to Jesus Christ but divided by theological beliefs. Because many Christians encounter members of non-Christian denominations in their daily lives, we have broadened the scope of this book to include descriptions of a number of these groups. These additional chapters examine the Jews, Mormons, Christian Scientists, Muslims, Buddhists, and other religious groups.

Since 1958, when the first edition of *Separated Brethren* was published, the Catholic world has witnessed the far-reaching impact of the Second Vatican Council and the Church's growing involvement in the ecumenical movement. These changes have been reflected in the thorough revision of each denominational description.

The two introductory chapters present an overview of American religious life and the basic theological differences between Catholicism and Protestantism. This was done to avoid restating fundamental Protestant principles — such as the sole sufficiency of the Bible — in subsequent chapters on particular denominations. Those who wish to use this book as a handbook for reference will want to keep this in mind. The chapters on denominations outline the history, doctrine, ritual, organization, and traditions of each group.

In completing the research for the writing and revision of this book, I relied heavily on personal interviews, official church publications, correspondence, published studies, and observation. If space permitted and I were not afraid of inadvertently omitting someone's name, I would like to acknowledge my indebtedness to the scores of ministers, church officials, and laity who generously gave of their time to enable me to get a current picture of the life of their denominations.

I would especially like to thank my wife, who read the manuscript chapter by chapter, offered innumerable suggestions, and maintained those conditions of domestic tranquility conducive to writing.

Some of the material on the Pentecostals, Unitarian Universalists, and Old Catholics originally appeared in *U.S. Catholic* magazine. Statistics generally were drawn from the 2001 edition of the *Yearbook of American and Canadian Churches* published by the National Council of Churches.

W.J.W.
Lafayette, Indiana
August 2001

CHAPTER 1

America's Religious Panorama

*More Than Two Hundred Fifty Churches
Enroll U.S. Members*

SHORTLY AFTER THE DISCOVERY OF AMERICA, THE UNITY OF WESTERN
Christendom was shattered by the Protestant Reformation. That bond
of common faith that had cemented the brotherhood of European
Christians for a millennium was broken, and altar was set against altar.
Christians remained brothers in the grace of baptism and in loyalty to
the person of Jesus Christ, but they became separated brethren.

After the dust of the Reformation and the Counter-Reformation
had settled, Protestantism consolidated its position in northern Germany, Scandinavia, Holland, Scotland, and England. Colonists and
missionaries from these areas would carry the new religion to other
continents. Meanwhile the Spaniards, Poles, Italians, French, Portuguese, Austrians, Hungarians, southern Germans, Irish, and other nationalities held fast to the ancient faith.

The apologetic exigencies of the times prompted controversialists
in both Christian camps to emphasize the separation more than the
brotherhood. They segregated and stressed points of doctrine on which
Protestant and Catholic disagreed. For the Catholic the possibility of
converting the Muslim was remote; the obstinate Jew clung to his religious beliefs in the shelter of the ghetto; the Protestant was the obvi-
ous target for theological debate and polemics.

Earlier the Great Eastern Schism had split Eastern and Western
Christians. Most of the Greeks and Slavs were in schism. Efforts at
the Council of Lyons in 1274 and the Council of Florence in 1439
failed to effect a permanent reconciliation. Theological differences
between East and West, however, were slight compared with those

engendered by the wholesale innovations of the Protestant Reformers. Moreover, the Eastern Orthodox retained a valid episcopacy, priesthood, Mass, and seven sacraments that Protestantism lacks.

Protestantism soon split into four main branches that persist to this day. The followers of Martin Luther disagreed with the Zwinglians and Calvinists on the Real Presence and other doctrinal issues. In England elements of Catholicism and Protestantism combined to form the Anglican communion. Finally, the left wing of the Reformation, the sects, developed into the various Baptist, Congregational, Mennonite, Disciples of Christ, Church of Christ, Holiness, and Adventist bodies. The four branches, then, are Lutheranism, Calvinism (Presbyterian and Reformed), Anglicanism, and Independent or Radical.

Through historical and geographical circumstances the fourth branch, variously known as Independent, Radical, Nonconformist, or Free Church, gained ascendancy in the United States. The despised sects won the battle of the American frontier. World Protestantism has been dominated by the other three wings, but the success of the radical wing in this country exerts a growing influence. Every second American Protestant is a Baptist or Methodist, although worldwide there are far more Lutherans than Baptists, Methodists, Congregationalists, and Disciples of Christ combined.

Estimates vary on the number of Christians in the world, but a reasonable set of figures would indicate 1 billion Catholics, 466 million Protestants, and 235 million Eastern Orthodox. Several million other Christians belong to the Lesser Eastern Churches. In the United States Protestants outnumber Catholics by about three to two.

More Americans are church members than ever before in our national history. The theocratic influence of the Protestant churches in colonial times obscures the fact that only one person in ten was a church member. This was only 16 percent of the population a century ago, but today it has risen to 63 percent. Protestantism, more or less static in Europe, now claims the allegiance of 35 percent of the U.S. population, compared with 27 percent in the late 1920s. When poll takers ask for religious "preference," they find that many more register a "preference" for Protestantism even though they are not on any church register.

What is significant in the growth of Protestantism in recent decades is that this growth has taken place outside of what is called "cooperative Protestantism." Generally "cooperative Protestantism" includes those denominations represented in the National and World Council of Churches: Methodists, Northern Baptists, most Lutherans, Episcopalians, Presbyterians, Disciples, and Black Baptists, for example. During the last two decades the number of Methodists, Disciples of Christ, Episcopalians, and Presbyterians has actually declined. The really amazing membership gains have been made by the Southern Baptists, Jehovah's Witnesses, Assemblies of God, Mormons, Nazarenes, Seventh-day Adventists, and Pentecostals.

While the sects emerged from the suppressed left wing of the Reformation, the Protestant Churches emerged from the right wing. The two terms, church and sect, are not precise. In general, however, the church refuses to cut the ties with the past, tends to seek state support and protection, considers all members of the nation in its constituency, baptizes infants, demands subscription to creeds and confessions, and adopts an episcopal or presbyterian form of government.

The sect denies what the church affirms. It usually latches on to one doctrine such as Adventism or Perfectionism, rejects infant baptism and often insists on immersion, advocates complete separation of church and state, prefers a congregational polity, appeals to the poor and uneducated, establishes personal conversion as the chief condition of church membership, enforces a Puritan morality, urges tithing as the divine method of fund raising, and dispenses with art and fixed ritual in worship.

A sect may become a church. As its members rise in social status, the sect often modifies its original stand. Methodism, for example, began as a sect within Anglicanism even though it never rejected infant baptism and retained an episcopacy in America. Today Methodism reveals all the characteristics of a church. Disaffected Methodists who preferred the milieu of the sect tended to drift into Holiness and

13

Pentecostal sects. We can observe the evolution of some sects into churches in our own day: The Church of the Nazarene has almost completed the transformation. Many sects peter out after the death of the leader or else remain numerically insignificant.

No other nation has witnessed the proliferation of Christian churches and sects that we find in the United States. European nations are likely to have one dominant Christian religion — Lutheranism, for instance, in Sweden or Catholicism in Spain — or two major denominations as in Germany and Holland. Estimates place the number of churches and sects in the United States at more than two hundred fifty.

Every European religious tradition has been transplanted to American soil. Yankee inventiveness sometimes extended into ecclesiastical realms and added further divisions and varieties. Historical circumstances in the young nation, combined with the Protestant principles of private interpretation of the Scriptures and the denial of religious authority, furthered the fragmentation.

When Lutheran immigrants came to the New World they brought their own pastors, languages, and church traditions. As a result the Germans, Swedes, Norwegians, Danes, Finns, and Slovaks organized separate and independent synods. Immigrants from Eastern Europe — the Albanians, Greeks, Russians, Bulgarians, Romanians, Serbs, Syrians, and Ukrainians — set up their own Orthodox denominations with close ties with the mother churches in Europe and Asia.

The Civil War and the issue of slavery further split many Protestant denominations into northern and southern branches. The Methodists reunited in 1939, but other such schisms persist: the American (Northern) Baptists and the Southern Baptists, the northern United Presbyterian Church in the U.S.A. and the southern Presbyterian Church in the U.S.

The conservative Churches of Christ broke away from the Disciples of Christ on a question of worship — they could not find scriptural justification for the use of a pipe organ in church. A serious schism was precipitated among the Mennonites by the problem of whether one man should wash and wipe the believer's feet in the foot-washing ceremony or whether one man should wash and another wipe. Mennonites also separated over the use of newfangled buttons instead of hooks-and-eyes.

Booker T. Washington once remarked that if you find a Negro who is not a Methodist or Baptist someone has been tampering with his religion. Practically all black Christians are Methodists and Baptists, and most of them are members of independent black denominations. Perhaps five hundred thousand black individuals belong to racially mixed Protestant churches, mainly the United Methodist Church. About two million Roman Catholics are black.

Nine of ten black Protestant worshipers are part of segregated denominations such as the African Methodist Episcopal Church, the African Methodist Episcopal Church Zion, the Christian Methodist Episcopal Church, and the two National Baptist Conventions. Many smaller denominations are composed entirely of black Christians.

Theological controversies produced Unitarianism, the Christian Reformed Church, and the Orthodox Presbyterian Church. Dozens of Fundamentalist and Holiness sects have arisen as a protest against the Modernism of the older denominations or as the personal vehicle of a popular preacher such as Aimee Semple McPherson.

A number of churches and sects are homegrown, including the Seventh-day Adventist, Christian Science, Church of the Nazarene, Disciples of Christ, Jehovah's Witness, Mormon, Polish National Catholic, Spiritualist, Worldwide Church of God, and Unity School of Christianity. The Adventists and Witnesses now find the bulk of their membership outside the continental United States; the Mormons also are engaged in an aggressive foreign missionary program.

This bewildering array of churches, sects, and cults should not mislead the student of the American religious scene. After all the denominations have been tallied the fact remains that nine out of ten American Protestants belong to one of the six great denominational families: Baptist and Disciples, Methodist, Lutheran, Episcopalian, Presbyterian and Reformed, and the United Church of Christ. Even counting separate denominations, we find that 90 percent of the Protestants in this country belong to the twenty largest denominations.

Since its founding the United States has moved from a situation in which most of the states favored established Protestant churches to one of religious pluralism. At the time the Declaration of Independence was signed, Roman Catholics numbered only some twenty-five thousand of the several million people in the new nation. Now Catholics constitute the largest single denomination in the United States (about sixty-one million), and one out of every four Americans identifies himself as a Catholic. Other religious traditions have taken their place in a society once characterized as pan-Protestant: Jews, Eastern Orthodox, Latter-day Saints, and many others who identify themselves as secular Humanists, Buddhists, Muslims, and more.

On the local level the average Protestant can attend a Methodist church one Sunday, a Baptist the next, a Presbyterian church after that and find himself more or less at home. As long as he stays within the predominant Puritan-Independent tradition, he can switch denominational affiliation with a minimum of accommodation and inconvenience. On the other hand, a monthly cycle of Christian Science, Anglo-Catholic, Southern Baptist, and Quaker worship would be conducive to multiple personality disorder. For the Protestant the choice of church affiliation may be based on family background, the personality and preaching ability of the minister, adequacy of the physical plant, proximity to home, social advantages, Sunday school, youth programs, or preference for one type of church polity over another.

Three types of church government predominate: congregational, presbyterial, and episcopal. We might mention that in practice the episcopal form is never so autocratic nor the congregational so independent as the labels suggest. Some of the most highly organized denominations in the country, such as the Seventh-day Adventist and Missouri Synod Lutheran, operate under a congregational or consistorial system. In at least a third of the Protestant denominations the congregation is theoretically supreme and recognizes no authority beyond itself. Besides the two churches just mentioned the Baptists,

Disciples of Christ, Churches of Christ, Quakers, Unitarians, and many Holiness groups are congregational in polity. The congregational-type church hires and fires the minister, whose position then depends on maintaining the goodwill of his parishioners. The congregation likewise holds title to all property, manages church finances, elects its own officers, and perhaps formulates its creedal statement.

The Episcopalians, Eastern Orthodox, and Methodists maintain an episcopal form of church government. In most cases the bishops are elected rather than appointed as in the Catholic Church.

The presbyterial system dispenses with bishops but exercises a measure of control over the local congregations by means of representative presbyteries. Clerical and lay delegates cast equal votes, and no individual holds an ecclesiastical office superior to another. Besides the Presbyterians themselves, other Protestants who are governed by this polity are those in the Reformed and Christian Reformed Churches, and the Assemblies of God.

Smaller groups such as the Salvation Army and the Volunteers of America follow a military organization adapted to religious life.

The average Protestant congregation is small, with fewer than three hundred fifty members (compared with more than eighteen hundred in the average Catholic parish). These parishioners may reside in any part of the city because they are not assigned to a specific church as in the Catholic parochial arrangement. Members usually make an annual pledge to support the church and its benevolences.

Architecturally the familiar Protestant church is a semicircular auditorium. A pulpit, organ, or altar may occupy the chief focal point in the chancel. A liturgical revival in Protestantism is introducing the cross, central altar, vestments for minister and choir, stained glass, sculpture, and ecclesiastical furniture common in Catholic churches. Episcopal and Lutheran churches have always employed art and music to greater advantage than churches in the Puritan heritage.

The 10:30 or 11 o'clock service is usually the main Sunday worship service, although larger churches may offer duplicate services at other hours. An usher escorts the worshipers to the pews. The typical

17

nonliturgical Protestant worship service lasts about an hour and consists of the invocation, Lord's Prayer, responsive reading, anthem, Scripture lesson, pastoral prayer, offering, hymns, sermon, closing prayer, and benediction. The sequence of these elements may vary according to the denomination or the wishes of the minister or congregation. Music is provided by both the trained choir and the congregation as a whole. Liturgical churches follow the Christian year and a fixed ritual resembling the Catholic Mass.

Communion is observed monthly or quarterly except by the Episcopalians and Disciples of Christ, who celebrate the Lord's Supper every week. Communion is distributed under both kinds; all denominations use bread but some use wine, some grape juice, and one (Mormon) water.

At an earlier hour the children will be listening to Bible stories, singing hymns, drawing, or playing games in the Sunday school. (Fewer than 360,000 attend Lutheran, Christian Reformed, Baptist, and Seventh-day Adventist full-time parochial grade and high schools.) Volunteer lay people conduct these Sunday schools, which attempt to provide at least a minimum of religious instruction. The larger city churches may employ a trained director of education to supervise the educational program for the various age groups.

The old-fashioned midweek prayer meeting has fallen into disuse except in the South and certain rural areas. Many of the churches sponsor annual revival services either in the church building or in a tent or rented hall. Church facilities may be used during the week for meetings, choir rehearsals, suppers, Boy Scout activities, dances, dramatics, study clubs, and the like. Union programs among various churches have been arranged for the Lenten season, Reformation Sunday, Thanksgiving, and other special events.

An increasing number of Protestant ministers are entering their profession with the benefit of college and seminary training. Some Baptist, Methodist, and Holiness clergy still are ordained with little or no education beyond high school or with no regular seminary training. On the other hand, the Lutherans, Episcopalians, Presbyterians, and

Congregationalists have always insisted on high educational standards for their clergy.

Few comprehensive studies have been undertaken on the social classes in American Protestantism. Those that have been published indicate there are more lower-class Episcopalians and more upper-class Baptists than popularly thought. Nevertheless, many denominations are more or less class-bound. The Episcopal, Presbyterian, Congregational, and Unitarian churches appeal to the wealthy and privileged; the Baptist, Assemblies of God, and Fundamentalist churches find their chief support among the common people in the South and in rural America.

In terms of income and education, Roman Catholics have made enormous strides since World War II. In both categories Catholics now rank above the national average. Thanks in part to the GI Bill, American Catholics have entered the highest ranks of government, industry, education, and entertainment. Their ranks include Supreme Court justices, university presidents and professors, physicians, senators, and other professions. Studies indicate that the 24 percent of the U.S. population that identifies itself as Catholic furnishes half again as many college and university students.

Protestants support home missions to the black community, American Indians, Asians, Puerto Ricans, and Mexican-Americans, but most of their missionary efforts are directed to foreign lands. For centuries after the Reformation the Catholic Church carried the burden of Christian missions alone. This Catholic head start in the mission fields is illustrated by the fact that today several times as many Catholics reside in mission territories as do Protestants. Since the Chinese missions have been abandoned, Protestant missionaries have turned their attention to Latin America.

Protestantism's success in Latin America has been phenomenal. It has been estimated that more Catholics have become Protestants in twentieth century Latin America than in all of Europe during the Reformation. In 1914 there were only one hundred thousand Protestants in Latin America; in 1960 membership exceeded ten million.

More converts enter Pentecostal churches than all other mainline Protestant churches combined.

The remarkable improvement in relations between Catholics and Protestants during the past decade is one of the rare examples of genuine reconciliation in the United States. In a nation divided between rich and poor, black and white, liberal and conservative, this religious reconciliation is a hopeful sign. The "Cold War" waged by rival Christian groups for more than four centuries has ended, and the major Christian churches have set their sights on eventual reunion no matter how long this may take.

The very first statement of the Decree on Ecumenism is: "The restoration of unity among all Christians is one of the principal concerns of the Second Vatican Council." Christians of many different traditions are finally listening to one another, praying with one another, respecting one another. Many years ago Cardinal Mercier of Belgium wrote: "To unite, we must love one another; to love one another, it is necessary to know one another; to know one another, we must meet one another." In the following chapters the author invites the reader to meet those whose beliefs and practices may be different from his or her own but deserve serious study and sympathetic understanding.

CHAPTER 2

Basic Differences Between Catholicism and Protestantism

Theological Disagreements Divide Western Christians

COMPARED WITH THE CHASM BETWEEN ATHEIST AND THEIST, BETWEEN Christian and non-Christian, the differences that separate Catholic and Protestant Christians may seem relatively slight. A Christian world that saw Christendom divided into two neat camps in Western Europe developed rival apologetics that emphasized the theological points of disagreement. Today in what some have labeled the post-Christian era, we find Western man offering his allegiance to dozens of religions and ersatz religions: communism, nationalism, scientism, secularism, hedonism, sentimentalism, cultism. The Weltanschauung of these devotees contrasted with the Christian philosophy of life puts the current picture into sharper focus and reveals the Christian camp as a besieged outpost in an aggressively hostile world.

To minimize the real differences between the Catholic and the Protestant interpretations of the gospel would be dishonest. But to fail to recognize the bonds of unity between separated brethren is also dishonest and shortsighted. Of course, we are speaking of those who believe in a personal God, the divinity of Christ, and other central Christian dogmas. Despite the profound differences between them, the Catholic and the Protestant Christian in the modern world are more often allies than antagonists.

Catholic and Protestant share a spiritual view that looks beyond material things to spiritual values, that reminds man to live for eternity as well as for time. They share a belief in God and a loyalty to the person of Jesus Christ. They accept the same Ten Commandments as rules of conduct, acknowledge that fallen man unaided cannot attain his own salvation but needs a Savior, honor and read essentially the same Bible, recite the same Apostles' and Nicene creeds, pray the same Lord's Prayer. According to Catholic teaching both are admitted to the life of grace through the sacrament of baptism, which may be administered by priest, minister, layman, or even Jew or Muslim. Bride and groom, whether baptized Catholics or Protestants, bestow the sacrament of matrimony on each other, which brings the necessary graces to their Christian homes and makes their marriage a truly sacramental union. The feasts of Christmas and Easter, the writings of the Fathers of the Church, devotional literature, and hymns form a common heritage for Catholic and Protestant Christians.

The Decree on Ecumenism of the Second Vatican Council declared "that all who have been justified by faith in Baptism are members of Christ's body, and have a right to be called Christian, and so are correctly accepted as brothers by the children of the Catholic Church" (Decree on Ecumenism, No. 3).

While insisting that membership in the Catholic Church is the ordinary channel of God's grace, Catholic theologians acknowledge that God is free to bestow His grace on whom He will. The Jansenist proposition that "outside the Church there is no grace" was long ago condemned by Rome, even though the grace that non-Catholics receive comes to them somehow in virtue of the Catholic Church.

Referring to churches and communions separated from the Catholic Church, the Decree on Ecumenism affirmed that they "have been by no means deprived of significance and importance in the mystery of salvation. For the Spirit of Christ has not refrained from using them as means of salvation which derive their efficacy from the very fullness of grace and truth entrusted to the Church" (No. 3).

As we examine the basic differences between Catholicism and Protestantism, we should keep in mind the distinction between fundamental and accidental differences. The latter are products of church discipline, historical development, and cultural adaptations that may be amended and changed as the Church sees fit. Fundamental differences touch the core of the Christian faith, dogmas God has revealed to mankind through His Son.

We can logically classify mankind into two groups: those who believe man was once better than he is today and those who believe he was once worse. Christians believe man was once better but forfeited his favored position through disobedience to God in the Fall. Social evolutionists deny the Fall and maintain that despite occasional temporary setbacks, man is getting better and better.

Although Catholics and Protestants attach great importance to the Fall, they disagree on the consequences of that Fall. We discover the first basic difference between the two Christian theologies in the view of man's nature after the Fall. Catholics believe that through the Fall man's natural and religious endowments were weakened. The first transgression by man's first parents lost for them and for their descendants those supernatural and preternatural gifts that were theirs in the Garden of Eden. These gifts included supernatural grace, potential bodily immortality, integrity, and impassability. Were it not for the promise of a Redeemer and the sacrifice of the Son of God on the cross, man would have been utterly unable to attain his supernatural end, the vision of God. But Catholics hold that these gifts were not due man but were free gifts of God that God withdrew; man, stripped of these gifts, remained man, and his nature, though his will was weakened and his intellect darkened, remained intact.

To use a necessarily inadequate example, the Fall was as though someone took back the million dollars he had given to another person who previously had only fifty cents in his pocket. Without the million dollars, the second person realized he had suffered a great loss, but he was still solvent. His situation had not changed to bankruptcy; his nature remained intact.

Luther, however, concluded that man's nature was totally corrupted by the Fall. This cardinal principle of Protestantism led logically to most of the other theological innovations. Man's nature is totally depraved and inclined only to evil, declared the German friar. Man is a sinner in whatever he does and all his actions are disgusting to God.

How can such a worthless creature be justified, be made pleasing to God? In an age when religion had become for all too many the mechanical performance of external devotions and Nominalism had undercut the orthodox positions of Thomism, Luther proclaimed his discovery of the truth that justification was by faith alone. Salvation is a free gift of God that man cannot merit. All is grace, pure grace.

Soon justification by faith became associated with three other principles not inherent in the original doctrine nor acceptable to the Church. These were the denial of free will, the doctrine of extrinsic justification, and the denunciation of all good works. Luther denied that man could cooperate with the actual graces God bestowed before justification. The Church, on the other hand, traditionally taught that man could reject God's graces through the exercise of his free will. By extrinsic justification the German Reformer taught that the act of justification is something entirely outside of man. Man remains a sinner, totally depraved, but God, so to speak, looks the other way. God covers man's sins with a cloak, but the sins remain. Justification never touches the inherently sinful nature of man.

Catholicism has always denied that good works without justification would avail to man's salvation. After justification, however, the good works a man performs, ethical or ceremonial, earn merit. Luther flatly denied the idea of merit and urged his followers to perform good works only as fruits or evidence of their justification. But no matter what they do, even in their loving God, they sin. The Church upheld the value of good works after justification in the firm belief that faith without works is dead.

It is one thing to deny Luther's positions on free will, extrinsic justification, and good works, but it is something else to suggest that man can merit his own justification by good works. He must cooperate with the actual graces he receives, do penance, seek the truth, but he cannot thereby earn his justification.

A serious complication has clouded theological argumentation since the Reformation. When the Reformers spoke of faith, they did not mean what the Church has always meant by the term. The Church defines faith as an intellectual assent given on the authority of another. For example, if a railroad conductor informs you that the next stop is Chicago and you accept his word, you have faith in him. If the Son of God declares that marriage is indissoluble or that baptism is necessary to salvation, you accept these statements because you have faith in Him. He has not proven these statements by mathematics or laboratory experiments but, because He is who He is, you accept them. Faith, then, is an assent to God's revelation. But to the founders of Protestantism, faith became a supreme act of confidence that God had spared you from hell and covered up your sins. Faith became an act of the will and the emotions for the Protestant but remains primarily an act of the intellect for the Catholic.

Early in his career Luther saw that the Roman Catholic Church would never accept his theological views. On the other hand, he soon witnessed Protestant extremists, the Anabaptists, denying any authority in religion or appealing to weird visions and revelations. Unable to appeal to the Roman Church for authority and unwilling to allow the fanatics to overthrow all religious authority, Luther claimed the supreme religious authority to be found not in a man or institution but a book — the Bible. Protestantism dethroned the Church and set up the Bible as the sole rule of faith. Only what the Apostles had committed to writing would be binding on Christians; that oral tradition handed down through the Church from apostolic times was denied. Eventually Protestantism became the religion of the book par excellence.

Catholic controversialists could point out that Christ was a preacher not a writer, that the first Christians never saw a complete Bible, that the Church herself compiled the New Testament and fixed the canon, that the rejection of oral tradition was purely arbitrary, that the Bible itself claimed no supreme authority, and that prior to the invention of printing most of mankind had no access to the Bible even if they could read. But the new religion erected the Bible as the sole rule of faith while vilifying the Church that had compiled, translated, and preserved the Bible through the ages.

Not only was the Bible the sole rule of faith, the source of all that was needed for salvation, but the individual Christian now had the right, the duty, to interpret the Bible for himself. The spectacle of hundreds of churches and sects in this country alone gives testimony to the fruits of this disastrous principle of private interpretation. Of course, the masses of the Protestant faithful never exercised this right and duty in the face of a state-supported orthodoxy. Someone has estimated that there are at least one hundred distinct interpretations of four words in the New Testament: "This is my body."

Catholics believe that the Church, under the ever-present guidance of the Holy Spirit, is the proper interpreter of Scripture. No matter how flattering to the man in the street, the invitation to become his own Bible scholar has always been illusory. Anyone with the slightest acquaintance with the Bible soon admits that a knowledge of languages, theology, history, and archaeology is a prerequisite to mastery of Scripture. Apparently Luther believed that once the layman was encouraged to read the Bible, fortified by the principles of the Reformation, he would come to the same interpretations as his fellow Christians. Religious history since the Reformation disproves this theory. Most Protestant communions sooner or later imposed on their constituencies official interpretations of the Bible, which only the most intrepid would dispute.

Searching their Bibles, Protestants came across numerous references to the Church. They knew that the Church of Rome had not adopted Luther's views. Evidently, then, the church must be an invisible rather than a visible body. The members of this invisible church would be known only to God; the head of this invisible church was not the pope, whom Luther branded the anti-Christ, but Christ Himself. Violent opposition to the See of Peter animated Protestantism for four centuries, but in recent years many Protestants have taken a more sympathetic stance toward the papacy. Catholics believe in one, holy, catholic, and apostolic Church, founded by Christ, whose visible head is the Vicar of Christ, the successor to St. Peter, the Holy Father, the bishop of Rome. This visible Church composed of saints and sinners has been the mother of billions of souls since its founding in Jerusalem.

Most Protestants refuse to recognize the Church as a divine institution with authority to teach; they see the Church as a fellowship of believers in Jesus Christ with access to the Word of God in the Scriptures. Roman Catholics and Eastern Orthodox hold that the message of salvation comes to the individual through the Church, which enjoys protection against error that no individual Christian can claim.

The traditional Christian sacraments were included in the Reformers' denunciation of good works. Luther reasoned, however, that two sacraments, baptism and the Lord's Supper, were specifically enjoined by Christ and would be observed out of obedience to His will. Penance, confirmation, holy orders, matrimony, and anointing of the sick were denied any sacramental meaning but were often retained as ceremonies of the church.

A simplified worship service patterned after the Catholic Mass but eliminating the idea of sacrifice was introduced. Not sacrifice but the preaching of the Word of God became the central feature of Protestant worship. Without a visible church, a Mass, and five of the seven sacraments, there was little need for a priesthood. Rather, all Christians were declared priests whose only ordination was baptism. Nevertheless some men (and eventually some women) were specially trained for the ministry, ordained in a rite of the church, and given a measure of authority over the congregation. To a great degree this doctrine of the priesthood of all believers suffered the same fate as private interpretation of the Scriptures and was compromised by organizational necessities. Catholics believe all men participate in some way in the royal priesthood of Christ as members of His Mystical Body but that some men are set apart and ordained for sacrifice.

Predestination preoccupied the Reformed branch of Protestantism for several centuries. Catholics flatly deny that absolute or double predestination that teaches that God has elected some to salvation and damned others to hell. This doctrine, so stated, leaves no room for man's free will and has been all but disowned by modern Protestants, even those who fall in the Calvinist tradition.

Protestants deny the doctrine of transubstantiation but differ among themselves on belief in the Real Presence. Lutherans, for example, believe in the Real Presence but propose that the bread and wine and the body and blood of Christ co-exist in the elements. Calvinists speak of receiving Christ in a spiritual and heavenly manner. Even after the prayer of consecration, the bread and wine remain bread and wine. The Methodists, Baptists, Disciples, and Mennonites consider the Lord's Supper a simple memorial service. Anglicans encompass a variety of views from transubstantiation to memorial service, and the Quakers and Salvationists have no Communion service.

Other Protestant positions were derived from the basic principles of total depravity, justification by faith alone, the Bible as the sole rule of faith, private interpretation of the Scriptures, and the priesthood of all believers. The existence of purgatory was denied; after death the soul was assigned to either heaven or hell. Prayers for the dead were useless and unscriptural. Devotion to Mary as the Mother of God and intercession of the saints were abandoned, although Luther kept alive a tender devotion to the Blessed Virgin until his death. The Reformer continued the practice of private confession all during his lifetime, but this too died out in the non-Anglican branches of Protestantism. Confession has been revived in German Lutheranism in recent years.

Perhaps the majority of Protestants in the United States can be classified as activist evangelicals, neither theological liberals nor fundamentalists. They probably hold most of the traditional Protestant principles we have discussed without hesitating to modify any particular position.

In many customs and practices the differences between Catholicism and Protestantism have narrowed since the Second Vatican Council in 1963-65. The Mass is now celebrated in the language of the people, and greater emphasis has been given to preaching and congregational singing. Lay people serve as lectors and eucharistic ministers. On occasion the laity receive both the bread and the cup. Permanent deacons, usually married men, are ordained to the clerical state; they are authorized to preach, baptize, conduct weddings and funerals, and so forth. A more pastoral approach characterizes the attitude toward Protestant-Catholic marriages. On the other hand many Protestants have reexamined the role of Mary in Christian life and have taken a fresh look at the institution of the papacy. The Eucharist has assumed a more central place in Protestant worship. Catholic and Protestant theologians have engaged in serious dialogue and have discovered far greater areas of agreement than would have been imagined only a few years ago.

After emphasizing that baptism "establishes a sacramental bond of unity which links all who have been reborn by it" (Decree on Ecumenism, No. 22), the Fathers of Vatican II examined the Protestant expression of Christianity.

"The daily Christian life of these brethren is nourished by their faith in Christ and strengthened by the grace of Baptism and by hearing the word of God. This shows itself in their private prayer, their meditation on the Bible, in their Christian family life, and in the worship of a community gathered together to praise God" (Decree on Ecumenism, No. 23).

CHAPTER 3

The Lutherans

'The Just Man Lives by Faith'

A GERMAN AUGUSTINIAN FRIAR TOUCHED OFF THE EXPLOSION THAT shattered the unity of Western Christendom in the sixteenth century. Except for the Eastern schism of 1054 and the minor defections of the Waldenses and Moravians, this unity had remained intact for almost fifteen hundred years after the death of Christ.

Soon after the initial revolt and the spread of its doctrinal teachings, the Protestant movement split into several camps that remain divided to this day. The followers of Martin Luther consolidated their position in northern Germany and Scandinavia, while the Reformed or Calvinists captured Scotland and Holland, parts of Switzerland, and for a while threatened to win France and England.

Today Lutheranism, with sixty-three million adherents, is by far the largest component in world Protestantism. This fact is sometimes obscured by the strength of the Baptist and Methodist denominations concentrated in the United States. Many of these Lutherans, especially in the Scandinavian countries, must be classed as inactive or nominal, as must millions of Catholics in France, Italy, Spain, and South America.

To understand Protestantism we must understand Lutheranism; to understand Lutheranism we must know Luther. To do this we must try to project ourselves into his age. Catholics occasionally point out what some Protestants seem willing to admit: the Reformation would have been an impossibility in the twenty-first century. The conditions in the Church that cried out for reform no longer exist. The refusal to see Luther in the context of his own era magnifies the enormity of his rebellion, because Catholics see so little — if any — justification for the dismemberment of Christendom.

The modern Church has been singularly blessed by a succession of saintly, capable, and devoted pontiffs. But Alexander VI, who is generally conceded to be the worst pope in history, occupied the papal throne in Luther's youth.

Not long before Luther's birth, three rival popes claimed the allegiance of the faithful, each excommunicating the other and his followers. The bishop of Rome had resided not in Rome but in Avignon in France for sixty-five years. To support the luxuries of the papal court, new schemes for taxes and revenues had to be devised. The successors of St. Peter installed their children and relatives in the highest Church offices, sold ecclesiastical positions to the highest bidders, and lived more like warlords than spiritual leaders.

Not all the abuses were confined to the papacy. The parish clergy, a huge clerical proletariat in Germany, had lost all ideals of celibacy, which had been made mandatory for Latin clergy in the eleventh century. They exacted such large sums for their services that the sacrament of extreme unction was commonly called the rich man's sacrament, too expensive for the dying poor. The upper clergy was composed largely of the sons of royalty for whom lucrative Church offices had been purchased. Monasteries grew lax and wealthy, and the monks earned the contempt of the people. Among the laity infidelity, illegitimacy, and superstition were rife. The educated classes turned to the pagan writers of Greece and Rome rather than to the Bible or the Church Fathers and fed on a wisdom of hedonism and sensuality.

We must not overstate the case. The age also produced its saints and devout Christians. Not all priests and monks were untrue to their vows. A few bishops called for reform of the manifold scandals. But after all these allowances are made, we must admit that the Church of Christ had fallen on evil days.

Into this situation was born a baby boy named Martin Luther after St. Martin, on whose feast day he was baptized. The boy knew poverty in his youth, but his father's fortunes improved, and he was able to study at three prep schools. At eighteen he transferred to the University of Erfurt to study not theology, but law. He won his master's degree in 1505.

At this point the course of Luther's life changed dramatically. While riding in a storm he was hurled to the ground by a bolt of lightning. In terror he cried, "St Anne, help me. I will become a monk." Evidently the reputation of the monastery he chose was such that a young man would consider it a logical refuge if he wished to consecrate his life entirely to God. Luther joined the strict Hermits of St. Augustine.

No one doubts that Luther determined to be a good religious. In fact, his self-imposed penances went far beyond the rules of the order. Professed in 1506, he was ordained a year later and only then began his study of theology. No religious order today would accept a candidate who sought entrance because of a vow made in fear of his life, and certainly no one would be ordained two years after entering as a novice and without theological preparation.

Father Martin was barely able to complete his first Mass as he contemplated the miracle he was about to perform. Subject to extreme states of depression and melancholia, the young friar was obviously a victim of scrupulosity. He would spend as long as six hours in the confessional attempting to recall all his sins. What if he had forgotten to confess some sin? What if he had violated some rule of his order and had forgotten about it? His weary but wise confessor finally told him, "Man, God is not angry with you. You are angry with God. Don't you know that God commands you to hope?" Luther continued to be haunted by the thought that he might lose his soul; efforts by his religious superiors to assuage his fears were useless.

He visited Rome briefly on official business for his order and returned with a lowered estimate of Italian Catholicism. From Erfurt he was transferred to the young university at Wittenberg, where he received a doctor of theology degree in 1512. Frederick the Wise had founded this university only eleven years before in a village of about twenty-five hundred. Luther became a professor of Scripture and began an intensive study of the Bible.

His theological system was taking shape. He was already teaching that through the Fall man's nature was radically corrupted. In essence man is a sinner, inclined only to evil, a possession of the devil. "Sin is not only a specific wrongdoing but also the basic condition of our fallen existence," decided Luther. All man can do is make a complete act of trust in God, who confers forgiveness on him through the merits of Christ.

Luther tormented himself with the question, "Where can I find a merciful God?" How could he be assured that he would be saved? While preparing his Scripture lectures he came upon a passage in Romans that he called the "door to paradise." He read, "The just man lives by faith." Here was the answer to his anxiety.

Luther used his conception of justification by faith as the key to interpret the rest of the Bible. It remains the basis of the experiential Protestant theology of consolation. St. James wrote that "Faith without good works is dead"; the Reformer dismissed this epistle as a "straw epistle."

When God gave mankind the Ten Commandments, He knew they could not be observed. They were given to humble man, to break his willful spirit and bring him to a complete act of faith in God's goodness and mercy. For the sake of His Son, Jesus Christ, God casts a cloak over man's sins and man, still a sinner, is justified.

Because every action of man is sinful, good works are sinful and of no avail for salvation even after man is justified. Perhaps Luther knew the traditional Catholic position that good works performed by man in the state of original sin are of no merit. He now denied the merit of any and all good works for justification.

Because Luther considered good works useless to salvation, we may not assume that he encouraged moral laxity. The just man will gladly perform good works and avoid evil for the glory of God.

The barefoot friar of Wittenberg developed his doctrinal position while busily engaged in a variety of other tasks. In a letter written to a friend in 1517 he wrote:

> "I really ought to have two secretaries or chancellors. I do hardly anything all day but write letters. . . . I am at the same time preacher to the monastery, have to preach in the refectory, and am even expected to preach daily in the parish church.

I am regent of the house of studies and vicar, that is to say prior eleven times over; I have to provide for delivery of the fish from Lietzkau pond and to manage the litigation of the Herzberg friars at Torgau; I am lecturing on Paul, compiling lectures on the Psalter, and, as I said before, writing letters most of the time. . . . It is seldom that I have time for recitation of the Divine Office or to celebrate Mass, and then, too, I have my peculiar temptations from the flesh, the world, and the devil."

The sale of indulgences was the occasion of Luther's open protest but quite incidental to his theological creation. No one denies that scandalous abuses of all sorts had crept into the granting of indulgences. Luther's own patron, Frederick, boasted a collection of relics said to include a strand of Jesus' beard, a nail from the crucifixion, a piece of the swaddling clothes, and a twig from Moses' burning bush. Those of the faithful who venerated all these relics and made a contribution could amass a total indulgence of 1,909,202 years and 270 days.

Pope Julius II granted a new indulgence to obtain funds for the building of St. Peter's in Rome. The preaching of such an indulgence resembled a modern parish mission, but the salesmen claimed to guarantee results even though the recipients were not in the state of grace. Frederick forbade the preaching of this indulgence in his province because it would compete with his own collection. But many Wittenbergers crossed the nearby border to obtain its extravagant promises from a Dominican priest by the name of Tetzel. Tetzel employed all the devices of the modern huckster in promoting this indulgence. A representative of the Fugger's banking house sat next to the coffer to collect his share of the proceeds as promised by the playboy archbishop of Mainz.

Luther nailed a list of ninety-five theses on indulgences to the church door in Wittenberg, the usual manner in which scholars invited debate. About these theses Luther would insist: "In all we wanted to say, we have said nothing that is not in agreement with the Catholic

Church and the teachers of the Church." The debate never took place, but the theses were widely circulated throughout Germany.

Soon Luther was driven to more radical positions, and he launched attacks on papal authority, infallibility, invocation of the saints. He presented himself as the champion of the German people, groaning under the demands of Rome.

At one stage the Reformer may have hoped that his new theology would find acceptance by the Church. Indeed, as we have seen in the preceding chapter, the positive principles of the Reformation are in complete harmony with the teachings of the Church. The Church was forced to condemn the negative principles of extrinsic justification, the wholesale condemnation of good works, absolute predestination, a personal religion that dispensed with the Church itself, and the denial of the role of tradition. Luther sought authority in a council rather than in the pope, but he finally settled for the authority of the Bible. We have seen that he ridiculed the Epistle of St. James because it contradicted his own theology. When he realized that the doctrine of purgatory and prayers for the dead were implied in the Second Book of Maccabees, he threw out that book. The Book of Esther he called a "superfluity of heathen naughtiness," and he relegated some Old Testament books (the Apocrypha) to the appendix. He nevertheless insisted that the Bible was the complete and infallible Word of God.

Among those who joined Luther at Wittenberg were two fellow professors: Carlstad and Melanchthon. Luther had refused to go to Rome at the pope's orders to answer charges of heresy, but Carlstad was challenged to a debate by Dr. John Eck at Leipzig. Luther's voluminous writings were receiving wide circulation through the relatively new medium of the printing press, and he grew bolder, denouncing the pope as the anti-Christ. While he lost the support of some Humanists such as Erasmus, he won a number of dissatisfied priests, monks, nuns, and lay people to his cause.

Three influential tracts went to the printer in 1520. In these tracts, *The Babylonian Captivity*, *The Freedom of the Christian Man*, and the *Address to the German Nobility*, Luther trimmed the number of sacraments from seven to three (he later eliminated confession as a sacrament).

His revolutionary theology was formally condemned by the faculties of the Universities of Paris, Louvain, and Cologne. When the papal bull threatening excommunication and citing forty-one errors finally reached Luther from Rome in 1520, he tossed it on the fire as admiring students sang the *Te Deum*. He was summoned before the civil Diet of Worms by the Emperor Charles V and asked to admit the authorship of his heretical books. Closing his defense, the defiant friar declared: "Unless I am convicted by Scripture and plain reason — I do not accept the authority of popes and councils for they have contradicted each other — my conscience is captive to the Word of God. I cannot and will not recant anything, for to go against conscience is neither right nor safe. God, help me. Amen." Assuming his sincerity, his stand on the supremacy of conscience was, of course, strictly orthodox, and St. Thomas Aquinas points out that anyone convinced that the Church is in error is bound to leave it.

At Worms Luther stood convicted of heresy, but the emperor promised him safe conduct back to his home in Wittenberg. The followers of Luther refused to accept the decision of what they called a rump court. En route a band of masked men kidnapped Luther and delivered him into protective custody at the castle at Wartburg. Frederick arranged this maneuver to forestall possible treachery because Luther was now an outlaw in the rest of Germany by order of the emperor. During his year in Wartburg Luther completed his translation of the New Testament into German. We should note, however, that before 1518 there had been fourteen translations into High German and four into Low German.

Back at Wittenberg Luther's two colleagues assumed the leadership of the snowballing Reformation. Priests, monks, and nuns began to marry; German replaced Latin in the liturgy; images were smashed; Masses for the dead were forbidden. When Luther returned home in the disguise of a bearded knight, he upbraided Carlstad for his violence and iconoclasm but otherwise applauded the changes.

When three laymen from neighboring Zwickau visited Wittenberg and began to denounce infant baptism, Luther was horrified. He repudiated any connection with these anarchistic Anabaptists while they, in turn, chided the Lutherans as compromisers. Because Luther maintained the necessity of faith for the reception of a sacrament, he was hard-pressed to present a convincing case for infant baptism.

The general disparagement of authority and the radical doctrine of the priesthood of all believers inflamed the German peasants and inspired the bloody peasant revolt of 1524-25. Rather than become their leader, Luther penned the vicious tract *Against the Murderous and Thieving Hordes of Peasants.* In this tract he advised, "Let everyone who can, smite, slay and stab secretly or openly, remembering that nothing can be more poisonous, hurtful or devilish than a rebel. It is just as when one must kill a mad dog; if you don't strike him, he will strike you, and the whole land with you." More than five thousand peasants were slain in the hopeless uprising. Luther, the peasant, turned his attention to the princes while the betrayed peasants listened with greater interest to the left-wing Anabaptists.

The marriage of parish priests was one thing, but that of monks was quite another. Seeing his Augustinian brethren in Wittenberg taking wives, Luther exclaimed, "Good heavens! Will our Wittenbergers give wives to monks? They won't give one to me." But they did. Nine Cistercian nuns arrived at the cloister in search of husbands, and Luther acted as matchmaker. After two years one ex-nun remained unmarried, Katherine von Bora. Urged to practice what he preached and to give his father a grandson, Luther finally married the former nun and established his household in the Augustinian monastery. Six children were born to the union, and the male succession continued until 1759.

Turning from the peasants for his support, Luther came to rely more and more on the German princes as "emergency bishops." Lutherans early dissociated themselves from secular affairs and have traditionally allowed the prince, emperor, president, or dictator to manage state affairs with a minimum of church interference or ethical judgment. The Reformation gave the princes an opportunity to seize coveted church property and to escape the inconveniences of an international Church.

The Diet of Spires in 1529 reaffirmed the verdict of Worms and insisted on liberty for Catholics in Lutheran areas but limited the further spread of the new religion in Germany. The Lutherans protested, giving rise to the term "Protestant." They had formerly preferred the term "Evangelical" and eventually came to be known as Lutherans despite Luther's wishes: "I beg that my name be passed over in silence, and that men will call themselves not Lutherans but Christians. What is Luther? My teaching is not mine. . . . How does it happen that I . . . have the children of Christ called after my unholy name? Let us root out party names and call ourselves Christians, for it is Christ's gospel we have."

Unlike the Reformed leader, Calvin, Luther left no systematic statement of his theology. His co-worker Melanchthon performed this task and represented Lutheranism at the Diet of Augsburg in 1530, called by the emperor to restore religious unity. Melanchthon prepared a conciliatory confession that softened the more abusive criticism of the ancient Church and went so far as to suggest that the adoption of vernacular in the liturgy would solve most of the differences. This Augsburg Confession remains the most authoritative Lutheran doctrinal statement. It also branded the Zwinglians, led by ex-priest Ulrich Zwingli in Switzerland, and the Anabaptists as heretics.

Of confession the Augsburg Confession declares: "Confession in the churches is not abolished among us; for it is not usual to give the body of the Lord, except to them that have been previously examined and absolved" (Article XXV). It maintained that children should be baptized, that the Body and Blood of Christ are truly present in the sacrament, and that "the Mass is retained among us, and celebrated with the highest reverence." Yet the Augsburg Confession also classified as "childish and needless works" such things as "particular holy days, particular fasts, brotherhoods, pilgrimages, services in honor of saints, the use of rosaries, monasticism, and such like."

Plagued by insomnia and constipation Luther nevertheless turned his tremendous energies to institutionalizing the Reformation movement. He translated the Old Testament and prepared his Larger and Smaller Catechisms. He composed several dozen hymns including "A Mighty Fortress Is Our God," the battle hymn of Protestantism. His revised liturgy emphasized preaching and congregational singing as integral parts of the Eucharist.

Toward the end of his life Luther found himself carried along by the revolution he had triggered. One of his young supporters, Philip of Hesse, tired of his wife and appealed to Luther to approve a divorce. This Luther refused, but he suggested that the prince take a second wife as in Old Testament days. Wife No. 2 was to be kept secret, but her mother objected and the Reformer then advised recourse to a lie. Luther's conduct during the peasants' revolt and his countenancing of bigamy are seldom defended by even his staunchest admirers.

Many results of his Reformation distressed him. He saw moral standards sink below those of former times and he lamented: "Avarice, usury, debauchery, drunkenness, blasphemy, lying and cheating are far more prevalent now than they were under the papacy. This state of morals brings general discredit on the Gospel, and its preachers, as the people say, if this Gospel were true, the persons professing it would be more pious."

As the years went by the Reformer grew intolerant of any who might venture to disagree with him. "He who does not believe my doctrine is sure to be damned," he announced. Toward the end of his life he penned two unfortunate attacks on the Jews and the papacy, illustrated with lewd cartoons. Referring to the Jews, he recommended, "That their synagogues be burned, their houses broken down and destroyed, and their rabbis forbidden to teach under pain of death."

Martin Luther died on February 18, 1546, in Eisleben, a village in Thuringia where he had been born on November 10, 1482.

Luther had not intended to found another church. In 1519 he would write to Pope Leo X: "Before God and all his creatures, I bear testimony that I neither did desire, nor do desire to touch or by intrigue undermine the authority of the Roman church and that of your holiness." He never considered himself outside the fold of the historic Catholic Church.

Centuries later the German priest Karl Adam would offer this appraisal of Luther:

"Yes, it was night. Had Martin Luther then arisen with his marvelous gifts of mind and heart, his warm penetration of the essence of Christianity, his passionate defiance of all unholiness and ungodliness, the elemental fury of his religious experience, his surging, soul-shattering power of speech, and not least that heroism in the face of death with which he defied the powers of the world — had he brought all these magnificent qualities to the removal of the abuses of the time and the cleansing of God's garden from weeds, had he remained a faithful member of his Church, humble and simple, sincere and pure, then indeed we should today be his grateful debtors. He would be forever our great Reformer, our true man of God, our teacher and leader, comparable to Thomas Aquinas and Francis of Assisi. He would have been the greatest saint of our people, the refounder of the Church in Germany, a second St. Boniface" (*One and Holy*, p. 25).

Another Catholic scholar, Willem Hendrick van de Pol, writes: "The integrity of his character and personality, the purity of his intentions, the unselfishness of his actions, the genuineness and depth of his piety and his extraordinary gifts of mind and heart are beyond any doubt of suspicion" (*World Protestantism*, p. 33).

Where the Swiss Reformers attempted to dispense with everything not specifically commanded or authorized by the Bible, Luther preserved whatever was not specifically forbidden by Scripture. The Lutheran Church retains more of the liturgy, church year, vestments, and church architecture than other continental Protestant churches. Luther halted the destruction of works of art that had been instigated by Carlstad.

Lutheranism soon hardened into a rigid orthodoxy that made the Protestant right of private interpretation inoperative. Conformity or excommunication was the choice after 1580. This orthodoxy went far beyond Luther in rejecting ancient practices such as confession and the veneration of Mary.

Various German princes abandoned Catholicism and cast their lot with the Lutherans. Eventually Lutheranism also became the state church of Denmark, Norway, Sweden, Finland, Iceland, Estonia, and Latvia. Today more than half the world's Lutherans live in Germany. There are approximately 7 million in Sweden, 4,300,000 in Denmark, 4,300,000 in Finland, and 3,200,000 in Norway.

Lutherans in America often have been considered religious isolationists by their fellow Protestants. For many years, they clung to the German and Scandinavian languages; contributed little to the propagation of the social gospel, liberal theology, prohibition efforts, and the ecumenical movement; and often educated their children in their own parochial schools. Their continental background gave them a more relaxed attitude toward beer drinking, smoking, dancing, and Sunday blue laws. A greater degree of cooperation between Lutherans and non-Lutheran Protestants can be observed today, although such groups as the Missouri and Wisconsin Synod Lutherans usually stand aloof from many ecumenical movements.

Lutheranism constitutes the third largest family in U.S. Protestantism, after the Baptists and Methodists. The three largest Lutheran bodies enroll more than 95 percent of the nation's nearly nine million Lutherans. About 5,178,000 belong to the mildly liberal Evangelical Lutheran Church in America, 2,594,000 to the Lutheran Church-Missouri Synod, and 411,000 to the very conservative Wisconsin Evangelical Lutheran Synod. Perhaps one hundred thousand others belong to a number of much smaller Lutheran synods.

In general Lutherans are scarce in New England and the South and strongest in the Midwest, with large constituencies in Minnesota, Wisconsin, Pennsylvania, Illinois, and Michigan. Most adherents come from German and Scandinavian backgrounds.

The first stable colony of Lutherans in this country was composed of Swedish immigrants in Delaware in 1638, but most of the descendants of these Swedes eventually became Episcopalians.

Henry Melchior Muhlenberg is known as the great patriarch of American Lutheranism because it was through his forty-five years' labor that the scattered German parishes were organized. Of his eleven children, all the men became ministers and most of the women married ministers. One son became a general and served under Washington.

A series of mergers, eight in all, culminated in the formation of the Evangelical Lutheran Church in America in 1988. Members of the new ELCA came from German, Swedish, Finnish, and other ethnic backgrounds. The ELCA belongs to the National and World Council of Churches.

A 1999 agreement between ELCA and the Episcopal Church, the result of thirty years of dialogue, allows full communion and affirms the full authenticity and validity of all existing ordained ministries in both churches. In 1997 the ELCA entered into full communion with the Presbyterian Church (USA), the Reformed Church in America, and the United Church of Christ.

Several boatloads of "Old Lutherans" from Luther's own province of Saxony landed near St. Louis in 1839. These ultraconservative Lutherans fought the proposed union with the Reformed in their homeland and waged war against all forms of Rationalism. In this country they soon drove their pastor from the community for alleged immorality and for assuming the powers of a bishop. Fortunately for the group a brilliant organizer, C.F.W. Waither, assumed leadership and can be called the real father of the Lutheran Church-Missouri Synod. The synod was formally organized in Chicago in 1849. Today the Missouri Synod is a nationwide church with its largest membership in Illinois.

The Missouri Synod Lutherans built their own parochial school system from kindergarten to university. They operate hundreds of grade and high schools, Valparaiso University, and one of the largest Protestant seminaries in the nation, Concordia in St. Louis.

Bitter disputes over biblical literalism have torn the Lutheran Church-Missouri Synod since the late 1960s. The conservative head of the synod, Dr. Jacob A.O. Preus, suspended the president of Concordia in 1974, charging him with "holding, defending, allowing, and fostering false doctrine." Most of the faculty and students set up a rival Seminary-in-exile, but Preus threatened disciplinary action against any district presidents who accepted Seminex graduates.

The Wisconsin Synod shares most Missouri Synod positions but also bans membership in the Boy Scouts and the Lutheran Men of America. From 1872 on, the Missouri and Wisconsin synods cooperated in the Lutheran Synodical Conference of North America, which included Norwegian and Slovak bodies. In 1963 the Wisconsin Synod criticized the Missourians as too liberal and severed its relations with Missouri.

Lutheran pastors receive the benefit of a thorough, classical theological education. A candidate for the Missouri Synod ministry, for example, often begins his studies after completing grade school. He attends one of eleven prep schools to take six years of pre-theological training through junior college. He then completes two more years of college, two years of theology, one year as a vicar in some larger parish or college student foundation, and a final year of theology before ordination. The course includes Latin, Greek, Hebrew, and German.

The Missouri and Wisconsin synods and other Lutheran bodies operate more than 2,000 grade and high schools for approximately 235,000 pupils. About one of every three students in these schools comes from a non-Lutheran home.

While the ELCA ordains women to the ministry, the Missouri and Wisconsin synods balk at this development. Women also have been ordained in Lutheran churches in Sweden, Denmark, and Slovakia.

Lutheran deaconesses undergo special training and staff foreign missions, hospitals, parish offices, and welfare homes. These women take installation vows and sometimes wear no distinctive garb but usually serve for life.

All Lutheran churches have regulations against membership in lodges, but only the Missouri and Wisconsin synods enforce these regulations strictly. Some older ELCA ministers are themselves high-ranking Masons, but ELCA ministers are now forbidden to join a lodge. Synodical conference churches carry on active campaigns against secret societies and continually warn their members against affiliation. Some synods have come out in favor of birth control, while other synods leave this matter up to the individual. Divorce with remarriage is allowed for such reasons as adultery and desertion because of "hardness of hearts." The ELCA permits Lutheran pastors to witness a marriage of any divorced person who shows "repentance."

Lutheran worship is liturgical to a greater degree than that of most Protestants. Lutherans observe the church year, wear vestments, and follow a set ritual. Their order of worship closely resembles the Catholic Mass from which it was adapted. The Common Service consists of silent prayer, hymn, confession of sin, declaration of grace, *Introit, Kyrie Eleison, Gloria*, collect, epistle and gospel, creed, hymn, sermon, general prayer, announcements, offering, hymn, the Our Father, and benediction.

The Lord's Supper is observed every Sunday by an increasing number of congregations. Others hold a Communion service at least once a month. The preface, *Sanctus*, Communion prayer, words of institution, and *Agnus Dei* are used in the Order of Holy Communion on these occasions.

Music has always played a prominent part in Lutheran worship; someone has estimated that there are more than one hundred thousand Lutheran hymns. Their hymnology is enriched by the compositions of Johann Sebastian Bach, a devout Lutheran.

Either a crucifix or a plain cross will be found on the Lutheran altar, which occupies the central position in the chancel. Candles, the Bible, and flowers often are found on the altar, and the altar hangings and vestments follow a color cycle that calls for white for Christmas, red for Reformation Sunday (the Sunday nearest October 31), violet for Ash Wednesday, and so on. Most ministers wear a cassock, surplice, and stole, and some use the historic chasuble. During the day some pastors wear a clerical collar and dark suit, but most wear ordinary business clothes. They prefer to be addressed as "Pastor" rather than as "Reverend" or "Mr."

European Lutheran churches follow an episcopal polity, but those in America have preferred a congregational system that allows the local church to own property, call pastors, and elect church officers but preserves doctrinal unity.

Relations between Catholics and Protestants in Germany, the homeland of the Reformation, have not been more cordial since the sixteenth century. Encouraging signs of better feeling between Lutherans and Catholics in the United States have been seen in recent years. Lutheran ministers and Catholic priests are engaging in theological dialogue. Lutheran choirs have sung in Catholic churches and Catholics may be found singing Luther's powerful "A Mighty Fortress Is Our God" at Mass.

Undoubtedly one of the most significant achievements in the history of ecumenism was the signing on October 1, 1999, of the agreement on justification. By justification Christians, Catholic and Protestant, sought to understand how sinful human beings are made acceptable to God. The document was signed by representatives of the one billion Roman Catholics and most of the world's Lutherans who belong to churches in the Lutheran World Federation.

After 483 years of theological dispute, the signers attributed the different views on justification more to a misunderstanding than any denial that salvation is a free and unmerited gift from God. The document states:

"Together we confess: By grace alone, in faith in Christ's saving work and not because of any merit on our part, we are accepted by God and receive the Holy Spirit, who renews our hearts while equipping and calling us to good works."

If agreement on this central theological position could be reached through prayerful dialogue, the prospect for further ecumenical progress is hopeful.

FURTHER READING

Adam, Karl, *One and Holy* (New York: Sheed and Ward, 1951).
Bainton, Roland, *Here I Stand* (Nashville: Abingdon, 1950).

Bergendoff, Conrad, *The Church of the Lutheran Reformation* (St. Louis: Concordia, 1967).

Loew, Ralph W., *The Lutheran Way of Life* (Englewood Cliffs, N.J.: Prentice-Hall, 1966).

Todd, John M., *Martin Luther* (Westminster, Md.: Newman, 1964).

Vajta, Vilmos, *The Lutheran Church Past and Present* (Minneapolis: Augsburg Press, 1977).

Van de Pol, W.H., *World Protestantism* (New York: Herder and Herder, 1964).

Wentz, S.R., *A Basic History of Lutheranism in America*, rev. ed. (Philadelphia: Muhlenberg Press, 1955).

CHAPTER 4

The Presbyterians

Calvinism Emphasizes the Sovereignty of God

LIKE THE EPISCOPAL CHURCH, THE PRESBYTERIAN CHURCH TAKES ITS name from its form of government. Elected elders rather than bishops rule the Presbyterian churches. But the larger church exercises supervision over the congregations through presbyteries or associations of churches in a given area. This representative system strikes a mean between the town-meeting democracy of the Congregationalists and the autocracy of the Episcopalians.

Theologically the Presbyterians follow the teachings of John Calvin, a French lawyer who systematized non-Lutheran Protestantism in the sixteenth century. Not all Calvinists — the Baptists and Congregationalists, for example — are presbyterian in polity; likewise, not all Presbyterians are Calvinist in theology. We should keep in mind that presbyterianism refers to a particular representative form of church government, while Calvinism refers to a theological emphasis centered around the absolute sovereignty of God, the helplessness of man, and, at least originally, predestination to heaven or hell.

The American Presbyterian Church is wealthy, sizable, influential, middle and upper class, generally conservative, often fashionable, and largely English, Scottish, and Scotch-Irish. Three denominations, the Presbyterian Church (U.S.A.), the Presbyterian Church in America, and the Cumberland Presbyterian Church, enroll 90 percent of the Presbyterian communicants. Presbyterian or Reformed churches predominate in Scotland, Northern Ireland, and Holland and claim large constituencies in Switzerland, South Africa, Germany, and Hungary. Most French Protestants or Huguenots adhere to a Reformed theology.

The World Alliance of Reformed Churches is made up of 175 Presbyterian, Reformed, and Congregational churches in 75 countries.

To trace the development of Presbyterianism, we must go back to the early days of the Reformation. While Luther led the revolt in Germany, an ex-priest, Ulrich Zwingli, established the new religion in Switzerland. Zwingli began to devour Luther's writings in 1518, and four years later he was denying the value of fasting and clerical celibacy. He petitioned his bishop for a release from the obligations of celibacy, and when this was denied, he married the widow with whom he had been living. A daughter was born four months after the wedding.

Zwingli soon parted company with the German Reformer on the question of the Real Presence of Christ in the Eucharist. This led to the split between Lutheran and Reformed Protestantism that continues to this day. Zwingli held the Lord's Supper to be nothing more than a simple memorial service, whereas Luther upheld the Real Presence while denying the doctrine of transubstantiation. The Swiss reformer stripped the churches of all art and music and established a theocracy at Zurich. He was slain in 1531 in a battle against the Catholic cantons.

Jean Cauvin, known to us as John Calvin, was the son of a minor French ecclesiastical official. A year after his father's excommunication Calvin turned from the study of theology to law, and in 1533 he embraced the new religious ideas of the Reformation. His reasons for leaving the Catholic Church were never explicitly stated, but he became the tireless propagator of the new religion. Fearing persecution, he left his native country. At Basle he composed his classic exposition of Reformation doctrine, the *Institutes of the Christian Religion*. He was twenty-seven at the time.

A reformer at Geneva, where Calvin had stopped to spend the night, persuaded him to stay and guide the Protestant community in this Swiss city of about fifteen thousand. Calvin agreed and set about establishing what might be termed a religious police state. Modeled after Old Testament theocracies, the Geneva city government employed harsh penalties, espionage, and religious sanctions to enforce a drab and severe religious code. Calvin fulminated against dancing, amusements, luxuries, feast days, indolence, and vestigial Catholic practices. After two years of this regime, the citizens rebelled and forced Calvin to leave.

He taught at Strasbourg for three years, married a widow, and finally received a second invitation to come to Geneva. During his exile he had perfected his presbyterian system of representative church government. Older and wiser, Calvin returned and undertook to transform Geneva into a model Protestant community. Thousands of religious rebels from Europe and the British Isles swelled the city's population and returned to their homelands with Calvinistic orientations.

Calvinism furnished the theological foundation for the Huguenots and for the more successful Reformed churches of the Netherlands. John Knox brought Calvinism to Scotland, and Scotland has always been the center of Presbyterianism. English divines banished by the Catholic Queen Mary found refuge in Geneva, and when they returned under Elizabeth they carried their Calvinism with them.

Classical Calvinism based its theology on five points, all of which have been drastically modified by modern Presbyterianism: (1) predestination or election, (2) limited atonement, (3) total depravity, (4) the irresistibility of grace; and (5) perseverance of the saints. In other words, Calvin taught that man's nature since the Fall is totally depraved. God elects some men to salvation and damns others to hell. Christ died only for the elect, who cannot resist God's grace and cannot backslide once they have received this grace of election.

"We assert that by an eternal and immutable counsel, God has once for all determined, both whom He would admit to salvation, and whom He would condemn to destruction," wrote Calvin. Calvinists generally relied on passages from St. Augustine to substantiate their views of absolute or double predestination. They deduced that unbaptized babies were certain to be cast into hell, and the American theologian and preacher Jonathan Edwards asserted, "Hell is paved with the skulls of unbaptized children."

The pure Calvinist impulse to reaffirm the absolute sovereignty of God and to expose the idolatry of acting as though God and man existed on the same plane was often misdirected. By 1741 Edwards was presenting the following picture of God the Father to his congregation: "The God that holds you over the pit of hell, much as one holds a spider, or some loathsome insect, over the fire, abhors you and is dreadfully provoked; His wrath toward you burns like fire; He looks upon you as worthy of nothing but to be cast into the fire; He is of purer eyes than to bear to have you in His sight; you are ten thousand times so abominable in His eyes, as the most hateful and venomous serpent is in ours."

The Catholic Church approaches the question of predestination with greater trepidation than Calvin. The Council of Trent called predestination "a hidden mystery." Catholicism upholds the doctrine that salvation is primarily God's work and His grace, but that man is not totally depraved. After justification he may offer the merits of good works for his salvation. Man possesses free will, and whether a man is saved or damned, he arrives at this state through the exercise of his free will. God condemns no one to hell; man condemns himself to hell by his sins. Calvinism finds itself in the position of implicating God with sin because if God damns a soul to hell, He also must force that soul to sin to deserve hell.

Whereas Luther claimed to preserve whatever was not specifically forbidden by the Bible, Calvin sought to reject everything that was not positively commanded. He impoverished the Reformed worship service when he discarded vestments, altar, images, paintings, organs, and hymns. God could be praised only by His own words; therefore, Calvin forbade any hymns but the psalms themselves. Today Presbyterians acknowledge Calvinistic excesses and have reintroduced Christian art and symbolism into their architecture, chancels, and liturgies.

Calvin adopted a position on the Eucharist slightly closer to Luther's than was Zwingli's, but like Zwingli he upheld a mystical rather than a substantial Real Presence. The Calvinist receives the bread and wine as a guarantee of the grace flowing into his soul from Christ in heaven.

Calvinism encouraged education, sobriety, thrift, political as well as religious democracy, philanthropy, capitalism, Bible reading, and the somber Sabbath. The Bible became an infallible rule of conduct, and the Calvinists accorded relatively greater emphasis to the Old Testament than did other Christians.

Max Weber and R.H. Tawney have suggested the positive relationship between Calvinism and the rise of capitalism. Calvinism stressed the secular vocation, lifted the bans against interest, offered investment opportunities to the many Protestant refugees in Geneva, and pointed out that the elect might well be identified by their material prosperity because God would favor His elect.

In striving to give all possible honor to God, Calvin eventually presented a God who arbitrarily damned souls to hell and forced men to sin, who condemned innocent babies to eternal torment, and who denied free will to both the elect and the reprobate. His followers today generally regard predestination as a "hidden mystery." The expected reaction against the harsher aspects of Calvinism came from the Dutch theologian Jacob Arminius, who reemphasized free will and inspired Wesleyan theology.

Afflicted by headaches and indigestion, Calvin nevertheless kept up an exhausting daily routine. In 1553 he consented to the burning of Spanish Unitarian Michael Servetus. Humorless, cold, and ruthlessly logical, Calvin had few close friends but was greatly respected. He shares with Martin Luther the title Father of the Protestant Reformation. Calvin died at age fifty-four.

Protestantism never made much headway in Calvin's native France. The politically inspired St. Bartholomew's Day massacre in 1572 involved the slaughter of thirty thousand Huguenots. The Edict of Nantes in 1598 granted them freedom of worship, but when it was revoked by Louis XIV in 1685 thousands of French Protestants, many of them skilled artisans, fled to other lands.

Among the Huguenot refugees who fled to America were the Du Ponts, whose descendants control a family fortune estimated at several billion dollars. The French Revolution decimated Protestant as well as

Catholic churches, and today French Protestants number fewer than one million.

The Reformed faith took deep root in the Netherlands, and the royal family of Holland and a majority of the people belong to one of the two main Reformed churches. Dutch colonists carried the Reformed Church to North America, South Africa, and the Dutch East Indies.

John Knox had been a Catholic priest, Protestant preacher, exile in England, and galley slave in the French navy before reaching Geneva. What he learned from Calvin during three years in that city he taught in his native Scotland, opposing the Catholicism of Mary Queen of Scots and the Anglicanism of the English. He helped dethrone Mary and maneuvered the Scottish parliament into establishing Presbyterianism as the state religion. Periodic attempts were made to overthrow Scottish Presbyterianism and substitute an episcopal system. Charles II sniffed, "Presbyterianism is not a religion for gentlemen." The church suffered a number of schisms over the issues of monarchy and lay patronage. A union of all major branches, however, was achieved in 1929 in the Church of Scotland.

Scotch colonists settled confiscated lands in Northern Ireland or Ulster, and soon that area of the island was mainly Scottish. These Scotch-Irish took their Presbyterianism with them to that Catholic island. Today Ireland, including the six northern countries, is one-fourth Protestant, mainly Presbyterian. Between 1729 and 1809 a steady stream of Scotch-Irish emigrated to America. One such immigrant, the Reverend Francis Makemie, is considered the father of Presbyterianism in this country. The Scotch-Irish influenced the course of American Presbyterianism more than any other nationality.

In England two groups pestered the Church of England: the Separatists and the Puritans. Both wished to purify the state church of such popish practices as the sign of the cross, the use of vestments and images, kneeling for prayer, feast days, and the like. The Separatists, however, believed that the Anglican Church was hopeless; they felt compelled to separate from this church and found another, purer church.

The Puritans were convinced that they could remain Anglican and bring about their reforms from within. Calvinism pervaded both parties, and most — but not all — of the Puritans were also Presbyterians, with a sprinkling of Congregationalists.

Eventually the Puritan party gained power in England and the episcopacy was abolished. "No bishop and no king" was their motto. Parliament called together 151 clergymen and laymen, most of whom were Presbyterians, to formulate a confession of faith. The delegates remained in session for five years at Westminster, threw out the Book of Common Prayer, and prepared the Westminster Confession of 1648, a Directory of Worship, a form of government, and a Larger and Shorter Catechism. Fourteen years later the Puritan Commonwealth under Cromwell gave way to the monarchy, and the Anglican hierarchy was restored.

The Westminster Confession remains the standard of faith for American, Scottish, and English Presbyterianism, but its statement on predestination has been modified from its original form: "By the decree of God, for the manifestation of His glory, some men and angels are predestined unto everlasting life, and others fore-ordained to everlasting death. . . . The rest of mankind, God was pleased . . . to pass by, and to ordain them to dishonor and wrath for their sin, to the praise of His glorious justice."

Presbyterianism in England crumbled in the eighteenth century as a result of government disabilities, Arian and Unitarian heresies, and a poorly trained ministry. Only later Scottish immigration saved Presbyterianism from extinction there. Even now the denomination counts only one hundred thousand adherents in that country.

Puritan ministers brought Presbyterianism to America when they followed the Separatists out of the Church of England. Some switched to Congregationalism in the Massachusetts Bay colony, but others remained Presbyterians. Makemie organized the first presbytery, an essential of that form of polity, in Philadelphia in 1706. Disagreement over the place of revivals in the church and interpretations of the Confession led to the New Side-Old Side division that lasted from 1741 to 1758.

Presbyterians were almost 100 percent behind the colonists in the American Revolution. In fact, the Revolution was known by many in England as the "Presbyterian Rebellion." This attitude was in contrast to that of the Loyalist Methodists and Anglicans.

Of the fifty-five signers of the Declaration of Independence, twelve were Presbyterians, including the only clergyman to sign: the Reverend John Witherspoon. Eventually six Presbyterians would occupy the White House: Presidents Buchanan, Jackson, Benjamin Harrison, Cleveland, Wilson, and Eisenhower. General Eisenhower delayed joining any church until he retired from active military service and entered politics.

The two Calvinist denominations, Presbyterian and Congregationalist, entered into a Plan of Union whereby congregations on the western frontier could maintain affiliations with both denominations. Although this Plan usually worked to the advantage of the Presbyterians, an Old School party within Presbyterianism complained of Congregational influence. This led to the schism of 1837, which was not healed until after the Civil War.

The United Presbyterian Church of North America represented an 1858 merger of two strict Scottish Presbyterian churches. Both had withdrawn from the Church of Scotland. Particularly before 1925 this denomination had been known for its espousal of classical Calvinism, opposition to secret societies, exclusive use of the psalms in worship, and closed Communion.

A merger of the United Presbyterian Church and the Presbyterian Church in the United States, the two largest Presbyterian bodies, was achieved in 1983. The resulting Presbyterian Church (U.S.A.) reports 3,574,000 members.

In the 1960s some Presbyterians began to voice concerns about the liberalism they saw in the Presbyterian Church in the United States. They objected to the denomination's support for ordination of women, abortion, membership in the National Council of Churches, and other issues. By 1973 some forty-one thousand people had left the larger church to find a more conservative spiritual home. In 1974 they formed the

Presbyterian Church in America, which now counts 279,000 members and offers a conservative alternative to the Presbyterian Church (U.S.A.).

Revivalism led in 1810 to the secession of the Cumberland presbytery, which had begun to ordain preachers lacking the proper educational qualifications. The Cumberlanders organized their own church after they were officially dissolved by the Kentucky synod. They preached an Arminian rather than a pure Calvinist doctrine, but it was no greater departure from Geneva Calvinism than that now held by the northern church. Most of the Cumberlanders rejoined the parent church in 1906, but the Cumberland Presbyterian Church, which refused to enter the union, reports eighty-seven thousand members.

While Episcopalians have debated ritualism and Methodists have debated the evils of smoking and drinking, Presbyterians have stoked the fires of theological controversy. They stood on the firing line in the leading Fundamentalist-Modernist battles that shook American Protestantism from 1910 to about 1925.

Two wealthy Presbyterian laymen in Los Angeles published the tracts that outlined the "fundamentals" of the Christian faith. More than three million copies of *The Fundamentals*, the articles of war against Modernism, the social gospel, and evolutionary theory, were distributed in 1910 and the years following. Presbyterian evangelist the Reverend Dr. (Westminster College) Billy Sunday enlivened tent and tabernacle with his colorful denunciations of Modernists, saloonkeepers, birth controllers, and Socialists.

Dr. Harry Emerson Fosdick, a Baptist, occupied the pulpit of New York's First Presbyterian Church. His frankly Modernist position and specific denial of the virgin birth prompted the General Assembly — at the top of the national Presbyterian structure — to invite him to become a Presbyterian (under its jurisdiction) or give up his position as pastor of a Presbyterian church. He followed the latter course and continued to expound his liberal theological views at Riverside Church.

Modernism continued to upset Presbyterian conservatism long after the main battle ended. A small group of conservatives followed Professor J. Gresham Machen of Princeton out of the mother church.

Machen, one of the ablest advocates of Fundamentalism and one of its few real scholars, organized the Presbyterian Church of America, but the courts made him adopt another name for his church, the Orthodox Presbyterian Church.

Presbyterianism has traditionally been strong in the Mid-Atlantic states of New York, New Jersey, and Pennsylvania, but it also enrolls large memberships in Ohio, Michigan, Indiana, Illinois, Iowa, and California.

Approximately sixty colleges and universities are related to the Presbyterian Church. Presbyterian seminary curricula still include Hebrew and Greek and more theology than most Protestant denominations offer their ministerial candidates. Princeton and McCormick in Chicago are two leading seminaries.

The whole number of the elect comprise the invisible church, according to Presbyterian thought; the visible church consists of "all those throughout the world that profess the true religion, together with their children, and is the Kingdom of the Lord Jesus Christ." The following description of the visible head of the Roman Catholic Church was revised by the northern Presbyterians in 1903: "There is no other head of the Church but the Lord Jesus Christ. Nor can the pope of Rome in any sense be head thereof; but is that anti-christ, that man of sin, and son of perdition, that exalteth himself, in the Church, against Christ, and all that is called God."

On the matter of predestination and free will, today's Presbyterian stands much closer to the original Catholic position than did Calvin. You would have to look to the tiny Presbyterian sects to hear absolute or double predestination preached. The drastic modification of the Westminster Confession is indicated in the 1903 interpretation of the northern church: "Concerning those who perish the doctrine of God's eternal decree is held in harmony with the doctrine that God desires not the death of any sinner, but has provided in Christ a salvation sufficient for all . . . men are fully responsible for their treatment of God's gracious offer . . . his decree hinders no man from accepting that offer . . . no man is condemned except on the ground of his sin."

Presbyterians do not consider baptism necessary for salvation but do urge that infants and adults receive the sacrament. The current theory on the fate of unbaptized infants who die differs from Edwards' grim description of hell's pavement. Presbyterians now assume that death in infancy is a sure sign of election, and that the soul of the infant will spend eternity not in hell or limbo but in heaven, even though unbaptized.

Each Presbyterian congregation elects about a dozen ruling elders and a teaching elder, all of whom are ordained church officials. The teaching elder is the minister, but theoretically he holds a position on a par with the other elders. The session, comprising the pastor and the ruling elders, is supervised by the presbytery or regional body to which it belongs. At least five sessions are needed to form a presbytery, which is composed of all the ministers and one ruling elder from each church. The presbytery examines and ordains candidates for the ministry, installs and removes ministers, settles doctrinal and disciplinary questions, checks the records of local churches, starts new churches, and the like. Except in the case of national or racial groupings, the presbyteries are plotted on geographical lines.

The synod performs the same function for the presbyteries that the presbyteries perform for the churches. Most synods are organized along state lines, with at least three presbyteries in each synod. The member presbyteries elect an equal number of ministers and ruling elders to the synod, which meets once a year.

The General Assembly tops the national Presbyterian structure and includes an equal number of pastors and elders from each presbytery. The powers of the Assembly include the right to suppress heresy and schism, reorganize synods, settle doctrinal and disciplinary controversies, and ratify mergers with other denominations.

Members of Presbyterian churches in the United States need not subscribe to the Westminster Confession or any other creed. Such a declaration of belief is required of ministers, ruling elders, and deacons, but even in these cases Modernist sympathizers may devise ingenious interpretations.

Controversy surrounded the proposal to adopt a new 1967 confession of faith to supplement the Westminster Confession of 1648. The new confession rejects a literal interpretation of the Bible and urges the application of literary and historical scholarship to Scripture study. It also disclaims the original Calvinist doctrine of predestination and affirms that salvation occurs when divine love heals the conflicts that separate man from God.

Presbyterianism has always made its greatest appeal to activist Anglo-Saxons. Americans looking for a church home may decide to affiliate with the Presbyterian Church, which they see as less nationalistic than the Lutheran, more fashionable than the Baptist, more democratic than the Episcopalian, less blue-nosed than the Methodist, and more traditional than the Disciples.

As we have seen, traditional Calvinist principles carry little weight in current Presbyterianism. Predestination, for example, may be the first thought a Catholic observer associates with this church, but it has become a historical curiosity for the average Presbyterian layman. The drab and barren Calvinist worship is being enriched by a return to the practices of the ancient Church. Here, more so than in many denominations, we find a huge gulf between the classical formulation and present-day beliefs.

FURTHER READING

Mackinnon, James, *Calvin and the Reformation* (New York: Russell and Russell, 1962).

McNeill, John T., *The History and Character of Calvinism* (New York: Oxford University Press, 1967).

Wendell, Francois, *Calvin* (New York: Harper & Row, 1963).

CHAPTER 5

The Episcopalians

*The Episcopal Church Reflects Dignity,
Diversity, and Discord*

A ROMAN CATHOLIC WHO HAPPENED TO VISIT AN "ANGLO-CATHOLIC"
church some Sunday morning would find himself in a familiar setting.
He would observe the holy water fonts, the confessional booths, the
stations of the cross, statues, and the sanctuary lamp. The officiating
Episcopal priest wears the traditional Christian vestments, the alb, stole,
cincture, and chasuble. The sermon at this Holy Communion or Mass
might concern the seven sacraments, fast-and-abstinence regulations,
or the Real Presence of Christ in the Eucharist. The visitor might
easily imagine himself in his own parish church.

But were he to continue his Episcopal itinerary, he might be puzzled
at his next stop. This second Episcopal church, three or three hundred
miles away, might resemble a typical Protestant chapel in architecture,
ecclesiastical furniture, vestment, and liturgy — little different from a
Congregational or Methodist church. The minister would be vested in
surplice and stole and the main worship service would be Morning
Prayer rather than a Communion service or Anglican Mass.

A third Episcopal church might resemble the first or second in appearance and liturgy, but the sermon soon would disclose a Rationalist
or Modernist slant that would find equal welcome in Unitarian circles.

Our Catholic visitor would have seen parishes representative of
the three main parties in Anglicanism: the High Church or "Anglo-
Catholic," the Low or Evangelical, and the broad or Modernist. The
Church of England and its American counterpart, the Protestant Episcopal Church, embrace a wider spectrum of doctrine and practice than
any major Protestant communion.

Claiming to be both Catholic and Protestant, Anglicanism combines the ritual and polity of Catholicism with a moderately Calvinistic theology. Episcopalians assert that they resist the "additions of Romanism and the subtractions of Protestantism." Episcopal theologians do not claim that theirs is the only Catholic Church, but that it constitutes one of four branches of the Catholic Church: Roman Catholic, Eastern Orthodox, Anglican, and Old Catholic.

Unlike most Protestant denominations, Anglicanism values the apostolic succession, the episcopacy, and the priesthood. Anglicans are happy to acknowledge the authority of the pope as the bishop of Rome but deny that his authority extends beyond the boundaries of his own diocese.

Anglicanism differs from the products of the Continental Reformation in that the motives for the separation of the Church of England from Rome were admittedly political rather than religious. No one suggests that Henry VIII severed the English ties with Rome and set himself up as head of the national church for spiritual reasons. Neither theological disputes nor a demand for the elimination of abuses played a prominent part in the English revolt.

One consequence of the purely political motivation has been that the Anglican Church retains more Catholic beliefs and forms than either the Lutheran or Reformed churches. And since the Oxford Movement of the past century, the Church of England has witnessed a revival of Catholic practices that has brought large sections of the establishment closer to Rome than at any time since the reign of Queen Elizabeth I.

Forty monks accompanied St. Augustine to Britain on a missionary journey commissioned by Pope Gregory around 597. St. Augustine found a handful of Christians in Wales and Western England, remnants of the Christian community that had flourished in Roman times, who had been pushed into corners of the island by pagan Angles and Saxons. He became the first archbishop of Canterbury.

For nearly a thousand years the Church in England recognized the supremacy of the bishop of Rome, as did the rest of Western Christendom. For example, Bede the Venerable wrote in A.D. 735: "The

Pope bears pontifical power over the whole world." In the eleventh century St. Anselm of Canterbury declared, "It is certain that he who does not obey the Roman Pontiff is disobedient to the Apostle Peter, nor is he of that flock given to Peter by God." In 1154 an Englishman, Nicholas Breakspear, was elected pope.

Episcopalians have good reason to object to Catholic controversialists who attempt to prove that their church was founded by the lustful Henry VIII. The monarch would have been an uncomfortable Episcopalian. A fair theologian himself, Henry penned a volume on the seven sacraments and a refutation of Lutheran errors that won him the title from the pope of "Defender of the Faith." English kings still bear this papal title.

Validly married to the Spanish princess Catherine of Aragon, the king became enamored of Anne Boleyn, a lady in waiting. Eager to marry Anne and provide a male heir for the throne, the king asked for an annulment, but the pope hesitated and refused.

His archbishop of Canterbury, Thomas Cranmer, took it upon himself to declare the marriage to Catherine invalid, and Henry announced himself to be the sole head of the Church of England in 1534. The Act of Supremacy stated that: "The Bishop of Rome hath not by Scripture any greater authority in England than any other foreign bishop." Lord Chancellor Sir Thomas More, among others, was executed for refusing to recognize the king's claim of spiritual supremacy. All of the English bishops except one, John Fisher, bowed to the king's wishes.

Although he suppressed some six hundred sixteen monasteries (to get needed funds) and murdered hundreds of bishops, monks, nobles, and women, the king never departed from orthodox Catholic teachings except for the question of papal supremacy. He insisted on Communion under one species, auricular confession, clerical celibacy, requiem Masses, and belief in transubstantiation. No Catholic wishes to present Henry as a Christian model, but he did hold fast to dogmatic positions and quashed efforts to Protestantize the national church. Cranmer was obliged to pack his secret Lutheran wife and children back to Germany.

Henry VIII removed the English church from obedience to the Roman see, but he never tampered with doctrine. Priests continued to offer true Masses and bishops ordained true priests during his rule. For the common man, Catholic life continued much as before the administrative quarrel. England was in schism. But rather than being the first Anglican, Henry was a disobedient and wicked Catholic.

The Protestant party captured the English church during the subsequent seven-year reign (1547-1553) of the tubercular boy-king Edward VI, the son of Henry and wife No. 3, Jane Seymour. Members of the Reformed faith flocked to England from the continent with their novel doctrines of justification by faith alone, two sacraments, and sole sufficiency of the Bible. Priests took wives, the Mass was abolished, and churches were stripped of works of art. Cranmer's Book of Common Prayer cut the sacrificial heart out of the Mass, and the revised ordination rite made no mention of the sacrificial powers of the priest.

Queen Mary, the daughter of Henry and Catherine, vowed to return the church to its Catholic heritage. For almost five years the English church was reunited with Rome; the Holy Father sent Cardinal Pole as his delegate to consolidate the reunion. The Protestant innovators were exiled, and Cranmer was burned at the stake. But Mary's efforts to reestablish the ancient faith failed and earned her the title "Bloody Mary" in Protestant history texts.

Matthew Parker, a married cleric with Lutheran sympathies, was consecrated in 1559 according to the defective Edwardian ordinal of 1552. Through Parker, all Church of England bishops claim to trace their apostolic succession. The defective form was employed from the accession of Queen Elizabeth in 1558 until 1662. By the end of this period all validly consecrated Anglican bishops had died, and the apostolic succession was broken.

Elizabeth, the daughter of Henry and Anne, again cut the ties with Rome. She abolished the Mass and reintroduced the oath of supremacy, although she called herself the Supreme Governor rather than the Supreme Head of the church. She stabilized what has become known as Anglicanism and could more logically be considered the founder of the Church of England than her notorious father. The Thirty-nine Articles were established as the doctrinal standard for the national church, now definitely in the Protestant camp. Queen Elizabeth and all members of the Church of England were excommunicated by Pope Pius V, an action Cardinal Newman and other Catholic writers have considered a blunder that only bolstered anti-Catholicism in the nation.

Successes over the hated Spanish and the destruction of the Armada, political astuteness, and economic prosperity contributed to the queen's popularity. The new religion shared the credit for the nation's good fortune. As critical of the dissenting Presbyterians and Congregationalists as of the Papists, the queen suppressed all non-Anglicans by force.

Eventually the Puritans, Anglicans who wished to purify their church of lingering popish practices, established a dictatorship under Oliver Cromwell. In the restoration Charles II again made the Anglican Church supreme.

The established church lost members to the energetic Baptist, Congregational, Quaker, and Presbyterian bodies; in the eighteenth century the Wesleyan revival led thousands out of the Anglican fold. Today the Church of England reports twenty-seven million baptized members; of those, ten million have been confirmed, and about one million attend church on Sundays. The Roman Catholic Church reports about two million active members in England.

A century after the start of the Wesleyan movement, the Church of England experienced a different sort of revival. The Oxford Movement called for a return to Catholic traditions, a renewed sacramental life, a greater appreciation of the church, the episcopacy, and the priesthood. John Henry Newman and other Oxford men sparked the movement that revitalized Anglicanism and gave birth to the High Church or Anglo-Catholic party. Newman himself submitted to the Catholic Church in 1845, inspired several others to follow him into the Church, and died a cardinal at the age of eighty-nine.

British colonists brought Anglicanism to American shores in the Virginia settlement in 1607. Completely dependent on the mother church and the Bishop of London, the American branch had no bishop or diocesan organization for 177 years. Candidates for the priesthood had to risk smallpox and shipwreck to return to England for ordination, and the colonials were unable to receive confirmation until after the American Revolution. That an episcopal church without bishops showed little vitality should not be surprising.

At the outbreak of the Revolution, most Anglican clergymen fled to England and Canada because they had taken an oath of loyalty to the king. Before the hostilities, the Church of England had been supported by taxes in seven southern colonies. In Virginia, for example, the law stipulated an Anglican clergyman's salary should be "1,500 pounds of tobacco and 16 barrels of corn." With this financial support gone, its clergy scattered and discredited, and its name closely associated with the recent enemy, the Church of England in the American colonies faced serious postwar problems.

The remaining Anglicans selected Samuel Seabury to be bishop. He spent a year in England seeking consecration, but the law forbade consecration of a bishop who was not a British subject. In desperation, Seabury turned to the outlawed Scottish Episcopal Church, which granted him consecration in 1784. Three years later the archbishops of Canterbury and York consecrated two Americans. A General Convention in Philadelphia in 1789 united the Anglicans in America into the Protestant Episcopal Church.

Few immigrants after the Revolution professed the Anglican faith, and the church was unable to hold its own on the frontier against the aggressive Methodist and Baptist preachers. By 1830 only thirty thousand Protestant Episcopal communicants could be counted, clustered on the Atlantic seaboard. During the Civil War the southern bishops organized a Confederate church, but in the calm after the war the two branches were reunited.

As in England, the High Church movement introduced more ritual and beauty into the liturgy. The use of incense and the question of vestments enlivened the ritualist controversy with Bishop John Henry Hobart of New York and William Augustus Muhlenberg, a convert from Lutheranism, upholding the High Church position. Between 1825 and 1855, thirty Episcopal priests entered the Roman Catholic Church.

Phillips Brooks, recognized as the greatest preacher in the Episcopal Church, guided the Broad movement from his pulpit in Trinity Church, Boston. This party represented Modernism and Rationalism in the Unitarian stronghold but has remained relatively small compared with the Anglo-Catholic wing.

A group of low churchmen seceded in 1873 to found the Reformed Episcopal Church. They abhorred all ritual and deleted such words as "priest, altar, sacrament, and holy communion" from their revision of the Book of Common Prayer. This church has declined in membership and now numbers fewer than sixty-four hundred.

The typical Episcopal minister can be called a Prayer Book clergyman who follows a middle course, avoiding the extremes of Anglo-Catholicism, evangelicalism, and Modernism. The Thirty-nine Articles, relegated to the appendix in the Book of Common Prayer, do not bind either priest or layman. At ordination Episcopal priests must declare: "I do believe the Holy Scriptures of the Old and New Testaments to be the Word of God, and to contain all things necessary to salvation; and I do solemnly engage to conform to the Doctrine, Discipline, and Worship of the Protestant Episcopal Church in the United States of America."

Most Episcopalians would consider the Apostles' and Nicene creeds a reflection of their creedal beliefs. Anglicans are accustomed to appeals to the teachings of the undivided Church, the Church that existed before the East-West schism in 1054. Despite the ordination declaration, the Anglican priest is unlikely to hold the Bible to be the sole rule of faith. He probably will add the tradition of the undivided Church and the use of reason to the Scriptures as rules of faith. Some do not use the term "purgatory," but they believe in a state of purification that they may call the Church Expectant.

In contrast to the positions of most of their Episcopal brethren, the Anglo-Catholics stress the Catholic heritage. Anglo-Catholicism is aggressive and articulate, which may lead some Roman Catholics to overestimate its strength within the Protestant Episcopal Church. The recent leader of the American Church Union, the chief Anglo-Catholic organization, estimates there are two hundred thousand Anglo-Catholics and adds that perhaps a million more may support specific Anglo-Catholic positions.

A Midwestern "biretta belt" of Anglo-Catholicism embraces the dioceses of Fond du Lac, Eau Claire, Milwaukee, Chicago, Quincy, Springfield, and northern Indiana. The dioceses of Long Island, Dallas, Fort Worth, Albany and San Diego also figure prominently in the movement. Nashotah House in Wisconsin trains many Anglo-Catholic priests.

Anglo-Catholics emphasize the seven sacraments, the Real Presence, fast and abstinence, auricular confession, prayers and requiem Masses for the dead, retreats, and invocation of the saints. They say the rosary, make the sign of the cross, genuflect, and address their priests as "Father."

Anglo-Catholicism revived religious orders in Anglicanism after a lapse of three hundred years. Eleven Episcopal orders for men and fourteen for women seek to follow the evangelical counsels of poverty, chastity, and obedience. These include the Holy Cross Order, the Society of St. John the Evangelist, and Episcopal Franciscans and Benedictines; and the Sisterhoods of St. Mary, the Holy Nativity, St. Margaret, St. Anne, and the Poor Clares. Besides the sisters, Episcopal deaconesses assist rectors in parish work or in any activity entrusted to them by a bishop. Anglican canon law recognizes the religious vocation of those men and women who bind themselves by vows in a religious community. The priests and monks conduct missions and retreats, engage in charitable and parish work, and publish magazines and tracts, while the Episcopal sisters generally operate girls' academies. One such Anglican community, the Society of the Atonement, entered the Catholic Church in a body in 1905.

With rules closely modeled on those of the Society of Jesus and the Congregation of the Mission (Lazarists), the Society of St. John the Evangelist was the first successful religious order for men in the Church of England. Popularly known as the Cowley Fathers, these Anglican religious came to the United States in 1870, five years after the founding of their community in England. Their spiritual formation centers around the Mass, the Divine Office, confession, and daily meditation.

Anglo-Catholics often find themselves in the awkward position of reinforcing the authority of Episcopal bishops whose views they consider heretical. One Episcopal bishop may encourage, another may tolerate, and another forbid such Anglo-Catholic practices as the use of incense and holy water in his diocese. The average Episcopalian seems to view the Anglo-Catholics with a mixture of suspicion and amusement. Many, of course, are completely unaware of the nature of Anglo-Catholicism and may not even have heard of Anglican religious orders.

Bishops govern the one hundred thirteen dioceses in the United States. They are elected by the clergy and laity of the diocese with the approval of the other bishops and a majority of the standing committees. Compulsory retirement for bishops is set at seventy-two. Every three years the House of Bishops and the House of Deputies convene in the General Convention. The latter House includes clerical and lay delegates.

The worldwide Anglican communion of seventy million Christians comprises a number of independent sister churches such as those of England, Wales, Scotland, Ireland, Canada, Australia and Tasmania, New Zealand, Burma and Ceylon, South Africa, the West Indies, and the United States. Besides these are the semi-autonomous churches of China, Japan, East and West Africa, and scattered dioceses and missions. The Anglican Church is largely confined to England and to former English colonies.

Every ten years the archbishop of Canterbury invites all Anglican bishops to meet at his residence, Lambeth Palace. The decisions of the Lambeth Conference do not bind independent churches or individual Anglicans.

The king or queen of England is technically the Supreme Governor of the Church of England (he or she automatically becomes head of the Presbyterian Church of Scotland after crossing the border from England). But the prime minister appoints the Archbishop of Canterbury, and the prime minister may be — and has been — a Unitarian, Baptist, or Presbyterian, and could conceivably be a Roman Catholic or Jew. When the church presented revisions to the Book of Common Prayer in 1927 and 1928, the House of Commons simply refused to accept the proposed revisions and the churchmen were helpless. The word "obey" was, however, deleted from the wedding ceremony.

The German church historian von Dollinger characterized the Anglican establishment in these words: "There is no church that is so completely and thoroughly as the Anglican the product and expression of the wants and wishes, the modes of thought and cast of character, not of a certain nationality, but of a fragment of a nation, namely, the rich, fashionable, and cultivated classes. It is the religion of deportment, of gentility, of clerical reserve."

Certainly in the United States the Episcopal Church counts a distinguished roster of communicants, among them George Washington, Alexander Hamilton, James Madison, John Marshall, Henry Clay, Patrick Henry, Daniel Webster, Admirals Farragut and Dewey, Robert E. Lee, Washington Irving, James Fenimore Cooper, Francis Scott Key, and Franklin D. Roosevelt.

Here as elsewhere the Episcopal Church caters to those in the upper class, and this class orientation limits its social ministry. Its settlement houses and home missions attract some of those in the poorer economic status. As in colonial times, it finds its chief strength on the Eastern seaboard.

Once labeled "the Republican party at prayer," the Episcopal Church has attempted to broaden its appeal in recent years. Many priests and laymen labor in inner-city missions among people far removed socially from the society leaders who also attend Episcopal churches.

Throughout its history in America, the Episcopal Church has refused to follow the Puritanical path of other Protestant churches and sects. Like the Lutheran Church, it has declined to join campaigns against liquor, tobacco, gambling, dancing, the theater, and the like.

The Episcopal Church has established relatively few colleges for its size: Hobart, Kenyon, St. Augustine, Trinity, and University of the

South. These, however, are first-class institutions. The church supports dozens of academies and prep schools, including some of the best-known in the country.

Twelve seminaries train Episcopal clergy. The church has been ordaining far more clergy than the number of parishes requires. Two-thirds of the seminarians come from non-Episcopal backgrounds, as do about half the active members of the church.

An international commission of Anglican and Roman Catholic scholars has been meeting for several decades to see what steps can be taken to reconcile Canterbury and Rome. The goal of the commission is "full organic union between our two communions."

This commission announced general agreement on the nature of the Eucharist in 1971 and on the character and function of the church in 1973. A later document envisaged the see of Rome as the center of unity in the Christian community, which would include a variety of legitimate diversities.

The Archbishop of Canterbury visited Pope John XXIII in 1960, and Archbishop F. Donald Coggan met with Paul VI in 1977. He surprised many by proposing intercommunion in the near future. Stressing the urgent need for evangelization, the archbishop said many people of good will outside the church are saying, "Talk to us about reconciliation when you yourself are reconciled."

Cordial relations between the Anglican communion and the Orthodox, Old Catholic, and Polish National Catholic Church have been strained by the decision to ordain women as priests. This action prompted the Polish National Catholic Church to sever ties with the Episcopal Church. The controversial ordination decision also put an obstacle in the path of eventual Anglican-Roman Catholic reunion. Intercommunion is observed with the Philippine Independent Church (Aglipayan), which traces its orders through Anglicanism, and with the Church of Sweden, a Lutheran body that preserved the episcopacy.

In 1982 Pope John Paul II became the first pope to visit Britain when he made a pastoral visit to England, Scotland, and Wales. He preached in the Anglican cathedral in Liverpool, declaring: "The restoration of unity among Christians is one of the main concerns of the church in the last part of the twentieth century. And this task is for all of us. No one can claim exception."

In this country the Episcopal Church (called the Protestant Episcopal Church until 1967) has faced many crises in recent decades. Some Episcopalians opposed the translation of the Book of Common Prayer into contemporary English in the 1970s. Many more objected to the ordination of women in 1976. At about the same time, the church adopted permissive attitudes toward abortion and divorce. Recent General Conventions have debated the ordination of active gays and lesbians to the priesthood and the blessing of same-sex unions.

Dissident Episcopalians have formed at least a dozen breakaway churches over these and other controversial issues: the American Episcopal Church, the Anglican Catholic Church, the Anglican Orthodox Church, the Diocese of Christ the King, and the Southern Episcopal Church, for example.

For these and other reasons, the Episcopal Church has seen a dramatic decline in membership. From a high of 3,647,000 communicants in 1966 the church has dropped to 2,364,000 members, one of the greatest declines of any denomination.

FURTHER READING

Albright, Raymond W., *A History of the Protestant Episcopal Church* (New York: Macmillan, 1964).

DeMille, George E., *The Episcopal Church Since 1900* (New York: Morehouse-Barlow, 1955).

Konolige, Kit and Frederica, *The Power of Their Glory: America's Ruling Class: The Episcopalians* (New York: Wyden Books, 1978).

Williamson, William B., *A Handbook for Episcopalians* (New York: Morehouse-Barlow, 1961).

CHAPTER 6

The Methodists

'All the World Is My Parish' — John Wesley

WHEN JOHN WESLEY LAUNCHED A REVIVAL OF EARLY EIGHTEENTH century Anglicanism, he began a religious movement that at one time reported the largest membership of any American church.

Today the world Methodist Council represents twenty-nine million members of some sixty churches that trace their heritage to Wesley and his brother Charles. Of these, more than half live in North America, which means Methodists are scattered rather thinly across the rest of the globe.

From a constituency of a few thousand at the time of the American Revolution (which Wesley himself opposed), the Methodists grew to make up the largest church in the United States by 1850. Later they were overtaken by the Roman Catholics and Southern Baptists, but the Methodist family of churches — the United Methodist Church (8,400,000 members), three predominantly black Methodist bodies, and several smaller churches — still ranks third in numbers.

Often characterized as the quintessential American denomination, the United Methodist Church has been accommodating in theology, optimistic, ecumenical, activist, and superbly organized. Over the years Methodism has moved from a church of the poor to what one Methodist bishop called "the chaplain to the middle class."

Some years ago *Life* magazine described the Methodist Church in these words: "In many ways it is our most characteristic church. It is short on theology, long on good works, brilliantly organized, primarily middle-class, frequently bigoted, incurably optimistic, zealously missionary and touchingly confident of the essential goodness of the man next door."

John Wesley, Methodism's chief founder, emerges as one of the noblest and most appealing figures in Protestantism. Catholics as well as Protestants admire his genuine piety, zeal, and organizational abilities. As the Catholic scholar Moehler has said: "Under other circumstances he would have been the founder of a religious order or a reforming pope."

Not noted as a theologian himself, Wesley founded a church that assigns to dogma a relatively minor role. If any attribute fits Methodism from Wesley's day to this, it is activism. The founder once remarked, "The distinguishing marks of a Methodist are not his opinions of any sort. His assenting to this or that scheme of religion, his embracing any particular set of notions . . . are all quite wide of the mark. Whosoever imagines that a Methodist is a man of such or such an opinion is grossly ignorant of the whole affair." Since 1924 American Methodists have been excused from subscribing to any statement of belief or creed. Instead they promise "loyalty to Christ."

Ranked with Luther and Calvin as one of the Big Three of the Protestant Reformation, Wesley differed from the other two in that the milieu in which he labored was not a Catholic but a Protestant land. Many of his admonitions have been forgotten, and certain developments in twentieth-century Methodism would certainly distress him, but we must turn to Wesley to gain an insight into this huge American denomination and the reasons for its success on this continent.

John was born in 1703 in a Church of England parsonage at Epworth. His mother, Susanna, had been one of twenty-five children; John was her fifteenth and Charles her eighteenth.

Life in the rector's large family was orderly and scholarly, and John in particular valued the guidance of his strong-willed mother. Eventually John and his brother Charles entered Oxford, where they organized a Holy Club in the amoral university atmosphere. Rules for the club included fasting on Wednesdays and Fridays, Bible reading, diligent study, two hours of daily prayer, frequent Communion, almsgiving, and visiting the poor and imprisoned. Adolescent scoffers labeled the members Bible Moths and Methodists because of their regular habits of prayer and strict self-discipline. John's favorite devotional book was *The Imitation of Christ* by Thomas à Kempis.

When the Holy Club, forerunner of Methodism, was disbanded the brothers volunteered for a mission to recently settled Georgia. Both had been ordained Anglican priests and adhered to the High Church party, which later nurtured the Oxford Movement. Their hope was to convert the Indians in James Oglethorpe's new American colony.

During the sea voyage to America, Wesley saw the lack of faith in his own heart as he witnessed a band of Moravians calmly singing psalms and hymns during a raging storm. These spiritual descendants of John Huss, the Czech heretic burned three centuries earlier, also had been sent from their German headquarters to spread the Christian message in the New World.

Wesley spent two unhappy years in Georgia. He found the Indians indifferent to the gospel. He himself was involved in the first of a series of unfortunate love affairs. Finally, a judicial body accused him of various church offenses such as insisting on confession before Holy Communion as dictated by his unbending High Church conscience. He returned home to England disappointed and frustrated. Wesley would later write: "I who went to America to convert others was never myself converted to God."

Still fascinated by the simple faith of the Moravians, he made contact with their missionaries in London. From them, especially from Peter Bohler, he accepted the doctrines of justification by faith alone and of instantaneous conversion.

One evening in 1738 Wesley attended a religious society meeting on Aldersgate Street. A lay preacher was reading Luther's preface to the Epistle to the Romans. "I felt my heart strangely warmed. I felt I did trust in Christ, Christ alone for salvation; and an assurance was given me that He had taken away my sins, even mine, and saved me from the law of sin and death," Wesley later related. This experience at 8:45 p.m. on May 24, 1738, marks the beginning of the Wesleyan revival in Protestantism. The young Anglican priest now felt he had received the same faith he had admired in the Moravian missionaries.

Few Anglican churches would admit the Wesleyan enthusiasts to their pulpits. Undeterred, the brothers took to the open air and began to preach in fields, barns, and private homes. They sought out the neo-pagan miners, factory workers, and slum-dwellers rather than the wealthy and offered them a warm, emotional message that had never come from the cold established church. They were joined by the eloquent George Whitefield, a Holy Clubber and the converted son of a saloonkeeper, who also had labored as an evangelist in Georgia but with greater success.

Wesley's idea was to form societies of the spiritually elite within the Anglican Church; the sole requirement for membership was an expressed "desire to flee from the wrath to come, and be saved from sins."

All three of the first Methodist preachers instructed their converts to remain within the Church of England. They had no desire to found another sect. Methodists were urged to receive the sacraments in the established church although they might gather to study Scripture, testify, sing hymns, and hear sermons in Methodist classes. They were encouraged to become a leaven in the Anglican Church, a sort of Protestant Third Order. Because few clergymen joined the revival, Wesley reluctantly consented to the use of licensed lay preachers.

Theology received scant attention. Practical religion was the goal. If any theological principle received emphasis, it was the insistence on man's free will in opposition to Calvinist predestination. This represented a return to Catholic doctrine, which denied that God elected some to salvation and damned others to hell.

Their doctrinal views approximated those of Jacob Arminius (1560-1609), a Dutch theologian who contradicted the absolute predestination taught at Geneva. Arminianism insisted that Christ died for all men, that He offers His grace to all men rather than to a body of the elect. As predestination has been relegated to the shelf in modern Presbyterian and Reformed theology, the sharp differences between Methodists and Calvinists have been blurred.

Assurance of salvation became another original Methodist tenet. Wesley taught that a man who has experienced a second blessing or entire sanctification can be absolutely sure he will reach heaven. Such a man can lose all inclination to evil and gain perfection in this life. Wesley never claimed this state of perfection for himself but insisted the attainment of perfection was possible for all Christians. Here the English Reformer parted company with both Luther and Calvin, who denied that man would ever reach a state in this life in which he could not fall into sin. Today the Wesleyan doctrine of perfection has been soft-pedaled by the United Methodist Church, but finds champions in the smaller Methodist bodies and the Holiness sects spawned by Methodism.

Because Wesley claimed a conversion he could pinpoint to the day, hour, and minute, he assumed that all genuine conversion is the instantaneous operation of the Holy Spirit. At one time Methodists expected all converts to testify to a miraculous and instantaneous conversion. This requirement has been abandoned. Adults joining the United Methodist Church today need not relate their spiritual experience nor admit to having such an experience.

From the night of the Aldersgate meeting until his death at eighty-eight, Wesley followed a backbreaking schedule of preaching, writing, traveling, and organizing his Methodist classes. Initially he was assisted by his Moravian friends, and he even made a trip to their headquarters at Herrnhut to observe their way of life firsthand. Within a few years he had broken with the Moravians over the practice of "stillness." In stillness the brethren suspended all work, study, and prayer and waited for a special blessing from God. The Wesley brothers also disagreed with Whitefield when he turned to Calvinism and began to mix Methodism and predestination.

Once asked by what authority he dared to preach in the open fields as a Church of England priest, Wesley replied, "To save souls is my vocation; all the world is my parish." He preached 42,000 sermons and covered an estimated 250,000 miles on foot and horseback throughout the British Isles. The democratic structure of Methodism was admittedly a facade during his lifetime; he ruled his society as an ecclesiastical dictator.

Never a successful suitor, Wesley finally married a shrewish widow with four children. Quarrels and humiliations marked the match, and they separated. He learned of his wife's death only after the funeral. It has been said that his only child was Methodism.

John's relations with his more conservative brother grew strained as he drifted further from the High Church orbit, which Charles never left. While Charles devoutly believed in the Real Presence and the apostolic succession, his older brother came to accept a symbolic interpretation of the Eucharist and undertook to ordain priests himself. Among Charles' sixty-five hundred hymns are the popular "Hark, the Herald Angels Sing" and "Jesus, Lover of My Soul." He has been called the poet of the revival; John, the organizer; and Whitefield, the orator.

Critics commonly charged the Wesleys with being Jesuits in disguise, bent on subverting the established church to the interests of the papacy. Certainly the Wesleys restored the positive principles of the Reformation to English and continental Protestantism and stripped Protestantism of its negative features. They opposed extrinsic justification, predestination in the Calvinist sense, and the depreciation of good works. To this extent the revival may be considered a return to the traditional Catholic positions.

Furthermore, they urged fasting and abstinence, daily prayer and devotions, and frequent Communion. They accorded an importance to good works that was foreign to Lutheranism. They not only taught that man is changed by justification and sanctification, but that he could attain perfection — a far cry from Luther's "sinful and sinning" Christian. Most of these Catholic inclinations were diluted and lost as Methodism accommodated the conditions of the American frontier.

Neither John nor Charles had much firsthand contact with Roman Catholicism; John had predicted the papacy would fall in the third decade of the nineteenth century. Charles' son Samuel became a Catholic at eighteen and was known as one of the foremost church organists in English history.

The first authorized Methodist missionaries were dispatched to the colonies in 1769, only ten years before the American Revolution and fully one hundred fifty years after the other denominations had staked out their claims. Francis Asbury stands as the greatest figure in American Methodism, and to his foresight and energy must be credited much of the amazing growth of this tardy denomination. Like Wesley he spent a great part of his life in the saddle. He perfected the system of circuit riders, devoted lay preachers who brought religion to the people in isolated cabins and frontier towns. Equipped only with Bible, hymn book, and a set of sermons, the riders preached six days a week, urging all who would listen to "flee from the wrath to come." Their main audiences were the poor and underprivileged. They conserved the effects of their conversions by setting up classes under class leaders.

Methodism suffered a near-fatal setback during the Revolution even though it gained some numerical strength. Many colonists looked on Methodism as an English importation, and their suspicions were buttressed by two pamphlets in which Wesley disowned the agitation for independence. "We Methodists are no republicans and never intend to be," wrote Wesley. All but one of the Methodist preachers sent to America by Wesley were Tories who fled to Canada or England during the war.

Discredited by their pro-British attitude during the conflict, the Methodists retained strength below the Mason and Dixon Line and recouped losses by concentrating on the expanding frontier. Here their zealous lay preachers could outnumber the college-trained Congregationalist, Episcopal, and Presbyterian ministers. Here their proclamation of man's free will made more sense to the independent frontiersman than the fatalism of Calvin. When Bishop Asbury began his preaching, Methodism counted scarcely a few hundred members in the American colonies; at his death he could survey a thriving church of two hundred thousand souls.

As in England, the Methodists were directed to receive baptism and Holy Communion from Episcopal priests. They soon petitioned to receive the sacraments from the same Methodist preachers who visited their homes and conducted their worship services. The Bishop of London refused to ordain preachers in the colonies, so in 1784 Wesley assumed the power to ordain ministers himself. When he ordained two men and sent them to America, Methodism moved from the status of a revival movement in Anglicanism to that of a separate church.

He justified his action by claiming that bishops and presbyters were identical in the primitive church, therefore priests such as himself could lawfully ordain other priests. He then consecrated Thomas Coke as superintendent for the Methodists in the United States, and Coke in turn consecrated Asbury. Both men assumed the additional title of bishop over Wesley's ineffective protests. Brother Charles dissociated himself from these actions and declared, "I can scarcely believe that in his eighty-second year my brother, my old, intimate friend and companion, should have assumed the episcopal character, ordained elders, consecrated a bishop, and sent him to ordain our elder preachers in America. . . . My brother has put an indelible stigma upon his name."

The Methodist Episcopal Church was organized officially at the Christmas Conference of sixty preachers in Baltimore in 1784. Wesley died proclaiming his loyalty to the church of which he was a priest: "I live and die a member of the Church of England, and none who regard my judgment will ever separate from it."

Wesley had prepared an abridgment of the Anglican Thirty-nine Articles that was accepted as a doctrinal statement by the Americans. They added another article to Wesley's twenty-four that recognized the independence of the colonies. Among other doctrines, the articles affirmed justification by faith, the sufficiency of the Scriptures, and the baptism of infants. "The Romish doctrine concerning purgatory, pardon, worshiping and adoration, as well of images as of relics, and also invocation of saints, is a fond thing, vainly invented, and grounded upon no warrant of scripture, but repugnant to the Word of God," according to the Wesleyan articles. The sacrifice of the Mass was termed a "blasphemous fable and dangerous deceit." Other sources of Methodist belief are Wesley's *Notes on the New Testament* and fifty-three collected sermons.

At the 1968 General Conference in Dallas, the United Methodist Church agreed to remove from its Articles of Religion "any derogatory references to the Roman Catholic Church."

A demand for greater lay participation in church government led to the formation of the Methodist Protestant Church in 1830. Slavery drove a deeper wedge into Methodism in 1844 when the Southerners seceded and formed the Methodist Episcopal Church, South. Reunion of the three branches was not realized until 1939, although no doctrinal issues were involved. At this time the southern faction was pacified by constructing a segregated Central Jurisdiction for 340,000 black members regardless of place of residence. The five white jurisdictions were mapped out on a geographical basis. This racial compromise struck many Methodists as a betrayal of Christian brotherhood, and the 1956 General Conference adopted a constitutional amendment to dissolve the black jurisdiction gradually.

The United Methodist Church came into existence in 1968 when the Methodist Church and the Evangelical United Brethren Church formed one church.

The reluctance of American Methodist bishops to sanction preaching in the German language had led to the formation of two independent German Methodist denominations: the United Brethren in Christ and the Evangelical Church. These two bodies, similar in doctrine, polity, and national origin, merged in 1946 to form the Evangelical United Brethren Church.

Philip Otterbein studied for the Reformed ministry in Germany and came to America in 1752. He began to preach Arminian doctrines and to conduct revivals and prayer meetings with Martin Boehm, a Swiss Mennonite preacher. Had there been no language problem, their converts would have been absorbed into Methodism. As it was, they formed their own United Brethren Church in 1800 with themselves as bishops. A minority seceded in 1889. The twenty-three thousand members of the United Brethren in Christ oppose secret societies and participation in war.

A development parallel to that of the United Brethren led to the founding of the Evangelical Church, once called the Evangelical Association. Jacob Albright, an ex-Lutheran, began to preach in eastern Pennsylvania, but his plan for a German Methodist branch was vetoed by the Methodist hierarchy. In 1803 he organized a separate church whose adherents were variously known as Albright people or Brethren or German Methodists. The greatest period of expansion of this body was during the administration of Bishop John Seybert, elected in 1839. A serious schism disrupted the denomination from 1894 to 1922, when the two factions reunited in the Evangelical Church.

Both the United Brethren and the Evangelicals generally confined their evangelism to the German population in this country. Of course, most of their converts came from Lutheran, Reformed, or Mennonite backgrounds. At the time of the merger in 1946 the United Brethren reported 450,000 members and the Evangelicals about half that number. By the time of the 1968 merger with the Methodist Church, the EUB Church was reporting 758,000 members, with particular strength in Pennsylvania.

The great majority of black Methodists are found in separate denominations outside the United Methodist Church, such as the African Methodist Episcopal Church, the Christian Methodist Episcopal Church, and the African Methodist Episcopal Zion Church. Together they enroll about four million members. Both the A.M.E. and A.M.E. Zion churches were organized before 1800 by black Methodists who resented discrimination by their white coreligionists. The C.M.E. church incorporated the black segment of the Methodist Episcopal Church, South, after the Civil War. These churches follow the same theology and polity as the United Methodist Church, but little intercourse exists between white and black churches.

By the middle of the nineteenth century most Methodists had become fairly prosperous and conservative. Methodism has followed the typical pattern from sect to church even though from the beginning it lacked two sectarian characteristics: congregational government and adult baptism. The upper middle class now dominates the United Methodist Church, once the church of the English workingman.

Puritan values helped American Methodists improve their economic and social status. As they practiced the virtues of sobriety, thrift, and industry, they moved from the lower to the middle class. Method-

ist pews often filled with bank presidents, professors, and businessmen; the factory worker and small farmer gravitated toward the Pentecostal and Holiness churches. Five Methodists have occupied the
White House: James Polk, Ulysses Grant, Rutherford B. Hayes, William McKinley, and George W. Bush.

A dozen smaller Methodist sects totaling about 190,000 members
include the Free Methodist Church, which still emphasizes entire sanctification and elects superintendents instead of bishops, and the equally
strict Wesleyan Church.

No religious body of Christians outside the Catholic Church is as
highly and efficiently organized as the United Methodist Church. Organizational problems and the social gospel receive the attention that
other churches direct toward theology and liturgy. Laymen play a large
part in Methodist projects, and a layman with any special talent can
find a suitable niche in Methodism.

National committees in the church are set up for missions, the
local church, education, evangelism, lay activities, Christian social relations, temperance, world peace, social and economic relations, hospitals and homes, chaplains, and pensions. Methodism is big business,
with more than $4 billion invested in thirty-six thousand churches
and institutions.

Despite its efficiency, the Methodist Church has not been growing. In fact it reports 2,600,000 fewer members now than before the
merger with the EUB church.

Full authority in church matters rests with the General Conference. This body, consisting of equal numbers of locally elected laymen
and ministers, meets every four years. Laymen were first admitted in
1872; before this the complaint of the Methodist Protestant faction
was probably justified. General Conference decisions are incorporated
in the 890-page *Discipline*, which roughly corresponds to the Code of
Canon Law.

Personal moral standards rule out alcohol and tobacco, although
lay members who indulge are no longer excommunicated. At one time
Methodism in this country also banned dancing, card playing, all forms

of gambling, and the theater, but these are now tolerated. Methodists led in the formation of the Women's Christian Temperance Union and the Anti-Saloon League and take a large share of the credit for the 18th Amendment and the Great Experiment. The United Methodist Church still officially lobbies for national prohibition, condemns beer and cigarette advertising on radio and television, and tries to ban beer from army and navy establishments.

One of Wesley's rules for his Methodist societies was directed against "drunkenness, buying or selling spirituous liquors, or drinking them, unless in cases of extreme necessity." Wesley himself drank beer and wine but not hard liquor. The total abstinence movement within the church started only about one hundred twenty years ago; before that, temperance meant moderation in drink.

Among Protestant denominations, Methodists take first place in hospitals and colleges. Some of their one hundred colleges and universities have all but severed ties with the denominations, but others remain definitely Methodist: Syracuse, Boston, Emory, Duke, Drew, Denver, and Southern Methodist. The church operates three hundred sixty schools and institutions of higher learning overseas. Methodists established the Goodwill Industries in 1907 to help handicapped persons help themselves by repairing and selling old furniture and clothes. The United Methodist Church runs seventy-two hospitals in the United States.

Nowadays most Methodist ministers who become full members of the annual conference hold a bachelor of divinity degree. Methodism also still depends on lay preachers whose training is received via correspondence and short courses. A ministerial candidate may attend any of the thirteen seminaries maintained by the church, among which are Garrett, Drew, Duke, Candler, Perkins, and Boston.

Hundreds of women are serving as Methodist ministers, but few have become pastors. The 1956 General Conference accorded full clergy rights to women. The several hundred deaconesses in this country receive a fixed salary, regular leaves of absence, and provisions for retirement. The Methodist deaconess movement has experienced little growth in recent years, but deaconesses operate a number of hospitals and homes.

Bishops are elected; their main duties are administrative. The forty-five active U.S. bishops ordain ministers, appoint them to parishes, and supervise church activities in their areas. The bishops are chosen at the Jurisdictional Conferences, consecrated by three bishops, and expected to retire between sixty-six and seventy. The Council of Bishops serves as the executive branch of Methodism, just as the General Conference is the chief legislative branch. Methodists hold that the difference between a bishop and an ordinary minister is purely one of administrative responsibility.

Wesley prepared a revised liturgy from the Book of Common Prayer, but it was never widely adopted. Methodists are liturgical individualists who resist all attempts to impose a uniform pattern of worship on the local congregation. As in most Protestant denominations, a trend toward beauty in the worship service has reintroduced gowns, candles, crosses, and a central altar.

A typical form of worship would be: call to worship, hymn, prayer of confession, silent meditation, words of assurance, Lord's Prayer, anthem, responsive reading, *Gloria Patri*, affirmation of faith, Scripture lesson, pastoral prayer, offertory, hymn, sermon, prayer, invitation to Christian discipleship, doxology, benediction, silent prayer, and postlude. An alternate form is used when the Lord's Supper is observed. One form of Sunday worship and two forms for the Lord's Supper are presented in the *Discipline*, but the local church need not use these liturgies.

Weekly Communion was one of Wesley's frequent spiritual prescriptions, but few Methodist churches today observe the Lord's Supper more often than quarterly or monthly. The communicants kneel at the altar rail and receive bread and grape juice in a Communion service. The Lord's Supper is considered a memorial: "The body of Christ is given, taken, and eaten in the Supper, only after a heavenly and spiritual manner." Yet some Methodists believe in the Real Presence and hold a High Church view of the sacrament.

Methodists deny that baptism produces sanctifying grace or takes away sin. The sacrament may be administered by sprinkling, pouring, or immersion, although sprinkling is most widespread. Infants as well as adults are baptized. Confirmation, which is not believed to be sacramental, is conferred by ministers.

The great bulk of Methodists reside in the United States. Within a few years after the founder's death, British Methodism split into half a dozen sects. These groups developed a nonepiscopal form of church government and never emphasized the Puritan concern for personal morals that has preoccupied their American cousins. The world's twenty-nine million Methodists cooperate in the World Methodist Conference.

Successful itself in reuniting the three main Wesleyan bodies, the United Methodist Church takes an active and prominent role in the ecumenical movement. A Methodist layman, Dr. John R. Mott, was instrumental in calling the World Missionary Conference in Edinburgh in 1910, which turned out to be the beginning of the Protestant ecumenical movement.

Methodism is distantly related to a score of other denominations, Arminian in doctrine and sometimes claiming the authentic mantle of Wesley for themselves: the Salvation Army, countless Holiness sects, and the General Baptists.

In many respects the Wesleyan revival represented a distinct reversal of Protestant direction in the eighteenth century. Wesley's emphasis on free will, his insistence on the need for good works, his doctrine of conversion, his encouragement of fasting and abstinence, frequent Communion, and the value of a personal devotional life set early Methodism on a path verging toward Catholicism.

Wesley himself, however, knew little of Catholic doctrine, and his picture of the sacraments and the theology of the Roman Catholic Church was often a caricature. His estrangement from the High Church position of his youth and the transplanting of Methodism to the American frontier carried the movement more directly into the Protestant camp.

Fruitful ecumenical dialogues have been held since 1970 by the United Methodist Church and the Roman Catholic Church.

The United Methodist Church in the early twenty-first century faces a number of problems: a shrinking membership base, an aging constituency (the average age of members is fifty-five), and a contentious discussion on the ordination of active gays and lesbians and the blessing of same-sex unions. Yet the church maintains a presence in almost every city and village in the United States, and despite its challenges, tries to rekindle the fires set by the Wesleys and Francis Asbury.

FURTHER READING

Davies, Rupert E., *Methodism* (Baltimore: Penguin Books, 1963).

Ferguson, Charles W., *Organizing to Beat the Devil.* (Garden City, N.Y.: Doubleday, 1971).

Langford, Thomas A., ed., *Doctrine and Theology in the United Methodist Church* (Nashville: Kingswood Books, 1991).

Outler, Albert C., *John Wesley* (New York: Oxford University Press, 1964).

Richardson, Harry, *Dark Salvation: The Story of Methodism As It Developed Among Blacks in America* (New York: Anchor, 1976).

CHAPTER 7

The Baptists

'No Human Founder, No Human Authority, No Human Creed'

AFTER THE REVEREND BILLY GRAHAM DELIVERED THE INVOCATION, Gov. Bill Clinton of Arkansas took the oath of office as the forty-second president of the United States. Sen. Albert Gore was sworn in as vice president. Jimmy Carter, the thirty-ninth president and last Democrat to occupy the White House, sat a few feet away. These four men had at least one thing in common — they were all Southern Baptists.

Like almost sixteen million other Americans, they belonged to churches affiliated with the Southern Baptist Convention, the largest Protestant denomination in the country. Only the sixty-two million Roman Catholics count more U.S. adherents. Taken together, the two dozen Baptist denominations in the United States comprise the largest faith family in American Protestantism.

While the older Episcopal, Presbyterian, and United Church of Christ (Congregational) churches have suffered precipitous declines in membership in recent decades, the Southern Baptists continue to grow. They report three times as many members as they did fifty years ago and are establishing three new congregations every day.

Originally confined to the states of the old Confederacy, the Southern Baptists now support churches in all fifty states and in many foreign countries. Meanwhile their cousins in the American Baptist Churches, once known as the Northern Baptists, have mirrored the membership decline of the other mainline denominations.

Baptists carry the Protestant principle of justification by faith alone to its logical conclusion. Because infants are incapable of such an act of faith, they cannot receive the grace of baptism. Hence, only those able to make a profession of faith in Christ may be admitted to baptism.

Likewise, because the Baptists deny the sacramental character of baptism in favor of a symbolic interpretation, they see immersion as the most dramatic symbol of burial and rebirth in Christ. Immersion is the ancient form of baptism and was practiced by the Latin rite of the Catholic Church until the twelfth century.

To define a Baptist, we may say he is a follower of Jesus Christ who has been baptized by immersion and belongs to a local congregation identified by the name *Baptist*. Some Baptists would add that he must be committed to the Baptist principles of religious liberty.

Besides baptism by immersion, perhaps the most distinctive characteristic of the Southern Baptists has been the autonomy of the local congregation. No outside authority can dictate to a local Baptist church, which can adopt its own constitution and bylaws, set liturgical forms, ordain pastors and deacons, hire and fire pastors, and expel errant members. The forty-one thousand churches voluntarily support missions, seminaries and agencies of the SBC but recognize no ecclesiastical authority beyond the local church.

Although they can now be found in every state of the union, Southern Baptists completely dominate the religious life of a dozen southern and southwestern states. More than 2,600,000 Southern Baptists live in Texas alone, and there are at least a million each in Georgia, North Carolina, and Tennessee. In 1942 California had only forty-one SBC churches; it now reports more than one thousand. In 1950 the Southern Baptists abrogated the gentlemen's agreement with the Northern Baptists and began to expand their territory above the Mason-Dixon line.

Many Southern Baptist churches in rural areas count only one hundred or two hundred members and may be pastored by a minister with no education beyond high school. But in the larger cities of the South, a Baptist church may take up an entire city block. The First Baptist Church in Dallas lists twenty-two thousand members.

Baptists view the Protestant Reformation as a job only half-done. Luther and Calvin, they believe, allowed too many unbiblical practices and beliefs to remain — such as infant baptism — to merit the allegiance of Bible-believing Christians. Baptists see the genuine Reformation as taking place in America with the rise of the Baptist movement. This was a movement that did away with all creeds, infant baptism, sacraments, the episcopal and presbyterial systems of church government, ritual in worship, and what Baptists regard as unscriptural modes of baptism.

Each Baptist congregation hires and fires its minister, sets its own worship patterns, and examines and baptizes members. In some congregations, the members choose and ordain their own ministers, although in others the ordination is performed by a group of Baptist churches.

Every third Protestant in the United States is a Baptist. If the Baptists counted infants and unbaptized children as members, they would almost equal the number of Roman Catholics in the United States. About a third of Baptists are black, and the bulk of black and white members live in the South. In Alabama, Georgia, and Mississippi almost 60 percent of all church members are Southern Baptists. Baptists constitute a majority of church members in ten of eleven states of the old Confederacy. The emergence of this radical, independent sect into a position of numerical superiority in this country has influenced American Protestantism in the direction of individualism, anti-ritualism, and sectarianism.

Most Baptists belong to one of the four largest groups: the American Baptist Churches in the U.S.A. (called Northern Baptist until 1950) with 1,500,000 members; the Southern Baptist Convention with more than 15,700,000; the National Baptist Convention of the U.S.A., Inc., the original black organization, claims 5,500,000; and a 1916 offshoot of the latter organization, the National Baptist Convention of America, which reports 3,500,000. Twenty-three other Baptist groups are represented in this country, many of them claiming only a handful of adherents.

The first Christian congregation, some Baptists believe, was the First Baptist Church of Jerusalem. But history does not tell us of any organized Baptist groups until the early seventeenth century. Their spiritual ancestors, once removed, were the Anabaptists of Reformation times who despaired of the theological positions of Luther, Zwingli, and Calvin. They yearned for a church of saints, not a church of saints and sinners. These Anabaptists called for a voluntary association of adult Christians rather than a state church into which all citizens were born and baptized. These early radical reformers also agitated for separation of church and state, complete sovereignty of the local congregation, communal living, pacifism, and biblical literalism. They were persecuted by both Protestants and Catholics. By 1535 the Anabaptist movement had been largely suppressed by force except for a remnant gathered by the ex-priest Menno Simons.

A refugee congregation of English Separatists in Amsterdam accepted the doctrine of baptism of believers from the Mennonites around 1607. John Smythe and Thomas Helwys shepherded this first English Baptist congregation in Holland, but Smythe himself left to join the Mennonites. A handful returned to England with Helwys and carried their Baptist principles with them. As these pioneer Baptists pondered the symbolic meaning of baptism, they began to prefer immersion rather than the pouring mode used by the Mennonites. The first church to baptize by immersion was a London congregation in 1638. Theologically most of the original English Baptists were Arminian, but Baptists of this persuasion now form a small minority because most Baptists have adopted a more or less Calvinist theology.

Some names that stand out in the history of the English Baptist movement are John Bunyan, author of *Pilgrim's Progress;* John Milton of *Paradise Lost;* Daniel Defoe, the creator of *Robinson Crusoe;* and William Carey, the pioneer Protestant missionary to India.

Roger Williams, the founder of the first Baptist church in America, remained a Baptist for only four months. A Nonconformist clergyman, he left England in 1630 and sought religious freedom in the Puritan Massachusetts Bay colony. Instead of freedom he found himself accused of heresy and exiled. American Indians gave him shelter, and he founded a settlement of his own at Providence. In 1639 he became convinced of the Baptist position and was rebaptized, but within a few months he resigned his pastorate of this first Baptist church in the New World. Williams continued to search for religious truth until his death.

Little expansion was undertaken during the first century of the Baptist movement in America. The Baptists would register tremendous gains in the late eighteenth and the nineteenth centuries by an appeal to the lower classes, black citizens, frontiersmen, and Southerners. Thousands of unschooled Baptist preachers carried the gospel to the settler in his cabin. These preacher-farmers found a rich soil on America's frontier for their principles of separation of church and state, church democracy, simple worship services, and freedom of conscience. They offered no creeds but the Bible itself. Defections by the Disciples and the Adventists amounted to nothing more than temporary setbacks to Baptist growth.

The Baptists brought the Christian gospel to men white or black. Today most black Americans are either Baptists or Methodists. Reverend Martin Luther King, Jr., pastored black Baptist churches in Montgomery, Ala., and Atlanta before spearheading the civil-rights movement in the 1960s.

Often called the problem child of American Protestantism, the Southern Baptist Convention is conservative and cautious in its cooperation with other churches. Statistics indicate it is the fastest growing major denomination; an average of a thousand new members are baptized every day. This denomination, today nearly 16 million strong, has grown from 325,000 in 1845, the year of its secession from the northern group over the issue of slavery.

The big southern slaveholders were usually Episcopalians or Presbyterians, but the Baptists lined up with them in opposition to abolition. When the Baptist Foreign Missions Society refused to appoint any slaveholder as a missionary, the southern churches seceded and formed their own convention. The Reverend Richard Furman, who wielded great influence in the South, declared that "the right of holding slaves is clearly established in the Holy Scriptures, both by precept and example."

In 1950 the Southern Baptists decided to expand their evangelistic efforts to all states of the Union. This strained relations with the Northern Baptists but transformed the Southern Baptist Church from a regional to a national one. For example, there are now dozens of Southern Baptist churches in the New York City area and more than one thousand in California. These churches attract not only transplanted Southerners but Baptists unhappy about the liberalism or tepidity of former church homes. In turn the American (Northern) Baptists have started congregations in such cities as Richmond, Dallas, and Tulsa.

In 1963 the Southern Baptist Church overtook the United Methodist Church as the largest single Protestant church in the nation. Its aggressive evangelistic campaigns, its well-organized Sunday school program, and its frank espousal of the "old-time religion" help to explain its success. Billy Graham, a Southern Baptist minister, succeeded Billy Sunday as America's best-known revivalist.

Many people hold outdated stereotypes of the Southern Baptists. James Sullivan, a recent president of the SBC, commented: "A world that had thought we were an ignorant, barefooted, one-galluffed lot was jarred out of its seat when it found out that our voluntary gifts in a year are approximately $1.5 billion, and that on an average Sunday our churches baptize about three times as many people as were baptized at Pentecost." They now operate the largest religious publishing house in the world and the largest seminary. As the New South has taken its place in education, wealth, and power, so have the Southern Baptists.

Aggressively missionary-minded, the Southern Baptists support three thousand missionaries in home missions; special efforts are made to convert migrant workers, Puerto Ricans, American Indians, Mexican Americans, and Jews. Their twenty-nine hundred foreign missionaries labor in eighty countries on four continents, with the largest mission fields in Japan, Nigeria, and Brazil.

Southern Baptists traditionally support complete separation of church and state but find no paradox in vigorous efforts to impose community blue laws, enforce prohibition, fight the legalization of gambling, or stop the teaching of evolution in public schools.

The convention meets once each year, but its decisions cannot commit the denomination, any congregations, or any individual Baptist to a particular position. As many as fifteen thousand "messengers" represent local churches at these annual meetings.

In contrast to the fast-growing SBC, the American (Northern) Baptist Churches in the U.S.A. have not kept up with population growth. Their 1,535,000 members are outnumbered by the Southern Baptists in Texas alone. The American Baptists have been more liberal, ecumenical, and socially involved than their southern brothers.

Northern Baptists founded such institutions as the University of Chicago, Carleton, Colby, Denison, and Kalamazoo. American Baptists support about three hundred missionaries in Burma, India, Bengal, Thailand, Japan, Okinawa, and the Philippines.

Ministers and laity switch allegiance from northern to southern branches of the Baptist family with a minimum of inconvenience, but differences remain in such things as open communion, ecumenism, and theology. Reunion seems doubtful.

Perhaps the best-known Baptist preacher in the nation besides Billy Graham is the Reverend Jerry Falwell, founder of the Moral Majority and pastor of the Thomas Road Baptist Church in Lynchburg, Va. His church does not belong to the SBC but represents a growing number of congregations that are independent of any larger Baptist affiliation. Many of these independent Baptist churches make effective use of radio and TV, operate fleets of buses for Sunday school, build huge church buildings, and grow through the ministry of charismatic and flamboyant preachers.

About seven million Baptists live outside the United States. Some of the larger bodies are found in Brazil (850,000), Nigeria (615,000), Burma (475,000), Korea (325,000), Zaire (534,000), and India (more than 1 million). Hundreds of thousands of Baptists live in the former Soviet Union.

Besides the major Baptist bodies, a score of smaller groups attract Baptists with a strong ethnic background or a dissatisfaction with the theological stance of the larger churches.

Two Baptist groups were formed to minister to converts from German and Swedish backgrounds. One is the North American Baptist Conference, with forty-four thousand members of German ancestry; the other is the Baptist General Conference, which was originally entirely Swedish. Today the BGC counts 134,000 members, but only about half its pastors are Swedish Americans. This small conference sends one hundred forty missionaries overseas.

Other Baptist churches serve members of French, Hungarian, Danish, Italian, Finnish, Norwegian, Polish, Romanian, Jewish, Mexican, and Czech ancestry. Some are bilingual; others conduct all services in a foreign language.

A few Baptists groups go back to the seventeenth and eighteenth centuries. The Seventh Day Baptists observe Saturday rather than Sunday as the day of rest and worship. Their first congregation was established in Newport, R.I., in 1672; they now number only fifty-two hundred.

With the slogan "Free grace, free will, and free salvation," the Free Will Baptists are strongly anti-Calvinist. They started in North Carolina around 1727. The issue of slavery split the Free Will Baptists, and in 1910 those above the Mason-Dixon Line merged with the Northern Baptists. Those in the South continued their separate existence and now number 197,000. Black members organized the United Free Will Baptist Church.

The seventy-two thousand Primitive Baptists oppose Sunday schools, mission societies, denominational organizations, and youth groups. They date their history to the early nineteenth century. Also known as "Hard Shell," "Anti-mission," and "Old School," they are strongly Calvinist in their theology. They claim to be completely faithful to the New Testament, so much so that if the Bible has no record of mission societies in apostolic times, there should be no such innovations in the twentieth century. Their ministers need no college or seminary training, and their churches usually serve the people of the backwoods areas of the South. The National Primitive Baptist convention is the black counterpart and claims a membership of 250,000.

The seventy-two thousand General Baptists, who formed their organization in 1870, represent the Arminian rather than the Calvinist theological orientation. Their seven hundred ninety churches in the South and Midwest admit all.

Catholics and Eastern Orthodox along with Luther, Calvin, and the Anglican divines allowed the baptism of infants who would later be expected to affirm the decision made by their godparents and parents. Some Catholics today may be surprised to learn that immersion is the preferred form of Catholic baptism. The General Introduction to Christian Initiation states: "Either the rite of immersion, which is more suitable as a symbol of the participation in the death and resurrection of Christ, or the rite of infusion may lawfully be used in the celebration of baptism."

Some newer Roman Catholic churches have been equipped with baptismal pools, but infusion (pouring) is still the more common method. Baptists usually immerse new members in baptisteries behind the pulpit, but they also use lakes and ponds, swimming pools, bathtubs, and hospital whirlpools. Someone has even devised a portable baptistery that can be taken to a prison.

In a recent year 12 percent of baptisms in SBC churches were administered to children six to eight years old and another 20 percent to those nine to twelve. Obviously these were not adults, but Baptists believe they are old enough to be "born again" and give the testimony required of all who seek baptism.

Except for some Modernists in the northern branch, the Baptists preach Christianity based firmly on the divinity of Christ and the central facts of His incarnation and redemption of mankind. They accept the doctrines of the Trinity, the virgin birth, original sin, heaven, and hell. In some areas they have carried Protestant principles to conclusions the original Reformers hesitated to draw. Unlike some denominations that have catered to the upper classes, the Baptists have worked with the humble people and have developed a spirit of personal evangelism. Estimates have placed two-thirds of the Baptists in the lower economic class. Yet the Rockefellers and a number of Texas oil barons also claim the Baptist label.

Given the extreme independence of each Southern Baptist church and the dedication to "soul competency" — the accountability of each believer to achieve his or her salvation without the mediation of church or sacraments — the question becomes: "Can someone believe anything and still be considered a Baptist?"

For a creedless church, the Baptist Faith and Message statement adopted at the 1963 convention is as close to a creed as the Southern Baptist Church is likely to come. Like any other Baptist confession, it has no binding force over a local church but reflects the beliefs of most Southern Baptists. The SBC affirms its belief in the priesthood of all believers but warns "It is, of course, a perversion of this doctrine to say that all views are equally valid, that you can believe just anything and still be a Baptist, or that the pastor has no unique leadership role."

The Baptist Faith and Message statement explains: "Baptists emphasize the soul's competency before God, freedom in religion, and the priesthood of the believer. However, this emphasis should not be interpreted to mean that there is an absence of certain definite doctrines that Baptists believe, cherish, and with which they have been and are now closely identified."

Catholics, Baptists and most moderate and conservative Protestants would share the same beliefs in God, the Trinity, heaven and hell, the incarnation and virgin birth, and Christ's resurrection from the dead. Some Christians would part company with the Baptists on their insistence on the complete autonomy of the local church, their rejection of the sacraments, the proper age and mode of baptism, and other practices.

A local Baptist congregation that somehow adopted a confession of faith that denied, say, the Trinity or the resurrection would find itself outside the pale of the SBC. Tension arises when a local church favors a position that disturbs a majority of other Southern Baptists but is not clearly heterodox. Some SBC churches have ordained women, for example, but most Southern Baptists disapprove; at least five hundred women have been ordained but only about thirty serve as pastors. A few churches have embraced Pentecostal practices such as speaking in tongues and spiritual healing that find little favor among their fellow Baptists. Two SBC churches were recently expelled for asserting that homosexuality is a valid lifestyle for Christians.

Each Baptist church sets its own form of Sunday worship, but the elements are common: prayers, hymns, a sermon, an offering and usually an invitation to nonmembers to come forward and accept Jesus as their savior. Baptists observe baptism and the Lord's Supper because they believe these actions were commanded by Jesus Christ. They are called ordinances rather than sacraments. Baptists, despite their name, do not consider baptism necessary for salvation. What is necessary is to be "born again," to experience in a personal way the assurance of salvation and to profess this faith. Only then can a believer ask for baptism.

All those who are born again, say the Baptists, are assured of their salvation and can never fall away from the state of grace. Putting it in a few words, they would say: "Once saved, always saved."

A local church will celebrate the Lord's Supper on a quarterly or sometimes monthly basis. This is seen as a symbolic act of obedience and a memorial. The doctrine of the Real Presence of Christ in the Eucharist as understood in Catholic Orthodox, Anglican and Lutheran churches is completely foreign to Baptist thinking.

As might be expected, the SBC promotes a conservative code of sexual morality. It teaches that God's plan for marriage is the lifelong union of one man and one woman but allows divorce in some situations.

In general the SBC condemns abortion. "Procreation is a gift from God, a precious trust reserved for marriage. At the moment of conception, a new being enters the universe, a human being, a being created in God's image. This human being deserves our protection, whatever the circumstances of conception." Elaborating on this official position, the Baptist author C. Brownlow Hastings explains: " . . . an abortion is justified only under very serious conditions: when there is a clear threat to the health or life of the mother or possibly in the case of a pregnancy as a result of incest or rape or manifest deformity of the fetus — cases that are extremely rare." *(Introducing Southern Baptists, pp.142-143).* Southern Baptists see birth control as simply a medical matter.

The SBC rejects homosexuality as a "valid alternative lifestyle" because the Bible condemns it as a sin. "It is not, however, unforgivable sin."

Tensions grew in the SBC when conservatives (called Fundamentalists by their opponents) took control of the denomination in 1979. The conservatives used biblical innerancy as the litmus test for Baptist loyalty and began to purge seminary officials and faculty who failed the test. By innerancy they meant that not only were the Scriptures the inspired word of God, but they also were free from all errors, including historical and scientific details.

The conservatives in control of the SBC also came out against female clergy and declared that a wife "should submit herself graciously to the servant leadership of her husband." Hundreds of women already had been ordained by their own SBC congregation. Moderates objected, appealing to the Baptist principle of freedom of conscience.

In 1991 thousands of Baptists, unhappy about the new directions of the convention, formed the Cooperative Baptist Fellowship. Soon about eighteen hundred congregations suspended their contributions to the SBC and directed their financial support to their own parallel agencies.

In 2000 Texas Baptists rebelled against the conservatives and voted to cut $5 million in support of SBC seminaries and missions. They represented 2,700,000 Baptists in that state and led some observers to believe the nation's largest Protestant denomination was on the verge of splintering.

Nancy T. Ammerman, a sociology of religion professor at Hartford Seminary and longtime student of the SBC, wrote that the decision by the Texas Baptists marks "the continuing fragmentation of the SBC into a complex cluster of regional and ideological alliances."

Even former president Jimmy Carter renounced his lifelong affiliation with the SBC, saying it had become increasingly rigid in its conservatism and had taken positions that "violate the basic tenets of my Christian faith." He joined the Cooperative Baptist Fellowship.

In 2001 the SBC ended thirty years of ecumenical dialogue with Roman Catholics. One Baptist seminary president commented "We're not ecumenists. We're evangelicals committed to share the Gospel." Another seminary official noted that "ecumenism is not a high priority for most Southern Baptists."

Perhaps the SBC may be able to avoid further schisms, but if not, many more Baptists probably will leave for more congenial spiritual homes.

FURTHER READING

Armstrong, O.K. and Marjorie Moore, *The Indomitable Baptists* (Garden City, N.Y.: Doubleday, 1967).

Baker, Robert A., *The Southern Baptist Convention and Its People* (Nashville: Broadman, 1974).

Hastings, C. Brownlow, *Introducing Southern Baptists* (New York: Paulist Press, 1981).

Hays, Brooks and John E. Steely, *The Baptist Way of Life* (Englewood Cliffs, N.J.: Prentice-Hall, 1963).

Jordan, Anne Devereaux and J.M. Stifle, *The Baptists* (New York: Hippocrene Books, 1990).

Odle, Joe T., *Why I am a Baptist* (Nashville: Broadman, 1972).

Torbet, Robert G., *A History of the Baptists*, rev. ed. (Valley Forge, Pa.: Judson Press, 1963).

CHAPTER 8

The Disciples of Christ and Churches of Christ

'No Creed But Christ'

THREE MAJOR AMERICAN DENOMINATIONS GREW OUT OF THE Campbellite revival of the nineteenth century, which was pledged to the twin objectives of Christian unity and the restoration of the church in its New Testament form. These are the Christian Church (Disciples of Christ), the Churches of Christ, and the Christian Churches and Churches of Christ.

Paradoxically the unity-minded Disciples movement simply added another denomination to the roster of Protestant churches and sects. In fact, later disagreement over the precise nature of New Testament Christianity led to the schism of the two other groups. Thus the Campbellite restoration movement already has contributed several more denominations to the crowded American religious scene.

Akin to the much larger Baptist denomination, the Disciples denomination also insists on baptism of adults by immersion. This insistence on adult baptism by a particular mode separates the Disciples from the vast majority of Protestants and doomed their efforts toward a reunion of Christendom to an early failure. Disciples observe the Lord's Supper every Sunday, while Baptists usually hold a Communion service only four times a year. This difference between fifty-two and four Communion services a year seems to be the main one distinguishing the Disciples from the American (Northern) Baptists.

Disciples pride themselves on being members of a creedless church. "No creed but Christ" is a familiar maxim, and they will admit to their fellowship and to their Communion table all baptized persons who wish to participate. Neither the Apostles' nor the Nicene Creed finds any place in the liturgy, and no Disciple, minister or layman, need affirm belief in any specific Christian dogma. As a result you will find Disciples who approach Unitarian positions and others who would be logically classified as Fundamentalists, although most of those in the latter category would likely gravitate toward the Churches of Christ. "Study your Bible and believe what you wish" would be typical Disciples advice to a potential convert who expresses some reservations about a point of traditional Christianity such as the virgin birth, Christ's miracles, or a literal heaven and hell.

The sectarian de-emphasis of any clergy-laity distinction continues to characterize the Disciples to a greater extent than most Protestant bodies. Lay elders and deacons may baptize, serve the Communion elements, and preach: For legal reasons only an ordained minister may perform marriages. The Disciples of Christ minister is simply an elder among elders, hired and fired by the local congregation. He may be called "Reverend" by outsiders, but Disciples themselves observe no ecclesiastical amenities when referring to their professional, full-time clergy. More and more pastors of the larger churches in the denomination now possess college and seminary degrees. Women are accorded full clergy rights, but few are serving as pastors.

The Disciples movement grew out of a coalition of a number of nineteenth century "back-to-primitive-Christianity" revivals, but the denomination owes its greatest debt to the Campbells, Thomas and Alexander. Thomas came to the United States from Ireland early in the century and became minister of a small Seceder Presbyterian church in western Pennsylvania. His liberal views and invitations to non-Presbyterians to partake of the Lord's Supper scandalized his colleagues, and in 1809 he and his followers withdrew from Presbyterianism and formed the nondenominational Christian Association of Washington County, Pa.

That same year his son Alexander arrived in this country and joined his father as a free-lance preacher. Both declared their guiding principle to be: "Where the scriptures speak, we speak; where the scriptures are silent, we are silent." Both Campbells thought it was possible and desirable to strip Christianity of all post-New Testament accretions. Every doctrine must be preceded by a biblical "Thus saith the Lord." Father and son offered this common-denominator Christianity as an antidote to rampant sectarianism.

Whereas the Christian Association was more of a fellowship than a church, the Campbells took the next step and organized a separate church at Brush Run, Pa., several years later. They also had been persuaded that adult baptism by immersion was the only valid baptism. They themselves were immersed in 1812. Their newly proclaimed stand on baptism drew them closer to the Baptists, and they affiliated with that denomination in a union that lasted seventeen years.

Son Alexander, who had assumed leadership from his father, edited the *Christian Baptist* magazine in whose pages he denounced creeds, clergymen, church organs, mission societies, seminaries, Sunday schools, Catholicism, and other "nonscriptural" innovations. Over the years the Campbells, champions of the doctrine of free will, grew restive in the Calvinist Baptist fold. They also objected to the labeling of the Baptist Church as a "denomination," because they called their own movement a "restoration" and "brotherhood." In 1830 the Campbells severed their Baptist ties, and from then on the Campbellites were known by the term "Disciples of Christ."

Meanwhile in Kentucky and Ohio, an ex-Presbyterian minister with Unitarian tendencies, Barton W. Stone, was urging Christians to discard all divisive doctrines and unite in one Christian body. Other anti-Calvinists in New England were forming similar fellowships of Christians.

Shortly after withdrawing from the Baptists, the Disciples entered into a union with the bulk of Stone's "Christians." Those "Christians" in the East who refused to enter the merger continued their corporate existence until 1931, when they fused with the Congregational Church into the Congregational Christian Church. By this time, the doctrinal views of the one hundred thousand "Christians" were indistinguishable from Unitarianism.

The common-sense approach of the Disciples, the ability of their evangelists, and the wide scope afforded laymen contributed to the denomination's success on the American frontier. Two preachers, Walter Scott in Ohio and Pennsylvania and "Raccoon" John Smith in Kentucky, won thousands of converts.

By 1860 the Disciples movement counted two hundred thousand members, although statistics on the early Disciples and Christian groups are unreliable. Because Campbell approved of neither slavery nor abolition, his church managed to avoid schism during the Civil War. By keeping intact during the conflict, the Disciples won an advantage over the sundered Baptists, Methodists, and Presbyterians.

Alexander Campbell, contentious and vain, delighted in challenging clergymen of rival denominations to debate current theological issues. He was bitterly critical of all ministers and priests, whom he accused of being the "cause of all division, superstition, enthusiasm, and ignorance of the people." In 1837 he engaged in a lengthy debate with Roman Catholic Bishop John Purcell of Cincinnati.

Henry Clay moderated a debate between Campbell and a Presbyterian divine in 1843 that lasted sixteen days. Each speaker examined the question of infant baptism in a series of sixty-four speeches.

Campbell's sixty theological volumes interest few today except perhaps Disciples ministerial candidates. He railed against mission societies but became head of the first national missionary board. He denounced seminaries and higher education and ended his career as president of Bethany College. He accused the clergy of greed and avarice and died the wealthiest man in West Virginia, a successful businessman, sheep raiser, and author. He scorned instrumental music, Sunday schools, choirs, and Bible societies as unscriptural and eventually incorporated all these devices into his own church.

He renamed his *Christian Baptist* magazine the *Millennial Harbinger*, and his extreme millennial views sometimes embarrassed his twentieth-century spiritual children. The Protestant churches must drop all sectarian barriers because the end of the world is nigh, warned the editor. Later he mellowed on this issue as on many others; he finally predicted that the Second Coming could be expected in about 2000.

Many of his followers failed to notice his many reversals of position; they remembered only his earlier injunctions. By 1906 the conservative and progressive wings had split into the Churches of Christ and the Disciples of Christ. Today the two branches are separate denominations with no formal and little informal fellowship or cooperation.

The outsider is understandably confused by the use of similar names. Disciples churches rarely include the term "Disciples" in their church name. They are commonly known as First Christian Church, or Main Street Christian Church, for example. Some Disciples churches also use the term "Church of Christ," but no Churches of Christ church is ever identified as a "Disciples" church. The Disciples *Yearbook* lists some unusual church titles: Plumber's Landing, Weeping Mary, Rock of Ages, Gum Neck, The Last Chance, Sinners Union, Dripping Springs, and Little Bethlehem.

Each congregation is completely autonomous. Each church interviews prospective ministers and hires and fires without supervision by any conference or administrative body. The individual church may be High or Low in its liturgy, Fundamentalist or Rationalist in theology.

Most Disciples churches are equipped with a built-in pool for immersion baptisms. A Disciples minister's manual suggests a supply of leaded robes for men and women, heated water, and banks of flowers around the pool.

The Disciples, unlike most Protestants, schedule a weekly Communion service. At this service the minister takes a seat while laymen preside. One elder briefly discusses the significance of the Lord's Supper, and the other elder offers the prayer over the bread and wine. The Disciples invite all those present to participate in the Communion service, but the Churches of Christ limit Communion to those duly baptized by immersion. The elders serve the bread and wine to the deacons, who bring the elements to the worshipers in the pews.

Some Disciples churches are known as "open membership" churches; these congregations will receive as full members transfers from other Christian denominations who have not been baptized by immersion. They will not themselves baptize infants or use any form but total immersion. Other Disciples congregations still insist on baptism by immersion of all who ask for full membership. Disciples theologians differ on the question of the validity of infant baptism.

Local churches may choose to join district and state conferences; most Disciples churches belong to the voluntary Christian Churches (Disciples of Christ) International Convention, with headquarters in Indianapolis. All who attend the annual convention may vote, and nothing the convention recommends binds an individual church or Disciple. This convention is a mass convention rather than a representative assembly. Local churches may or may not contribute funds for the support of the convention.

Probably no Americans were more surprised and shocked than the members of this rather staid mainline denomination to discover that the instigator of the mass murder and suicide of more than nine hundred people at Jonestown, Guyana, was an ordained Disciples of Christ minister. The Reverend Jim Jones was ordained in Indianapolis in 1964 and remained a minister in good standing despite his bizarre actions until his death. In fact, the Peoples Temple congregations in California and Guyana were two of the five largest churches in the Disciples of Christ denomination.

In the aftermath of the tragedy the Reverend Kenneth Teegarden, general minister and president of the denomination, explained that "the congregational autonomy of a denomination such as ours, and the resultant tenuous relationships, with many local churches, of which we have 4,416, left us with a bare knowledge that the Peoples Temple of Redwood, California, had a Guyana colony and no appreciation of the fanaticism that could have led to the human destruction that took place." He added: "Under our church polity, it is neither possible, nor has it been desirable, to conduct investigations of the activities or ministries of local congregations." Nevertheless some Disciples of Christ are certain to recommend some procedures to disaffiliate congregations that stray as far from Christian orthodoxy as the Peoples Temple.

Almost all of the 879,000 Disciples of Christ live in half a dozen southern and Midwestern states. The Disciples report only seven churches in the New England area; there are only a few hundred individual Disciples in Wisconsin and a few thousand in Minnesota. Yet in such states as Indiana, Ohio, Kentucky, Illinois, Texas, Oklahoma, and Missouri, the Disciples play a major role in church life.

A traditional suspicion of higher education stunted the denomination's expansion in this area, although Butler, Drake, Phillips, and Texas Christian are Disciples institutions. For a denomination of its size in the United States, the Disciples's one hospital, six homes for the aged, and six orphanages reveal only a slight interest in social-welfare institutions.

President James A. Garfield was a former Disciples preacher. Poet Vachel Lindsay also was a member of the church. President Lyndon B. Johnson joined the Disciples of Christ as a teen-ager and maintained membership in the Johnson City, Texas, congregation. President Ronald Reagan usually attended a Presbyterian church but maintained membership in a Disciples congregation in California.

The fundamentalist Churches of Christ keep no records and are even more loosely organized than the Disciples because they have no annual convention and no local, state or national associations. Concentrated in Tennessee, West Virginia, the Ozark areas of Missouri and Arkansas, and the plains of central Texas, the members of the Churches of Christ can be found in all fifty states and sixty-five foreign countries. But they are hardly visible in the northeast and north central parts of the country.

Students of the Churches of Christ movement list at least five distinct groups. They differ on such matters as the proper form of worship, the support of church colleges, the use of the common versus the individual Communion cups, the operation of Sunday schools, and the use of various translations of the Bible. Total membership of the Churches of Christ has been estimated at 1,500,000.

All music is *a cappella* because they find no mention of organs in the Bible (or, for that matter, hymn books, pews, electric fans, and the English language). Their periodicals are carefully identified as "unofficial" and their colleges as "nonsectarian."

Because of the belief that the Church of Christ represents a restoration of New Testament Christianity rather than a Reformation of the church, most members of the Churches of Christ refuse to accept the label "Protestant." In practice this group has been considered a Protestant body in census tabulations.

What holds the fifteen thousand congregations together are such things as the support of broadcasting and evangelistic activities, the colleges that stand in the Restoration tradition, and the various periodicals. Hundreds of congregations contribute to the $1.6 million annual budget spent by the Highland Avenue Church of Christ in Abilene, Texas, to broadcast the "Herald of Truth" program on five hundred radio and one hundred fifty TV stations. Since 1955 the Churches of Christ have been placing newspaper ads offering correspondence courses in the Bible.

The closest thing to a convention is the annual Bible lectureship on the campus of Abilene Christian College. This event has drawn as many as ten thousand people, and those invited to deliver the lectures wield considerable influence in the movement.

Colleges associated with the Restoration movement take pains to point out that they are not official church institutions, but they claim to present Church of Christ teachings and insist that all college trustees belong to the church. These institutions include Pepperdine, Abilene Christian, David Lipscomb, Oklahoma Christian, and Lubbock Christian. Harding College describes itself as a bastion of capitalism and a center of anti-communism. Its current catalog includes these requirements for all its students: at least one Bible course each semester, daily chapel attendance, attendance at church Sunday morning and evening, and abstention from drinking, gambling, and dancing. Women may not smoke; male students may smoke but only in their own rooms or in the rooms of fellow tobacco addicts.

In general the Churches of Christ do not forbid smoking and drinking, although elders would consider it their duty to admonish anyone guilty of drunkenness. The only scriptural reason for divorce is adultery, and only the innocent party in such a situation is free to remarry.

Some ministers refuse to perform a second marriage for any divorced person. Women's liberation has made no visible inroads in the movement; women cannot qualify as ministers, elders, or deacons.

While the Pentecostals also claim to have restored the practices of the early church — speaking in tongues, healing, prophecy, and so forth — the Churches of Christ level heavy guns at the Pentecostal phenomenon. They believe all the gifts of Pentecost ceased at the end of the apostolic era; those who claim such gifts today are either deluded or seduced by Satan. When singer Pat Boone and his wife reported their belief in glossolalia and spiritual healing, their own Church of Christ disfellowshipped them.

The breakaway of the Churches of Christ in the early years of the last century was not the only schism in the Campbellite movement.

While the schism in the early part of the twentieth century grew out of the debate on the use of musical instruments in worship, another schism focused on church government. A desire for a stronger national organization led to a restructuring of the Disciples of Christ in 1968. Those who opposed the move formed what is now known as the Christian Churches and Churches of Christ.

Far more theologically conservative than the Disciples, the churches that grew out of the 1968 dispute sponsor an extensive missionary program in more than fifty countries, have established thirty-eight colleges and three seminaries, and operate a number of social service agencies. They report 1,071,000 members.

No mainline Protestant denomination has experienced as drastic a decline in membership as the Disciples of Christ. This church has lost more than half the members it reported in 1965. Much of this can be attributed to the 1968 split and to the defection of Disciples to more conservative Restoration bodies.

FURTHER READING

Adams, Hampton, *Why I am a Disciple of Christ* (New York: Thomas Nelson, 1957).

Beazley, George C., Jr., *The Christian Church (Disciples of Christ): An Interpretative Examination in the Cultural Context* (St. Louis: Bethany, 1973).

Garrison, W.E. and A.T. DeGroot, *The Disciples of Christ* (St. Louis: Christian Board of Publication, 1954).

CHAPTER 9

The United Churchmen

The United Church of Christ Born in 1957 Merger

ALTHOUGH A NUMBER OF DENOMINATIONAL MERGERS HAVE BEEN completed in recent years, most of these could be termed family reunions rather than marriages. Churches that had divided over some issue such as slavery or language came together to form a united church once more. Other churches that represented almost identical constituencies found common grounds for forming a single denomination.

In this respect the formation of the United Church of Christ in 1957 was unique in American Protestantism. Congregationalism, a product of English Separatism, came to these shores with the Pilgrim Fathers and became a virtual state religion for the New England Yankees. On the other hand, the Evangelical and Reformed Church, a fusion of two German denominations in 1934, found its adherents among the descendants of German immigrants in Pennsylvania and the Midwest. Congregationalism rested upon the complete autonomy of the local congregation and refused to recognize the power of any bishop, synod, or council over the congregation. The Evangelical and Reformed Church operated under a modified presbyterian system of church government. Congregationalists refused to bind members or churches with creeds, while the Evangelical and Reformed was committed to uphold the Heidelberg Catechism, Luther's Shorter Catechism, and the Augsburg Confession.

In some parts of the country the local United Church of Christ congregations still may be identified by the older names. In New England, for example, some UCC churches will be known as Congregational. What adds to the confusion is that more than four hundred Congregational Christian churches refused to join the 1957 merger;

they retain the Congregational name and have formed associations of like-minded churches.

Opposition by a minority of Congregationalists blocked the merger through court action for five years. Opponents of the union contended that they would be untrue to their most distinctive Congregational belief by uniting with a presbyterian church such as the Evangelical and Reformed. They lost their case, and the proponents of the union obtained large majority approvals in their respective church councils.

This youngest Protestant denomination numbers about 1,140,000 communicants in the United States and represents the same type of ecumenical approach whose counterpart we find in the older United Church of Canada and the Church of South India. To understand this new religious synthesis called the United Church of Christ, we must examine the backgrounds of its two diverse components.

For the origins of Congregationalism we must look to the Separatist movement in England, and for the Evangelical and Reformed Church to continental Calvinism and to attempts in Prussia to blend Lutheranism with Calvinism.

"No bishops" had been the battle cry of English Presbyterians who preferred a representative form of church polity that nevertheless exercised a measure of control and supervision over member congregations. This did not satisfy everyone. More radical wings of the Separatist movement denied any authority over the local congregation. "No head, priest, prophet, or king save Christ" was their motto. Each church, composed of the predestined elect, should be free to frame its own creed or no creed and to choose its own minister and church officers. Furthermore, they agreed with the more moderate Puritans that all vestiges of popery be driven from the church. These radicals came to be known as Independents or Congregationalists.

Persecution drove many Congregationalists to tolerant Holland, among them the future Pilgrims. Perhaps the most flourishing community was that at Leiden under the pastorate of the gentle John Robinson. This congregation had been organized by poor people of the hamlet of Scrooby who finally sought refuge in Europe's religious sanctuary.

As time passed these English Separatists found economic conditions harsh in their new home, and they saw their children adopting the customs of a foreign land and intermarrying with the Dutch. They wished to preserve their English heritage. A group decided to sail to the New World where they could reestablish their religious community, though the majority remained in Holland with their pastor. They arranged transportation through some merchant adventurers; by the time they set sail from England on the Mayflower, the majority of the one hundred one passengers were non-Separatists. When they sighted Cape Cod in 1620 the adult males among the Separatists signed the Mayflower Compact, but once ashore the distinctions between the Congregationalists and the "Strangers" disappeared.

Starvation, cold, and disease faced the Pilgrim Fathers, but they buried their dead and labored to build their colony at Plymouth. Half the settlers died within six months. Later, wealthy Puritans, originally non-Separatists, landed at nearby Salem. Between 1628 and 1635 more than twenty thousand Puritans arrived at the Massachusetts Bay colony. They eventually exchanged their own presbyterian preferences for the congregationalism of their Pilgrim neighbors. The two settlements merged in 1691, and Congregationalism became the established religion of the New England colonies.

Only church members could vote (1,708 voters out of 15,000 settlers in the Massachusetts Bay colony). Everyone was required to pay taxes for the support of the established church. This special status was not abrogated in Connecticut until 1818, in New Hampshire until 1819, and in Massachusetts until 1834.

While it may not be entirely fair to say that the Pilgrims came to this country to worship God in their own way and make everyone else do likewise, they certainly were not champions of religious freedom. They came to the New World to find freedom for themselves, rather than to provide it for others. Persecuted in England, they became self-righteous persecutors in America. Dissenters were firmly invited to leave. Four Quakers were hanged on Boston Commons. Heresy and witchcraft were vigorously extirpated, and Puritan treatment of Roger Williams and the Baptists, Anne Hutchinson, the Quakers, and any episcopal sympathizers is well-known. The Salem witchcraft trials of 1692 found a theocracy in religious frenzy. Nineteen men and women were hanged in Salem for trafficking with the devil.

The Puritan theocracy forbade dancing, card playing, smoking, mincemeat pies, the observance of Christmas, and all musical instruments save the drum, trumpet, and Jew's-harp. "No one shall travel, cook victuals, make beds, sweep house, cut hair or shave and no woman shall kiss her children on the Sabbath Day," declared the Puritan divines. But just as the Congregational heirs of Puritanism jettisoned strict Calvinism for theological liberalism, so they also abandoned Puritan morality to the Methodists, Baptists, and Holiness sects.

Despite the excesses and witch trials and bigotry, the Puritan theocracy made an enormous contribution to American life. The Puritans developed the town meeting system. They established standards of sobriety and the industry that helped American men and women tame a continent. They furnished the minutemen and gave us the Thanksgiving holiday.

An observer in the early nineteenth century probably would have assumed that Congregationalism or the "New England Way" would continue to be the largest and one of the most influential churches in the nation. That it lost this preeminence to become one of the smaller major denominations was the result of several factors.

Early in the 1800s, Congregationalism split into two parties: Trinitarian and Unitarian. The Unitarians lopped off all but one of Boston's fourteen congregations, captured Harvard and the original Pilgrim church at Plymouth, and dominated the religious scene in eastern Massachusetts.

Another reason for Congregationalism's decline was the Plan of Union, which was devised in 1801 to minimize denominational competition in the West but usually worked to the advantage of the Presbyterians. Before its repudiation in 1852, the Plan is said to have resulted in a loss of two thousand Congregational churches outside New England to the better organized Presbyterians. Until the 1957 merger, Congregationalism remained primarily a New England institution with smaller memberships in New York, Ohio, Illinois, Iowa, and California.

Reliance on state recognition and support led to complacency in Congregational ranks, and the upstart Methodists and Baptists forged ahead to become the leading Protestant denominations in the country. Like the Presbyterians and Episcopalians, the Congregationalists insisted on an educated clergy and lacked the trained manpower to compete with the Methodist circuit riders and the Baptist preachers.

Congregationalists organized the American Board of Commissioners for Foreign Missions in 1810 and dispatched the first missionary team to India in 1812. Others went from New England to South Africa, Ceylon, and Turkey. Descendants of Congregationalist missionaries to Hawaii not only converted many of the natives, but also obtained control of much of the economy of the islands.

Few Congregationalists held slaves, but many supported abolitionism. Harriet Beecher Stowe, daughter of a Congregationalist minister, wrote *Uncle Tom's Cabin*. After the Civil War the Congregationalists set up five hundred schools for black individuals in the former Confederate states and founded such institutions as Howard, Fisk, Hampton Institute, Dillard, and Tougaloo.

Congregationalism always has demonstrated a concern for higher education; church members founded Harvard, Yale, Dartmouth, Bowdoin, Amherst, Smith, Williams, Oberlin, and forty other colleges, most of which have since passed from church control. When Harvard capitulated to Unitarianism, the Congregationalists founded Andover seminary to inculcate orthodox Calvinism. The educational level of Congregationalists, clergy and laity, has traditionally been among the highest of all Protestant groups.

In 1931 the Congregationalists merged with the one hundred thousand-member Christian Church, sometimes known as the Baptist Unitarians. This group denied the divinity of Christ and rejected all creeds as it arose from the same religious ferment that produced the creedless Disciples of Christ and Churches of Christ. The first overtures for a merger were made in 1895. The new church was known as the Congregational Christian Churches.

Calvinism originally formed the theological basis of Congregationalism, although the Congregationalists minimized formal creeds and confessions. Then, as now, the local congregation could compose a creed of its own, adopt the Apostles' Creed, or remain creedless.

Theoretically the power of the local Congregational church was unlimited. It could fix doctrine and ritual, hire and fire ministers, choose its own officers. Theory and practice differed, and there are those who maintain that a Congregationalist had no more freedom than a Methodist or Lutheran. Strict educational and moral standards for the ministry were enforced, and a church had to be accepted by the churches in its district before it could use the title "Congregational." Group pressure sometimes can bring about more uniformity and conformity than elaborate governmental structures. Beyond the local churches were the associations, the conferences, and the General Council. The decisions of these regional, state, and national bodies had no binding power on the congregations. The problem of preserving the essentials of Christianity in a congregational polity was never solved, and in many cases the essentials were not preserved. A few Congregational churches could be characterized as Fundamentalist, but most taught a mixture of liberalism, Modernism, social gospel, and Unitarianism.

Early Congregational worship and architecture were severely plain: lengthy sermons, Bible reading and psalms, unadorned meeting houses. Christmas was called a popish holiday, and its observance cost the celebrant five shillings. Today Christmas finds a place in the Congregationalist year as well as the Puritans' own contribution to the calendar, Thanksgiving Day. Organs and hymns gradually were introduced, and the service was shortened from three hours to one.

At the time of the merger with the Evangelical and Reformed Church, the Congregational Christian Churches counted 1,342,000 adult members, mostly in New England. Each Congregational Christian Church was free to accept or reject the union with the Evangelical and Reformed Church.

Whereas almost all Evangelical and Reformed congregations joined the United Church of Christ, hundreds of Congregational Christian churches refused. The National Association of Congregational Christian Churches reports sixty-six thousand members. These churches believe basic congregational principles were compromised by the merger with the Evangelical and Reformed body. Another group, the Conservative Congregational Christian Conference, claims 40,000 members in 236 churches.

The Evangelical and Reformed Church itself was the youngest of the major denominations, tracing its beginning as a single church to a union in 1934 of two German-Swiss churches. As separate churches, the Reformed Church antedated the century-old Evangelical Synod by almost three hundred years.

Not all areas in Germany that abandoned the ancient faith accepted Lutheranism. Certain sections such as the Palatinate adopted a Reformed theology in the Heidelberg Confession of 1563. This confession attempted to strike a middle course between Lutheranism and Calvinism that differed mainly on the doctrine of the Real Presence.

A number of Palatinates left their homeland for America after the devastation of the Thirty Years' War. A Reformed minister, Michael Schlatter, organized these scattered German settlements in Pennsylvania, but the American church remained under Dutch control until 1793. In the early 1800s two groups led by Philip Otterbein and John Winebrenner seceded and started churches of their own: the United Brethren in Christ and the Church of God.

A merger of two German Reformed synods in 1863 and the wider use of the English language strengthened the Reformed Church in the United States (not to be confused with the Reformed Church of America, a Dutch body). Units of the Hungarian Reformed Church were absorbed in 1924.

The other party in the 1934 union, the Evangelical Synod of North America, represented the 1817 union of the Reformed and Lutherans in Prussia. King Frederick William III desired religious unity in his realm and decreed the union as a solution for religious differences between the Reformed and the Lutheran majority. He chose the three hundredth anniversary of Luther's revolt for the royal decree.

Members of this United Evangelical Church of Prussia began to enter the United States almost a century after the Reformed cousins. They formed their church in 1840. Although most of the charter members were Lutherans, this church has drifted far from orthodox Lutheranism, and its absorption into the United Church of Christ is evidence of the extent to which it had accepted more liberal theological assumptions.

Both participants in the 1934 merger were organized by German immigrants; both employed the German language in their pioneer days; both preached a Lutheran-Reformed theology; both were governed by a presbyterian polity. At the time of the merger in Cleveland, the Reformed Church counted 348,000 members and the Evangelical Synod, 281,000. An unusual feature of this action was that the two denominations united first and worked out the details later. Church boards were not consolidated until 1941.

Three of the most distinguished Protestant theologians in the United States were ordained Evangelical and Reformed ministers: Reinhold and H. Richard Niebuhr and Paul Tillich. The Niebuhrs grew up in an Evangelical and Reformed parsonage, and Tillich transferred his membership from the German church.

Pennsylvania, Missouri, and Ohio were the Evangelical and Reformed strongholds; a large proportion of the members resided in these three states and two others: Indiana and Illinois. In this respect, Evangelical and Reformed membership complemented the New England strength of Congregationalism.

Calvin Coolidge was the only U.S. president who was a Congregationalist, although members of this tradition have furnished more than their share of public servants. Some Congregationalists have won fame by founding new religions: Mary Baker Eddy, founder of Christian Science, and Charles Taze Russell, organizer of the Bible groups that became known as Jehovah's Witnesses.

The United Church has become more of a national church than either of the former denominations, although it has scarcely any adherents in the South and few black members. The growth of the separate parties to the merger has hardly kept pace with the increases in population in this country.

The two churches in the 1957 merger then reported a combined membership of 2,192,674. By 2000 this had fallen by almost 772,000 adherents, attributable in part to the defection of congregations that opposed the merger.

The spiritual heirs of the Puritans and the continental Lutheran-Reformed Protestants belong to one of the most liberal churches on the American scene.

FURTHER READING

Horton, Douglas, *The United Church of Christ* (New York: Thomas Nelson, 1962).

Kohl, Manfred Waldemar, *Congregationalism in America* (Oak Creek, Wis.: Congregational Press, 1977).

Starkey, Marion, L., *The Congregational Way* (Garden City, N.Y.: Doubleday, 1966).

CHAPTER 10

The Quakers

Follow the Inner Light

QUAKERS, MEMBERS OF THE RELIGIOUS SOCIETY OF FRIENDS, OFTEN consider themselves representatives of a third form of Christianity, neither Catholic nor Protestant. At other times they concur with many non-Quakers who see Quakerism as Protestantism carried to its logical conclusion.

Luther rejected the pope, the visible church, five of the seven sacraments, the value of tradition as a rule of faith, and the sacrificial element in worship. Calvin dispensed with the rule of bishops and minimized the role of music and art in worship. Congregationalists did away with centralized church government of any kind, and Baptists damned infant baptism as unscriptural.

The Quakers dispensed with all sacraments, all ritual, and any professional ministry. On the other hand, the familiar Protestant formulae — total depravity, justification by faith alone, and the sole sufficiency of the Scriptures — are foreign to Quaker thought. Further, the Quakers declare that the ultimate religious authority rests in no church, tradition, or Bible, but within each individual.

An understanding of the Quaker's Inner Light is essential to an understanding of this radical but influential phase of the English Reformation. By the Inner Light each man must follow, the Quakers do not mean conscience. Conscience itself is illumined by the Inner Light. This Inner Light is rather the immediate influence of the Holy Spirit, that which is of God in each soul. Like most mystics, the early Quakers found themselves helpless to express their experiences in words.

In some basic theological positions Quakerism comes closer to Roman Catholicism than to Protestantism. The Quaker rejects the classical Lutheran view of human nature as totally depraved as a consequence of original sin. Most Quakers would uphold the inherent goodness of man. They believe that perfection and freedom from sin are possible in this life. The founder of the Society of Friends early preached against the Calvinist doctrine of predestination; Quakerism denies that God has divided mankind into the elect and the damned. Finally, the Quaker does not ascribe to the Bible the same final authority as do Protestants.

Quaker writer Rufus Jones probably spoke for most of his coreligionists when he said: "Friends are not much interested in abstract theories and statements about God. They prefer to begin with personal experience of Him."

The Friends have never been numerous; there are probably about as many in the world today as there were in 1700. In the United States, the Quakers belong to three major and several smaller groups: 104,000 in the Religious Society of Friends, 41,000 in the Friends United Meeting, and 32,000 in the Friends General Conference.

Most of the customs and mannerisms that once set them apart from the world as a "peculiar" people have disappeared. The group mysticism of the English lower classes has become a respected denomination for the middle-class American. Their witness against war and their active interest in social questions continue, and they have won the universal admiration of their countrymen.

Like Luther and Wesley, the founder of the Quakers had no intention of founding another church or sect. George Fox (1624-1691) had little opportunity to attend school or study. He was apprenticed to a shoemaker at the age of twelve but developed a dissatisfaction with his religious life and that of his Puritan neighbors. One day as a youth of nineteen he was shocked at the sight of two clergymen engaged in a drinking bout at a fair. He said he heard the voice of God in a vision tell him: "Thou seest how men give themselves over to vanity. Forget about them. Keep aloof from them and in the future be as a stranger to them."

He decided to break with home, friends, church, and trade and began four years of wandering about England. Fox came to the conclusion that man arrives at truth not by study or Bible reading or listening to sermons but by following the Inner Light whereby God speaks directly to each soul. Of what use, then, are learning and ritual and church organization? Quakers take the year 1649 as their founding date.

The young enthusiast found many converts for his views among the dozens of sects that dotted the English countryside: Seekers, Ranters, Baptists, and mystics of all types. He found many who disliked the Anglican establishment and kindred spirits who had reacted against the harshness of Calvinism.

The Quaker founder believed God granted the Inner Light to all; Fox had no place in his system for elect and reprobate. He denied that man was depraved and set up perfection and freedom from all sin as a spiritual goal. Even the atonement was rejected because the Quakers believed that no one, not even God, could atone for another's sins. They reverenced the Bible but considered it *a* Word of God and not *the* Word of God.

Imprisoned for a total of six years, Fox endured dogged persecution throughout his life. Once condemned to death for his religious views, he missed execution only through the intervention of powerful friends. Nevertheless he maintained a full schedule of preaching and won many followers, especially in northern England.

On one occasion he was brought before a judge and accused of blasphemy. Fox startled the magistrate by shouting, "The time has come for even judges to quake and tremble before the Lord." "Oh," mocked the judge, "so you are quakers, are you?" The name stuck, although it has never been officially adopted and the term "Friends" is sometimes preferred. Fox's converts had previously called themselves "Children of Light" and "Friends of Truth."

Quaker ideas of social equality contributed to their persecution in seventeenth-century England. They refused to acknowledge any special privilege among men, which meant they would doff their hats to no human and address no one with the then-complimentary "you." Instead they used the plain "thee" and "thou." They opposed taking oaths on biblical grounds and as implying a double standard of truth, one for the marketplace and one for the courtroom. Objecting to the pagan origin of the days of the week, they renamed Sunday "First Day," Monday "Second Day," and so on. Simple dress, simple speech, sober habits were prescribed. Participation in war was strictly forbidden. Music, art, fiction, and the theater fell under Quaker ban. As a result of their attitudes, more than thirteen thousand Quakers were imprisoned and hundreds died in prison during the Stuart Restoration and the reign of Charles II.

At their meetings for worship neither preaching nor ritual had a place. The only ritual was silence. Quakers waited quietly for inspiration from God, and occasionally one or another of the assembled Friends would stand to testify or present a religious thought. Because they abhorred ritual of any kind, they neither baptized nor observed the Lord's Supper.

The Quaker withdraws to the silence of the weekly meeting only to find spiritual nourishment and inspiration to go back into the world. There is no such thing as a Quaker hermit or a Quaker monastery where contemplatives cut themselves off from men and affairs.

In all Quaker meetings the members seek decisions not by majority rule but by the "sense of the meeting," which means unanimity. Women hold equal power and status with men.

Elders and overseers are appointed to serve each monthly meeting. The elders arrange for worship, marriages, and funerals, while the overseers assume responsibilities for the pastoral care of members. The clerk is the chief administrative officer of the meeting.

A Quaker bride and groom repeat their marriage vows during a meeting for worship after obtaining the consent of the meeting to the union. Each declares: "In the presence of the Lord and of these our friends, I take thee, . . . to be my wife (or husband) promising with divine assistance to be unto thee a loving and faithful husband (or wife) so long as we both shall live." Then all those present sign the marriage certificate as witnesses.

Pioneer work in the social field was undertaken by the Quakers, and millions of people have benefited from their efforts. They were among the first to urge proper care for the poor, aged, and insane; they fought slavery and battled for just treatment of the American Indians; they promoted temperance, prison reform, and equality of the sexes.

Two other names besides Fox are associated with Quaker history in a special way: Robert Barclay, the theologian of Quakerism, and William Penn, the founder of Pennsylvania.

Barclay was Fox's Melanchthon. He drew up the systematic presentation of Quaker doctrine. A Presbyterian in his youth, Barclay was sent to Paris to study under his Catholic uncle who taught at a Jesuit college. The Jesuit Fathers taught Barclay scholastic philosophy, Catholic theology, the Church Fathers, Latin, and French. Fearing his conversion to popery, Barclay's parents withdrew him from the college. Back in England he finally joined the new Quaker movement in 1666 and employed his Catholic-sponsored education in the interests of this mystical sect. His chief work was *Apology for the True Christian Divinity.*

Penn, son of an English admiral, had embraced the principles of Quakerism and planned to establish a haven for his persecuted brethren. The king owed Penn's father a large sum of money and was happy to settle the debt by chartering a tract of land in the New World to Penn in 1681.

The first Quaker missionaries to America, two women, had been condemned as witches and sent back to England within five weeks of their arrival. The Massachusetts Puritans resisted and harassed the revolutionary Quakers in every way possible. Four intrepid Quakers who followed the women were hanged on Boston Commons, and their coreligionists were imprisoned, whipped, and tortured.

Penn arrived in his colony in 1682 and found Swedes, Englishmen, and Dutch already settled. He assured them that they would be governed by their own laws as before. Following his religious convictions, he soon concluded a model treaty with the American Indians. He granted freedom of worship to all Christians, including Catholics, and laid out the streets of his City of Brotherly Love, Philadelphia.

Meanwhile, in England the Act of Toleration of 1689 released the Quakers from some of the harsher penalties, and by the time of Fox's death two years later there were at least fifty thousand Friends in the British Isles.

Quakers prospered in the American colonies, and by 1700 Quakers owned not only Pennsylvania but New Jersey and Delaware, controlled Rhode Island and the Carolinas, and had strength in New York and Maryland. They constituted the greatest single religious community in the New World at this time.

Eventually the Quakers not only lost dominance in the colonies but shrank to comparative numerical insignificance in American religious life. They lost political control of Pennsylvania in 1756 when they voluntarily relinquished their seats in the state assembly rather than vote for war against the Shawnee and Delaware Indians. Schisms, doctrinal disputes, lack of trained leaders, Quietism, defection, membership purges, and a reluctance to proselytize furthered Quaker decline.

Quietism infected the movement for many decades. This enervating philosophy, which has appeared in many religious systems, teaches that God operates in man only when man silences all his usual activities: prayer, study, and work. Its infection of Quakerism might have been anticipated. As a result of this philosophy, planning, and organization are neglected. Such Catholic Quietists as Molinos, Fénelon, and Madame Guyon were popular among the Quakers. Membership dipped from sixty thousand in 1700 to seventeen thousand half a century later.

The movement depended almost entirely on birthright members who might grow indifferent to the original Quaker message. At other times purges crossed hundreds of names from the membership rolls. No replenishing evangelistic campaigns were conducted.

But the most serious organizational disruption of Quakerism sprang from the schism led by Elias Hicks. A Modernist theologian bordering on Unitarianism, Hicks apparently rejected the divinity of Christ and the existence of original sin. He led a large group of rural Quakers from the main body in 1827. The Hicksites never adopted Hicks's theology in total, but this split handicapped Quaker activities for nearly a century until the original differences melted away. A smaller group called the Evangelical Friends, or Wilburites, broke away in 1837 in the expected conservative reaction.

It was not easy to be a Quaker. They were expected to wear a distinctive garb (see the Quaker Oats package), oppose all wars, refuse to swear oaths, adopt peculiar habits of speech, ignore the traditional Christian holidays, and marry within the group. The periodic purges expelled backsliders. Even today no orthodox Quaker gambles, plays the stock market, or drinks.

Quakers early opposed slavery in all its forms. Led by the gentle John Woolman, they dismissed all slaveholders from their ranks and threw their weight behind the abolitionist crusade. Today they continue to fight segregation and racial intolerance.

Eventually compromises diluted Quakerism. The silent meeting often gave way to a programmed meeting differing only slightly from a simple Protestant service. Next came professional pastors. Those groups with programmed services came to be known as Friends Churches in contrast to the original Friends Meeting.

Officially the Quakers continue to oppose war, but as more young Quakers volunteered for military service the attitude toward soldier-members softened. Estimates put eight thousand Quakers in the armed forces during World War II, one thousand as noncombatants, one thousand as conscientious objectors, and one hundred in prison. Those who did serve in the military services were no longer ostracized, as they would have been in the earlier days of the sect.

The peculiarities that once set Quakers apart from the rest of the community have become private family customs.

The monthly meeting for worship and business is the basic unit of Quaker polity. This meeting convenes for silent or programmed worship, keeps records of births, deaths, and marriages, appoints committees, and conducts the necessary business. These meetings come together in quarterly meetings, and they in turn comprise the yearly or Five Years meetings, of which there are thirty-one in the United States and Canada.

Largest of these Quaker bodies is the Society of Friends (Friends United Meeting), which reports about forty-one thousand members in five hundred churches. This is a union of twelve autonomous yearly meetings in the United States, Canada, East Africa, Cuba, and Jamaica. It maintains headquarters in Richmond, Ind., and was once known as the Five Years Meeting.

The Hicksites form the Friends General Conference. Although this group never officially adopted the theological platform of Elias Hicks, its members tend to be more Rationalist and Modernist in their outlook. The General Conference is made up of thirty-two thousand Friends in ten yearly meetings in Baltimore, Canada, New England, Illinois, Indiana, New York, and Philadelphia.

In 1965 four independent yearly meetings — Ohio, Kansas, Oregon, and Rocky Mountain — formed the Evangelical Friends Alliance. They favor an evangelical Protestant theology, sponsor revivals, and seek associations with Holiness churches. They give their membership at eighty-six hundred.

At least a dozen other Quaker bodies report smaller memberships; all told these groups enroll about ten thousand members.

Most American Quakers will be found in Pennsylvania, North Carolina, Indiana, Kansas, Ohio, and California. Outside the United States and England, the largest number of Friends live in Kenya, Madagascar, Bolivia, Peru, Ireland, Central America, and Australasia. About twenty-two hundred men and women belong to the Wider Quaker Fellowship. They sympathize with Quaker positions but do not wish to cut ties with their own churches.

Representatives of the various Quaker branches formed the American Friends Service Committee in 1917. Since then the committee has spent millions of dollars on war- and disaster-relief work, rehabilitation, and care of conscientious objectors. Many non-Quakers contribute to the committee's financial support. Together with the Friends Service Council (London), it received the Nobel Peace Prize in 1947.

The Quakers operate ten small but distinguished colleges, including Swarthmore, Earlham, Friends University, and Whittier. Quaker businessmen founded both Cornell and Johns Hopkins, but neither university has been church-affiliated. Quaker pastors receive training at a number of interdenominational seminaries. A Quaker seminary has been opened at Earlham.

This relatively small denomination has seen two of its members reach the White House in this century: Herbert Hoover and Richard Nixon. Other well-known American Quakers have included John Greenleaf Whittier, R. H. Macy, and Susan B. Anthony.

Quakerism flourished during the lifetimes of its original triumvirate: Fox, Barclay, and Penn. Since then it has accomplished much in the way of social action and philanthropy but has hardly held its own in membership. Millions of Americans applaud Quaker activities but never seriously consider joining the sect, and no one ever asks them to do so.

With few members and few converts, the Quaker movement in this day demonstrates what even such a small band of people can do to serve mankind. The Quakers are mystics, but they do not ignore the world while they cultivate their own spiritual lives. As Penn wrote: "True godliness does not turn men out of the world but enables them to live better in it, and excites their endeavors to mend it."

FURTHER READING

Bacon, Margaret H., *The Quiet Rebels: The Story of the Quakers in America* (New York: Basic Books, 1969).

Brinton, Howard, *Friends for 300 Years* (New York: Harper & Brothers, 1952).

Hall, Francis B., ed., *Friends in the Americas* (Philadelphia: Friends World Committee, 1976).

Sykes, John, *The Quakers* (Philadelphia and New York: Lippincott, 1958).

CHAPTER 11

The Perfectionists

Christians Seek 'Baptism of the Holy Spirit' in Numerous Holiness Churches

Several dozen churches comprise the Holiness movement, which grew out of post-Civil War revivals. These revivals stressed Wesley's doctrine of entire sanctification or Christian perfection, which had been quietly eased out of the regular Methodist churches.

Today these numerous Holiness groups are characterized by emotionalism, swingy gospel hymns, faith healing, strict morality, premillenialism, revivals, and camp meetings. We can distinguish two branches of the Holiness movement, a right and a left wing, Perfectionist and Pentecostal.

Included in the Perfectionist wing are such bodies as the Church of the Nazarene, Church of God (Anderson, Ind.), and the Christian and Missionary Alliance. The Pentecostal wing embraces those groups that maintain that speaking in tongues, glossolalia, is a necessary and natural accompaniment of the baptism of the Holy Spirit.

All these groups, from the sedate Church of the Nazarene to the most primitive sect, believe they have restored the biblical and Wesleyan doctrine of entire sanctification to its proper and central position in the Christian life.

According to the theology of Holiness or, as it has been termed, the theology of the Holy Ghost, a Christian can receive a subsequent blessing after justification that frees him from all sinful desires. His nature is then freed from all depravity wrought by original sin. Whereas repentance is considered the prime requisite for baptism, consecration is the main requisite for holiness. All Christians are called to this holiness experience, an instantaneous transformation wrought by faith.

No one denies that Wesley, departing from the pessimism of Luther and Calvin regarding human nature, taught the doctrine of Holiness, and that his teaching on this subject has all but been disowned by modern Methodists. Many would deny that Wesley's teaching was carried to the extremes of some Holiness enthusiasts in the United States. By the end of the Civil War, the doctrine was seldom mentioned in Methodist circles. When the postwar revivals renewed interest in Holiness, the devotees of the movement first formed prayer groups within the existing churches and eventually broke away to form their own congregations. A pastoral letter in 1894 from the Methodist bishops criticized aspects of the Holiness movement and hastened the departure of many from the Methodist Episcopal Church.

More radical or ecstatic elements claimed that the gifts showered on the Apostles at Pentecost were necessary signs of holiness. They especially encouraged speaking in tongues, which the Nazarenes, for example, have never countenanced.

One of the largest Perfectionist bodies of the Holiness movement, the Church of the Nazarene, represents a merger of a number of smaller sects whose members were drawn from Methodism. These congregations sprang up around the country between 1890 and 1900, and the formal organization was completed at Pilot Point, Texas, in 1908. The original merger brought together 10,400 members; this church now claims 627,000 members in more than 5,100 congregations. The word "Pentecostal" was deleted from the church name in 1919, and all Nazarene colleges have dropped the "Holiness" designation from their names.

The Church of the Nazarene closely resembles Methodism in theology, polity, and worship. All Nazarene ministers and local church officials must testify that they have experienced instantaneous entire sanctification. They believe in divine healing but do not disparage or ignore medical science. Their moral code exemplifies the Puritan attitudes of most Holiness sects. For example, their general rules for church membership condemn "profaning the Lord's Day, either by unnecessary labor, or business, or patronizing or reading of secular papers, or by holiday diversions." Another section bars "songs, literature and entertainments not to the glory of God; the theater, the ballroom, the circus, and like places; also, lotteries and games of chance; looseness and impropriety of conduct; membership in or fellowship with oathbound secret orders or fraternities."

Nazarenes invariably rank high in per capita donations to the church among Protestant denominations. General superintendents take the place of Methodism's bishops and are elected to four-year terms. The church operates eight small liberal arts colleges in addition to Bible schools and a graduate theological seminary; headquarters are maintained at Kansas City, Mo. Ministers are ordained after completing a four-year college Bible course, but many now enroll for graduate work at the seminary.

Both the Free Methodist (62,000 members) and Wesleyan (112,000) churches have continued to uphold entire sanctification and should be included as part of the Holiness movement.

Now highly organized, the Church of God (Anderson, Ind., 234,000 members) was begun as a protest against church organization and shares a distaste for the term "denomination." It prefers to be called the Church of God Reformation Movement but adds the geographical location of its headquarters to distinguish it from the innumerable Church of God sects. Daniel S. Warner, a thrice-married Winebrennarian preacher, began this sect in 1880. His second wife attempted to wrest control of the sect from the founder, but he managed to retain control and obtained an uncontested divorce. Headquarters were moved to Anderson in 1906, where the church also maintains a college and publishing house. Like the Nazarenes, the members of this church are moving in the direction of church status. A full-time professional ministry, growing emphasis on education, and development of church organization accelerate this evolution.

Although most Holiness leaders came from Methodist and Baptist backgrounds, the founder of the Christian and Missionary Alliance, A.B. Simpson, was a former Presbyterian preacher. Members of other Protestant denominations support the evangelistic work of this organization much as they lend support to the Salvation Army. Like the Army, the Christian and Missionary Alliance has developed into a denomination itself with a particular emphasis on poor communities and foreign missions. It reports 345,000 members in more than 1,900 U.S. congregations.

Membership growth in the various Holiness churches continues to outstrip the more traditional Protestant denominations, and these members put most other churchgoers to shame in the category of financial sacrifice. But the amazing growth in the Holiness tradition has been among the Pentecostals rather than the Perfectionists.

FURTHER READING

Redford, M.E., *The Rise of the Church of the Nazarene* (Kansas City, Mo.: Nazarene Publishing House, 1951).
Smith, John W.V., *A Brief History of the Church of God Reformation Movement* (Anderson, Ind.: Warner Press, 1977).

CHAPTER 12

The Pentecostals

Gift of Speaking in Tongues Claimed by Pentecostals

"Golam kebah shakar elemont."

"The Lord is praised on the highest mountains," interprets an earnest young woman sitting near the front of the small Pentecostal chapel.

"Folant remdad marino," continues the dignified gentleman, who might well be an insurance salesman or real-estate broker.

". . . and in the depths of the oceans," explains the interpreter.

This is a religious experience for the members of the congregation, even though an observer hears nothing but incoherent mumbling. The gentleman is thought to have received the baptism of the Holy Spirit and is now giving evidence of this gift by speaking in tongues.

The tongue-speaker, the interpreter, and the other Pentecostals are convinced that the gifts bestowed on the infant Church on the day of Pentecost have been restored to this church in these latter days. And paramount among these gifts is glossolalia, or the gift of speaking in a language the speaker has never known or studied. "They were all filled with the Holy Ghost, and began to speak in other tongues, as the Spirit gave them utterance" (Acts 2:4).

The millions of Pentecostals around the world do not agree on every detail of theology, but all Pentecostals believe every Christian can expect a second baptism, subsequent to conversion. Furthermore, each spirit baptism is demonstrated by some form of motor manifestation of ecstasy, almost always speaking in tongues. A few are privileged to receive the gift of tongues to be exercised throughout their lives; most speak in tongues only at their second baptism.

A common statement of Pentecostal belief would be that proclaimed by the Assemblies of God: "All believers are entitled to, and should ardently expect, and earnestly seek, the promise of the Father, the Baptism in the Holy Ghost and fire, according to the command of our Lord Jesus Christ. . . . This experience is distinct from and subsequent to the experience of the new birth" *(Statement of Fundamental Truths, 7).*

Furthermore, "The Baptism of believers in the Holy Ghost is witnessed by the initial physical sign of speaking with other tongues as the Spirit of God gives them utterance (Acts 2:4). The speaking in tongues in this instance is the same in essence as the gift of tongues (I Cor. 12:4-10, 28) but different in purpose and use" *(Statement of Fundamental Truths, 8).*

Linguists have difficulty identifying these tongues when they have been tape-recorded and studied. To this objection the Pentecostals point out that there are more than twenty-eight hundred languages being spoken around the world, and that no one linguist or even a corps of linguists could possibly recognize more than a handful.

Since the start of the Pentecostal movement around 1900, this branch of Christianity has grown at a remarkable rate. Dismissed for years as "holy rollers," the Pentecostals have forged ahead by energetic missionary activity.

Some scholars put the world Pentecostal membership in the tens of millions. Most Protestants in Latin America belong to Pentecostal churches rather than mainline churches such as the Baptist and Methodist.

Pentecostal manifestations such as tongue-speaking have appeared in such churches as the Episcopal, Lutheran, Catholic, and Presbyterian. These so-called neo-Pentecostals prefer to remain in their own churches and exercise their gift of tongues in prayer circles or private devotions.

Glossolalia was first reported outside the Pentecostal churches in 1960 when the rector of a fashionable Episcopal church in Van Nuys, Calif., began to speak in tongues. The resulting controversy led to the rector's resignation, but soon glossolalia made its appearance in other churches: Methodist, Lutheran, Reformed, Baptist, Presbyterian, Episcopal. Roman Catholics — priests, sisters, laymen — have reported the reception of the gifts of Pentecost, including speaking in tongues; students of the movement estimate as many as five hundred thousand Catholics participate in charismatic prayer groups.

The first manifestation of Pentecostalism among Roman Catholics occurred at Duquesne University in 1967, when four members of a prayer group reported they had received the baptism of the Holy Spirit and accompanying gift of tongues. The movement spread to the University of Notre Dame and to several Newman Centers. Today as many as twenty thousand Catholic charismatics gather for annual sessions on the Notre Dame campus, and their numbers include bishops and hundreds of priests and religious.

Catholic prayer groups meet in churches or private homes, where they read Scripture, pray, sing, offer testimonials, and engage in speaking in tongues and healing. Theologians from the Catholic tradition are less likely to claim that the tongues are actually foreign languages; they may consider the sounds a type of "ecstatic" speech the Christian uses when ordinary words fail to express his or her praise of God.

The amazing growth of Pentecostalism and its aggressive missionary programs have prompted some writers to call Pentecostalism the cutting edge of Protestantism.

Norwegian scholar Nils Bloch-Hoell has called Pentecostalism "the primitive Christianity of the less educated." These churches appeal mainly to those of limited income, social standing, and education, but millionaires and professors also can be found in the ranks of Pentecostal and neo-Pentecostal groups.

A three-year study at the University of Minnesota concluded that the Pentecostal movement is not limited to "the discontented, the deprived, or the deviant." Professor Luther P. Gerlach, who directed the study, stated: "Our own judgment is that most of them are outstandingly stable individuals." He attributed the rapid growth to several factors: An effective recruitment system usually through friends or relatives, a simple master plan from the Bible that gives members a high degree of confidence, a flexible organization, and an experience (speaking in tongues) that produces a fervent commitment to the cause.

Most Pentecostal churches are storefronts or small rented halls or buildings, but you can also find Pentecostals worshiping in contemporary church buildings in middle-class suburbs. One of the most influential Pentecostal groups, the Full Gospel Business Men's Fellowship, appeals to professionals and businessmen of Pentecostal and neo-Pentecostal persuasion.

The roots of Pentecostalism can be found in the Wesleyan revival of the eighteenth century. John Wesley taught that committed Christians could expect to receive a baptism of the Holy Spirit subsequent to conversion that would enable them to achieve perfection or complete holiness. Over the years this doctrine of entire sanctification received less and less attention in mainstream Methodism; only the tiny Free and Wesleyan Methodist churches put any great emphasis on Perfectionism or "holiness."

After the Civil War some American Methodists took a renewed interest in Holiness. Bloch-Hoell observes, "The Holiness Movement in which the Pentecostal Movement had its main roots, was a Puritan reaction against a supposedly stiffening institutionalism and secularism in the greater American churches" (*The Pentecostal Movement,* p. 12). The Methodist bishops tried to constrain Holiness enthusiasm, but thousands of Holiness people seceded. They formed separate churches, of which the largest is the Church of the Nazarene.

Speaking in tongues rarely was reported in Christendom from 100 A.D. to 1800. Some heretical groups such as the Montanists claimed this gift, and glossolalia appeared among the Quakers, Shakers, and members of the Catholic Apostolic Church (Irvingites). Article 7 of the Mormon Articles of Faith claims the gift of tongues for the Latter-day Saints, but its exercise has been circumscribed since some early unfortunate experiences.

A Methodist minister in the Holiness tradition, Charles F. Parham, opened a small Bible school in Topeka, Kansas, in 1900. The school's only textbook was the Bible, and the students were drawn from Methodist, Holiness, and Baptist backgrounds. Parham believed in the baptism of the Holy Spirit and asked his forty students to search the

Scriptures to see whether they could discover any physical evidence of this second baptism. The students completed their assignment and came to the conclusion that the one consistent evidence that this baptism had been received was that the baptized began to speak in tongues.

Parham and the students prayed earnestly that they would receive this baptism of the Holy Spirit and give evidence by speaking in tongues. On Jan. 1, 1901, Miss Agnes Ozman spoke in tongues at a school prayer meeting and became the first person to demonstrate glossolalia in the Pentecostal revival.

Others followed Ozman, and soon many of the students as well as the minister were speaking in tongues. Parham taught that the modern church should possess all the gifts of Pentecost, that every Christian could expect to receive a second baptism, and that every Christian so baptized should give initial evidence by speaking in tongues. This remains the common belief of all Pentecostals and of most neo-Pentecostals. For the next few years, Parham and his students carried the Pentecostal message to various communities in the South and the Southwest.

Now the scene shifts to Los Angeles. In 1906 the city had a population of about 230,000, mostly recent arrivals. A black woman who belonged to the Church of the Nazarene invited a Holiness preacher of her race to deliver a series of sermons in Los Angeles. Preacher W.J. Seymour had attended a Pentecostal Bible school in Houston. He accepted the invitation to come to California.

After one sermon the more conservative Nazarenes closed the door on Seymour. The preacher then began to instruct potential converts in a private home; later his followers took over a ramshackle building at 312 Azusa Street that had been used as a livery stable.

The Azusa mission in the Los Angeles ghetto became the worldwide center of early Pentecostalism. By the end of 1906 the movement claimed thirteen thousand adherents in the United States and Canada and had outposts in India, Norway, and Sweden. At first the Pentecostals tried to spread their doctrine in the established denominations, but they soon were forced to organize separate churches.

Holiness preachers from around the country came to Los Angeles to receive their second baptism. They planted the new ecstatic religion in New York, Chicago, and other cities. Norwegian Pentecostal T.B. Barratt, who introduced the revival to Europe, received his baptism at the mission.

Today dozens of distinct churches fit into the Pentecostal category, besides numberless storefront Pentecostal chapels.

Best known of these is probably the Assemblies of God. Despite the fall from grace of its two most prominent evangelists — Jimmy Swaggert and Jim Bakker — the Assemblies of God has enjoyed steady growth. Its current membership of 2,525,000 is about five times what it was in 1960.

The Assemblies of God was organized in Hot Springs, Ark., in 1914 and now reports members in every state and seventy-five foreign countries. It operates sixteen Bible institutes and colleges in this country and eighty such schools overseas. The sect supports 1,100 foreign missionaries.

The Assemblies of God does 80 percent of all evangelical work on American Indian reservations, has commissioned thirteen missionaries to convert the Jews, provides fifty ministers to the deaf. It offers correspondence Bible courses for prisoners and works with teen-age gangs. Some four hundred local congregations conduct religious services in jails.

The Assemblies of God maintains its headquarters in Springfield, Mo., where its printing plant produces more than eleven million tons of literature every day. This is also the home of the main college of the Assemblies: Central Bible College. Probably the best known member of the Assemblies of God today is John Ashcroft, who was appointed attorney general by President George W. Bush; he previously had served in the Senate.

Black Christians participated in the birth and early spread of Pentecostalism, and several of the larger churches are composed entirely of black members. The Church of God in Christ was founded in the 1890s as a Holiness church, but founder C.H. Jones brought his followers into the Pentecostal fold.

This body had only 31,000 members in 1936 and now claims a membership of 5,500,000. If accurate, this would mean that the Church of God in Christ has more adherents than all the other Pentecostal churches in the United States put together.

Another black church, the Apostolic Overcoming Holy Church of God (twelve thousand members) was founded in 1916 by a former Methodist minister. Members not only speak in tongues but also engage in ecstatic dancing during revival services. They follow a Puritan ethic that discourages the usual vices as well as slang, the use of snuff, and idle talk.

Many churches bear the name Church of God, and most of these hold Pentecostal views. The first Church of God started after a revival in Tennessee in 1886 and now maintains headquarters in Cleveland, Tenn. It has 753,000 adherents in this country and Canada and about as many in the missions. Its overseer, A.J. Tomlinson, was impeached in 1923; this led to numerous schisms.

A Unitarian Pentecostal church, the United Pentecostal Church, is said to enroll about three hundred thousand members. It denies the doctrine of the Trinity and insists that Father, Son, and Holy Spirit are one Person and that Person is Jesus Christ. This position also is known as the "Jesus Only" doctrine. Converts who previously had been baptized in the name of the Trinity must be rebaptized in the name of Jesus only.

The flamboyant Los Angeles evangelist Aimee Semple McPherson founded the International Church of the Foursquare Gospel, which is classified as a Pentecostal body. She employed every kind of publicity device to attract people to her huge Angelus Temple. Less Puritanical than most Pentecostals, she was married three times. Bloch-Hoell discusses this aspect of Aimee Semple McPherson, "who, in the course of a few years, developed from a strictly puritanical matron to a luxury-loving and extravagant grande dame" (*The Pentecostal Movement*, p. 117).

Her son, Rolf, served as president of the church from his mother's death in 1944 until his retirement in 1998. The Foursquare Church reports 238,000 members and sponsors an ambitious mission program.

Baptism of the Holy Spirit is usually sought in a prayer meeting, which may well last three hours. The individuals prepare themselves by prayer, fasting, Bible reading, and hymn singing. The baptism may come when a minister or others in the congregation lay hands on the individual.

Pentecostal churches are usually bare auditoriums devoid of altar, art, vestments, candles, and liturgical appurtenances. The piano lends itself better to gospel hymns than the organ, although a trumpet, piano accordion, or even drum may accompany the pianist.

Doctrinally the Pentecostals are Protestant Fundamentalists who rely on a literal interpretation of the Bible. They abhor higher criticism of the Scriptures and condemn the teaching of evolution as unbiblical.

Pentecostals accept the Trinity, original sin, the divinity of Jesus, the virgin birth, the resurrection. In some areas of theology as in their view of human nature they come closer to Roman Catholicism than to classical Protestantism, but Pentecostals usually view Catholicism as a corrupt and superstitious form of Christianity.

A prominent Pentecostal theologian comments:

"As regards salvation by justification, we are Lutherans. In baptismal formula, we are Baptists. As regards sanctification, we are Methodists. In aggressive evangelism, we are as the Salvation Army. But as regards Baptism in the Holy Spirit, we are Pentecostal, inasmuch as we believe and preach, that it is possible to be baptized in or filled by the Holy Ghost just as on the day of Pentecost."

An attempt to provide some unity in world Pentecostalism was made in 1947 by organizing a world conference. Since 1958 the conference has been called the Pentecostal World Conference; it meets every three years.

Pentecostals sometimes participate in local ministerial associations but usually boycott the National Council of Churches and the World Council of Churches. Some Pentecostal churches support the National Association of Evangelicals.

Some Pentecostals fear that the World Council may be leading unwary Protestants back to Rome, is infected with a Modernist theological bent, and has been infiltrated by Communists. One prominent Pentecostal scholar, Dr. David Du Plessis, attended the Second Vatican Council as an observer but did not represent any particular Pentecostal church.

Puritanism influences the moral code of Pentecostal churches. A Jesuit priest observes that the Pentecostal convert in Latin America gives up drinking and smoking, saves his money, puts in a full day's work, avoids luxuries and is sought after by employers as a sober and conscientious employee. Many Pentecostal bodies forbid liquor, tobacco, mixed bathing, dancing, bobbed hair, cosmetics and jewelry, secret societies, labor unions, the theater, card playing, and motion pictures. Although most Pentecostals belong to the lower economic class, they live frugally and can therefore afford to support the extensive missionary and evangelistic programs of their churches.

In a short history of one hundred years Pentecostalism has grown to become a major force in world Protantism. Its growth rate and its devotion to missionary work indicate it hardly has reached its peak. Adherents find a fellowship in Pentecostal churches that they never found in the older churches.

Students of the movement, and especially of the phenomenon of tongue-speaking, adopt one of three attitudes. One school, which includes many other Fundamentalists, condemns Pentecostalism and tongue-speaking as the work of demons. Another school accepts the possibility of genuine glossolalia. A third school considers glossolalia a purely psychological phenomenon. They believe under certain emotional stresses individuals can lose control of their vocal powers and utter sounds others call tongues.

The authenticated cases in which a person actually speaks a foreign language interpreted by someone who knows the language are extremely rare. Usually the sounds bear no relation to a known language. The mysterious powers of the subconscious cannot be ruled out in the few authenticated cases; an individual might be speaking a language used by a neighbor or heard on a radio and stored in the subconscious until released in an emotional and religious ecstasy. Similar natural explanations also can account for most of the healings produced by Pentecostal preachers.

Few religious movements as young as Pentecostalism can report as amazing a numerical growth. The next decades will be decisive for the movement. The influence of the neo-Pentecostals, the worldwide ecumenical movement, the higher educational standards for Pentecostal ministers, and the advances in medicine and psychology will affect the Pentecostal revival.

FURTHER READING

Bloch-Hoell, Nils, *The Pentecostal Movement* (New York: Humanities Press, 1965).

Damboriena, Prudencio, *Tongues As of Fire: Pentecostalism in Contemporary Christianity* (Washington and Cleveland: Corpus, 1969).

Harrell, David Edwin, *All Things are Possible: The Healing and Charismatic Revivals in Modern America* (Bloomington, Ind.: Indiana University Press, 1975).

Hoekema, Anthony, *What About Tongue Speaking?* (Grand Rapids, Mich.: Eerdmans, 1966).

Nichol, John T., *Pentecostalism* (New York: Harper & Row, 1966).

Ranaghan, Kevin and Dorothy, *Catholic Pentecostals* (Paramus, N.J.: Paulist Press Deus Books, 1969).

Sherrill, John L, *They Speak With Other Tongues* (New York: McGraw-Hill, 1964).

Simson, Eve, *The Faith Healer* (New York: Pyramid, 1977).

CHAPTER 13

The Seventh-day Adventists

*A Prophetess Combines Fundamentalism and
Recrudescent Judaism*

AT FIRST GLANCE, SEVENTH-DAY ADVENTISTS SEEM TO BE SIMPLY
conservative Protestants who emphasize the Second Coming of Christ
and go to church on Saturday instead of Sunday. Closer examination
reveals several basic departures from traditional Protestant theology
and practice.

While Catholics and most Protestants agree man's soul is immortal, Adventists insist man is mortal. Man does not *have* a soul; he *is* a
soul. At death the soul enters a state of deep sleep or unconsciousness
until the Second Coming, when those who have accepted Christ as
their Savior will receive immortality. The wicked are resurrected one
thousand years later at the close of the millennial reign of Christ and
are annihilated by fire together with Satan.

Therefore, while the righteous may receive the gift of immortality
and the wicked may be brought back to life briefly before their cremation, man's nature is basically mortal. Justin Martyr, a convert, apolo-
gist, and teacher who was beheaded in about 165, championed the
view that the souls of the just enter heaven only after the resurrection.
Echoes of this belief may be found in present-day Eastern Orthodoxy.

Adventists believe that the followers of Christ will be raised from
the dead and reign with Him in heaven for a millennium. During this
time the Earth will be depopulated, a wilderness and prison for the devil.

Adventists attribute the belief that people go to heaven or hell
immediately after death to the infiltration of pagan mythology into
Christianity. They attempt to prove from the Bible that the dead are
asleep until the Second Coming.

At the close of the millennium the Holy City, New Jerusalem, will descend to Earth. In it will be Christ and His faithful. From its walls they will witness the resurrection and final destruction of the wicked. Then they will dwell for eternity in an Earth made pure once more.

Catholics and Protestants, on the contrary, teach that man has both a body and a soul. His soul is immortal. At death each man is judged and assigned to heaven, hell, or purgatory. (Protestants generally reject the idea of a place of temporary punishment and purification.)

The Catholic Church teaches that the Second Coming of Christ will precede the Last Judgment. The millennium is not a literal one thousand years, but indicates the entire period between the Incarnation and the Last Judgment. At the resurrection man's soul is reunited with his body, with special characteristics of glory for the saved. The Earth will be destroyed.

Adventists propagate their eschatological doctrines with an aggressiveness and sense of urgency that has brought them a good measure of success. To many they appear as prophets of gloom and doom. Embarrassed by several awkward date-setting episodes in their pioneer days, they carefully avoid such pitfalls today. Their revivalists and preachers, however, produce all types of natural catastrophes, wars, A- and H-bombs, modern inventions, and moral lapses as evidence that mankind is living in the latter days.

Total abstinence from liquor and tobacco is not only recommended but considered a sure test of Christian faith. Any who have not eschewed cigarettes and beer are refused baptism; adherents who lapse into such habits are promptly excommunicated.

The movement likewise commands an observance of the Jewish dietary laws, forbidding the eating of pork and other unclean flesh itemized in the Old Testament. In fact, for health reasons, most Adventists are vegetarians.

The Seventh-day Adventist and Mormon churches are the two best-known denominations to base their financial structure on the tithe. Adventists expect each member to tithe his gross income, as this is the divine plan for church support as revealed in the Bible. The basic tithe or 10 percent goes to the support of the ministry. Over and above this, other offerings provide for church buildings, maintenance, parochial schools, publishing plants, missions, relief work, and more. Many Adventists contribute twenty percent or more of their income to the church; virtually all members in good standing tithe.

With funds received from tithes, the Seventh-day Adventist Church employs some seventy-five thousand men and women as missionaries, teachers, printers, medical personnel, and the like. This means that one Adventist out of every seventy-five is a full-time salaried employee of the church. Salaries of these church workers, even college presidents and physicians, fall far below what they could receive in secular employment.

Statistics consistently show the Adventist Church at the head of the list of Protestant denominations in per capita contributions. A recent year indicated a per capita contribution of $1,088, probably many times that of American Catholics. This should be multiplied by a factor of three or so to obtain the average family contribution: about $3,000.

Their observance of the seventh-day has become almost an obsession. Their literature insists time and again that man's most important responsibility in this life is the correct choice of God's seal (the Saturday Sabbath) or the beast's sign (Sunday). Those who changed the Christian observance from the Judaic Saturday to Sunday are branded as tools of Satan. Christians who persist in keeping Sunday as the Lord's Day become accomplices in this nefarious plot to disobey God's own commandment.

Because history plainly records that the Catholic Church changed the Christian observance in memory of Christ's resurrection on Easter Sunday, Adventists hold the popes and "Romanism" responsible for deception. However, Protestants find themselves far more vulnerable to Adventist attacks on this score because they hold the Bible to be the sole rule of faith. "Search your Bible from Genesis to Revelation and show me any authorization for a Sunday Sabbath observance," challenges the Adventist.

Catholics point out that the word Sabbath means "rest," and the third commandment commands man to rest every seventh day and to offer special worship to God. The Jews chose Saturday for their Sabbath, while the early Christians chose Sunday. Writing in the fourth century, St. Augustine comments, "The Apostles and their contemporaries sanctioned the dedication of Sunday to the worship of God."

Adventists, preoccupied with what they consider the letter of the law, reason that because all other Christian churches have tampered with God's commandment without biblical leave, these churches must be apostate. Thus the Seventh-day Adventist Church alone constitutes the remnant church in these last days. This charge in the face of today's "live and let live" ecumenism arouses bitter feeling among other Protestants. Some of the harshest anti-Adventist tracts circulate among Fundamentalists who would otherwise find common cause with the Adventists.

The Seventh-day Adventists operate the largest Protestant parochial school system in the world. More than one million students from grade school through college attend fifty-eight hundred Adventist schools.

In higher education in this country it supports twelve coeducational colleges and two universities — Andrews University in Berrien Springs, Mich., and Loma Linda University at Loma Linda, Calif. The latter concentrates largely on medical education, annually turning out some three hundred physicians, dentists, and graduates in related fields. Andrews University's major emphasis is the training of theologians, though degrees in other liberal arts areas also are granted by both institutions.

Adventism is growing rapidly. Worldwide membership has surpassed 10 million; of these 840,000 live in the United States. The extraordinarily generous support from tithing enables the sect to finance a missionary, publishing, and educational effort out of proportion to its numbers.

It all began during the early decades of the nineteenth century when some Protestant clergymen and laymen began to study Bible prophecy. Many calculated that the Second Coming was at hand and would certainly occur during their lifetimes. Someone has estimated that three hundred Anglican ministers and twice that number of Nonconformists in England were heralding the imminent personal return of Christ in the 1820s and 1830s. This enthusiasm found converts in England, the continent, and the New World.

William Miller, a War of 1812 veteran, a converted Deist and Baptist farmer-preacher, spearheaded the American version. Miller concentrated on the Books of Daniel and Revelation. His chief discovery was that the twenty-three hundred days in Daniel 8:13-14 meant years. Figuring from the year 457 B.C., the date of the commandment to restore Jerusalem, he announced that the Second Coming could be expected in 1843. He began preaching this news in 1831.

People flocked to the movement from the old-line Protestant churches, and hundreds of ministers enrolled under Adventism's banners. But 1843 came and passed. The date was revised to Oct. 22, 1844. By this time at least fifty thousand people were known as Adventists, and Miller issued a call that his followers come out of "Babylon." By Babylon he meant the other Protestant communions. Many sold their possessions, settled their affairs, and awaited the Great Day. The press helped to publicize the event. But Oct. 22, 1844, also came and passed.

Disillusioned, thousands abandoned religion entirely as a monstrous hoax; others drifted sheepishly back to their former church homes in "Babylon." Miller died lonely and forgotten, expelled by the Baptists in 1845. But a tiny band of diehards in Washington, N.H., remained true to Adventism and reopened their Bibles to see what had gone wrong. They were First-day Adventists.

This group of New England Millerites formed the nucleus of the present Seventh-day Adventist Church. They insisted, despite rather convincing evidence to the contrary, that the 1844 date was correct. Finally, one of their number hit upon the explanation that the error was not in the date but in interpreting the date in terms of an earthly event. What really happened on Oct 22, 1844, was that Christ had entered the most holy place in the heavenly sanctuary. Here He offered His blood as the purchase price for man's redemption.

This explanation rescued the wobbly movement from complete collapse. Satisfied that they had not been deceived by Miller, the group rekindled their Adventist hopes and resolved never again to set a date for the Second Coming.

All the leaders in the reorganized Adventist church, including Joseph Bates, James White, and his wife, Ellen White (née Harmon), had been closely associated with the pre-1844 Millerites. Of this trio, Mrs. White became the undoubted leader. Never a church officer or minister, she was and is considered a prophetess by Seventh-day Adventists. She dictated many of her twenty books and three thousand articles while in a trance, and her writings are held to be inspired.

Mrs. White, a Methodist in her early youth, guided the Seventh-day Adventist Church for nearly seventy years, dying in 1915. She has been elevated to a role comparable to that of Mrs. Eddy in Christian Science. Here again Adventists cross swords with fellow Fundamentalists, who reject Mrs. White's visions and inspiration altogether.

By 1855 the church had gained enough adherents in Michigan to establish a national headquarters in Battle Creek. The present name of the church was adopted in 1860. In 1903 headquarters were shifted to Takoma Park, a suburb of Washington, D.C.

From a visiting Seventh-day Baptist the Adventists picked up their second distinctive doctrine. Prophetess White confirmed this doctrinal standard by announcing that an angel had shown her the tablets of the Ten Commandments with a great halo of light surrounding the defiled fourth (Catholic third) commandment.

The 1906 religious census reported a Seventh-day Adventist membership of 62,111. Fifty years later this enrollment had quadrupled in this country, with even greater gains outside the continental United States. Few denominations have done as well. The church registers its largest membership in California, Oregon, Michigan, Washington, and Florida.

Standards of personal conduct among Adventists are strict. Of course, no Adventist may drink or smoke. Other prohibitions include card playing, dancing, attendance at the movies or theater, costly or immodest apparel, jewelry, and lodge membership. Use of coffee, tea, and pepper is discouraged.

They observe the Sabbath from sundown Friday to sundown Saturday. Adventists attend Sabbath school and church services on Saturday and abstain from all buying, selling, and unnecessary labor. Most food is prepared Friday before the Sabbath begins as in Orthodox Jewish households. Bible reading and study of church publications are recommended for the rest of the Sabbath.

Converts are instructed in the essentials of Adventism, and must promise to tithe, observe the Sabbath, and practice total abstinence before they are admitted to baptism. Baptism of adults by immersion is the rule.

Their worship service resembles that of other nonliturgical Protestant denominations. A foot-washing ceremony in separate rooms precedes the quarterly observance of the Lord's Supper. To Adventists this constitutes merely a memorial service; all those attending are invited to the Communion table. Only grape juice is used.

Incidentally, the Seventh-day Adventists refuse to observe Easter, which they claim is a pagan and unscriptural holiday.

Seventh-day Adventists once attempted proselytizing campaigns incognito, not revealing sponsorship of revivals and community meetings. Now, however, their evangelists are instructed to identify their services, and the hidden sponsor is the exception rather than the rule. Their widespread "Voice of Prophecy" radio program and "Faith for Today" TV series also are now presented with Adventist credit lines.

No church sponsors a more ambitious foreign mission program. Adventist medical, educational, and religious work is now carried on in 189 countries. The only nations not penetrated by indefatigable Seventh-day Adventist evangelists are Afghanistan, Crete, and Vatican City. An ex-priest by the name of M.B. Czechowski inaugurated Adventist evangelism in Europe in the nineteenth century. Today four out of every five Seventh-day Adventists reside outside the United States, an indication the success of this missionary endeavor. For example, the entire population of Pitcairn Island (of *Mutiny on the Bounty* fame) has embraced the faith.

Health reform became a plank of the Adventist platform after a revelation to the prophetess in 1863. Members show a concern for health seldom found among other Fundamentalists. In their chain of 136 hospitals and sanitariums and 232 clinics, Adventist doctors, nurses, dietitians, X-ray technicians, and dentists care for more than five million patients each year. Seventh-day Adventist institutions graduate one hundred physicians and twelve hundred nurses annually. Although they emphasize drugless healing and hydrotherapy, they do not neglect surgery or modern medication. *Life and Health* magazine features popular health articles with a Seventh-day Adventist twist regarding alcohol and tobacco.

An Adventist layman, Dr. J.H. Kellogg, invented a breakfast cereal and changed the menus at millions of American breakfast tables. Adventists started the pioneer Battle Creek (Mich.) sanitarium for treatment of nervous disorders and introduced the techniques of hydrotherapy and physical therapy.

A flood of literature pours from fifty-six Adventist printing presses, of which thirty-four are overseas. About 75 new book titles are issued yearly, in addition to 348 periodicals in 300 languages. A bimonthly magazine entitled *Liberty* advocates separation of church and state and serves as an organ of the National Religious Liberty Association. Adventists oppose tax-supported welfare measures for parochial school pupils, including their own. Their publications regularly blast Sunday blue laws urged by fellow Protestants.

Adventist scholars are thoroughly anti-evolutionist and have supplied this school with some of its most respected controversialists, such as Professor George McCready Price. They believe the Earth was created in six literal days.

Seventh-day Adventists are not pacifists and do not seek exemption from military service. They call themselves "conscientious cooperators" rather than "conscientious objectors"; they do not avoid army service but object to bearing arms. To prepare their young men for medical duty, the sect operates thirty-five training programs each year.

Local church government is technically congregational. The district conference appoints pastors and coordinates area activities, and the General Conference wields great power. Pastors are called "Elder" or "Pastor." Seminary training is required for ordination, but many receive a bachelor's degree in theology from a church college that serves the purpose. Women as well as men serve as grade school and Bible class teachers.

Adventists do not consider themselves bound by a creed. Nevertheless, the annual *Yearbook* includes a statement of "Fundamental Beliefs of Seventh-day Adventists." They reject predestination and seem to stress man's cooperation in the work of justification more than most evangelicals.

Not all Adventists whose faith survived the Millerite debacle were attracted to Seventh-day Adventism. A number of smaller Adventists bodies are listed in religious directories. The largest of these, the Advent Christian Church, reports twenty-six thousand adherents. It upholds the conscious state of the dead and the eternal punishment of the wicked; it observes the Sunday Sabbath.

The Seventh-day Adventist doctrines of soul-sleep after death and the annihilation of the wicked have been appropriated by Jehovah's Witnesses, whose founder, Russell, received his introduction to millennialism in Adventism. However, Seventh-day Adventists differ from their Watchtower cousins in a number of respects, among which are the Saturday Sabbath, the character of the millennium, military service, voting and civic responsibilities, and the tithe.

The Seventh-day Adventists play no part in the contemporary ecumenical movement because they believe their church alone qualifies as the remnant church and obeys all God's commandments in a literal way. They do not, however, claim to be the only true Christians. In their *Questions on Doctrine* we read: "We fully recognize the heartening fact that a host of true followers of Christ are scattered all through the various churches of Christendom, including the Roman Catholic communion" (p. 197). The same Adventist text declares: "We respect and love those of our fellow Christians who do not interpret God's Word just as we do."

FURTHER READING

Froom, L.R.E., *The Prophetic Faith of Our Fathers* (Washington, D.C.: Review and Herald, 1946-54, 4 vols.).

Gaustad, Edwin S., ed., *The Rise of Adventism* (New York: Harper & Row, 1974).

Herndon, Booton, *The Seventh Day* (New York: McGraw-Hill, 1960).

Noorbergen, Rene, *Ellen G. White: Prophet of Destiny* (New Canaan, Conn.: Keats, 1972).

Numbers, Ronald L., *Prophetess of Health: A Study of Ellen G. White* (New York: Harper & Row, 1976).

Seventh-day Adventists Answer Questions on Doctrine (Washington, D.C.: Review and Herald, 1957).

CHAPTER 14

Other Protestants

*American Protestantism Comprises More Than
220 Churches and Sects*

EVERY SECOND AMERICAN PROTESTANT IS A BAPTIST OR METHODIST, and 80 percent of the Protestant Christians in this country belong to the thirteen largest denominations. Nevertheless, we find hundreds of smaller groups that are classified as Protestant for census and tabulation purposes. Some of these are Protestant only in the sense in that they are not Catholic: Mormonism, Christian Science, Unitarianism, Spiritualism, and others. Many are subdivisions of denominational families such as the Two-Seed-in-the-Spirit Predestinarian Baptists and the Lumber River Annual Conference of the Holiness Methodist Church. Scores of sects belong to the Holiness and Pentecostal family, and some are unique, such as the "House of God, Which is the Church of the Living God, the Pillar and Ground of Truth, Inc.," and the "House of David."

This chapter will examine a number of significant but smaller churches in the Protestant tradition. These include the Moravians, the Mennonites, the Reformed and Christian Reformed, the Brethren or "Dunkers," the members of the Salvation Army, and the Mission Covenanters. All of these churches represent more or less distinct traditions and could not conveniently be grouped with other denominations.

The Moravians

One of the two Protestant bodies that predate the Reformation, the Moravian Church received its inspiration from John Huss, a Bohemian priest and rector of the University of Prague who was burned at the stake for heresy in 1415. (The other pre-Reformation Protestants are the Waldenses in northern Italy.)

Huss appealed to the authority of the Bible alone, rejected the doctrine of purgatory and the invocation of the saints, and demanded the cup for the laity. His followers disagreed among themselves after his execution, but a small group organized in 1457 as the Unity of the Brethren or Unitas Fratrum. They wielded influence in Bohemia, Poland, and Moravia for more than two centuries. By the time Luther was nailing his Ninety-five Theses to the Wittenberg church door, this Bohemian Protestant Church numbered about 175,000 members in 400 congregations.

The Counter-Reformation and the Thirty Years' War all but obliterated the Hussites, most of whom were absorbed into the Catholic, Lutheran, and Reformed churches. A few diehards kept alive Hussite beliefs and traditions, and this underground church found a distinguished leader in the educator John Amos Comenius.

Count Nicholas Ludwig von Zinzendorf, a Lutheran layman, sponsored the Moravian revival in the eighteenth century. He turned over a corner of his Saxony estate to a nucleus of the Unitas Fratrum, nominally Catholic, with the thought that they would act as a leaven in the Lutheran establishment.

Eventually the Moravians at Herrnhut became a separate church and chose Zinzendorf as their bishop. The first large-scale Protestant missionaries, they worked among black slaves on St. Thomas Island in the West Indies beginning in 1732 and among the American Indians in Georgia in 1735. As we have seen, a band of Moravian missionaries traveling to the New World impressed John Wesley, the founder of Methodism, with their piety and faith. Moravianism multiplied its influence on Protestantism through Wesley and the Wesleyan revival.

Bethlehem and Nazareth in Pennsylvania and Salem in North Carolina became centers for American Moravianism. Zinzendorf himself visited this country in 1741, and for many years Moravian settlements in America were closely supervised from the German headquarters. Changes in the middle of the nineteenth century brought autonomy in church government to the American members.

Today the Moravian Church in America includes two provinces. The fifty congregations in the southern province are within one hundred twenty miles of Winston-Salem and enroll about twenty-one thousand members. The northern province takes in the rest of the country and reports twenty-six thousand communicants in ninety-five congregations.

Total Moravian membership worldwide exceeds 507,000, including 56,000 in the United States. American Moravians maintain missions in Alaska, Nicaragua, and Honduras, while other Moravians staff missions in ten other areas. Herrnhut itself is now a village of two thousand in Germany, while Bethlehem, Pa., has become a steel city of seventy-five thousand.

This church follows a church year and a liturgical form of worship, but the Moravian churches themselves have no altars. A distinctive Moravian custom is the love feast, which consists of coffee and buns; the Lord's Supper is observed half a dozen times a year. The Moravian liturgies for Christmas Eve, Holy Week, and Easter Dawn attract many people because of their beauty and solemnity.

Besides the major Moravian body in the United States, there is the thirty-two-hundred-member Unity of the Brethren. Until 1962 this group was known as the Evangelical Unity of the Czech-Moravian Brethren in North America. It enrolls descendants of immigrants who began arriving in Texas in 1850 and is similar to the Unitas Fratrum.

A small component of world Protestantism, the Moravian Church has made an important contribution through its missionary programs, its influence on other Protestants such as Wesley, and its liturgy and hymns.

The Mennonites

Once the Reformation sundered the unity of Western Christendom, more radical groups than the Lutherans and Reformed urged a complete return to what they considered primitive Christianity. Chief among these sects were the various Anabaptist bodies, which insisted that infant baptism was unscriptural. Adults who had been baptized as infants had to submit to rebaptism, hence the name Anabaptist.

These early Anabaptists became the object of intense persecution by state and church officials. The first martyr in 1527 was bound hands to knees, rowed to the middle of a lake, and dumped overboard to drown. Later, thousands of others throughout Europe would be broken on the rack, left to rot in prison, beheaded, and burned.

The Anabaptists taught nonresistance to evil, which meant they refused to serve in the army. They preferred an untrained and unsalaried ministry chosen by lot and believed the church should be a brotherhood of believers without hierarchy or titles. They would not swear any oaths or hold any public office.

Menno Simons, a Catholic priest for twelve years, left the Church to join the conservative Anabaptist wing. He systematized its organization and theology and provided such outstanding leadership to these despised Anabaptists that their movement became known by his name, the Mennonites.

Around the world some 480,000 adults belong to the Mennonite family of churches; of these the largest number are North Americans. But this is a spiritual family plagued by schisms since its earliest days. Over the centuries Mennonites have quarreled over whether a second band of suspenders constitutes worldly luxury and whether one or two people should wash and wipe the feet in the foot washing ceremony. In the United States alone, the estimated 217,000 baptized Mennonites belong to at least 19 different church bodies.

Many of the most serious divisions have sprung from the use of the ban or "shunning." The Anabaptists always have sought to establish a voluntary church of saints, in contrast to a state church that embraced saints and sinners, children and adults, believers and mere conformists. To preserve the exclusive character of their congregations, the Mennonites have resorted to excommunication more than most churches.

The Amish, for example, enforce the ban to the extent that an excommunicated husband cannot eat at the same table or have sexual relations with his wife. He is completely ostracized from the community and his own family. Moderate and progressive Mennonites still enforce excommunication and strongly discourage marriage outside of the religious family but do not apply the ban as the Amish do.

Jacob Amman, a Swiss bishop, thought the church was not strict enough in enforcing the ban. He traveled around the Mennonite communities urging a return to traditional ways, and his followers began to withdraw from the main body in 1693. No Amish remain in Europe, but they can be found in Pennsylvania and several Midwestern states.

In Holland the number of Mennonites has declined from an estimated 160,000 in 1700 to fewer than 38,000 today. They may have diluted their Anabaptist principles in the eyes of many American Mennonites, but they have prospered and sit on the boards of some of the largest Dutch corporations, hold distinguished professorships, serve in the cabinet, and contribute members out of proportion to medicine and the sciences in that country.

Outside North America and the Netherlands, the largest bodies of Mennonites are reported in Russia (40,000), India (30,000), Zaire (40,000), Germany (11,000), and Indonesia, (21,000).

Lancaster, Pa., became the center for Swiss Mennonites in the United States, although later immigrations brought the church to the Midwest. Mennonites are universally respected as scrupulously honest and God-fearing. Despite a reluctance by some to adopt mechanized farming methods, they are known to be excellent farmers.

The two largest Mennonite bodies voted to merge in 2001. The Mennonite Church and the General Conference Mennonite Church will form the new Mennonite Church, USA, with 125,000 members.

Almost half the Mennonites in the United States belong to the Mennonite Church, whose members once were known as the Old Mennonites. These ninety-two thousand Mennonites occupy what might be considered a middle ground between the ultraconservative Amish and the progressive General Conference Mennonite Church. But all Mennonites in North America share a relatively conservative theology in the context of contemporary Protestantism.

The Mennonite Church finds its strength in Pennsylvania, Virginia, Indiana, Ohio, Iowa, and Ontario. This group supports eleven high schools, three colleges, a hospital, two nursing schools, three children's homes, and four homes for the aged. Most of its members are farmers, but a growing number are going into other occupations such as teaching, medicine, and business.

Membership in this church has quadrupled since 1900, mostly through a high birth rate. Its ranks have been augmented by former Amish who have become dissatisfied with the sect's strict rules. It sponsors the Mennonite Hour, which is carried by several hundred radio stations and maintains two hundred twenty overseas missionaries.

A statement of doctrine declares: "That mixed marriages between believers and unbelievers are unscriptural, and marriage with divorced persons with former companions living constitutes adultery." These Christians also hold that it is unscriptural to "follow wordly fashions, engage in warfare, swear oaths, or join secret societies."

A somewhat more progressive stance characterizes the General Conference Mennonite Church, organized in Iowa in 1860. This church always has sought the union of all Mennonites and has fostered seminary training for ministers, foreign missions, and church publications. It has thirty-six thousand members in the United States and almost seventeen thousand in Canada; an estimated two-thirds are of Dutch ancestry and the rest, Swiss.

Russian-German immigrants who began to enter America in 1874 organized the Mennonite Brethren of North America. Most members now live in Kansas and Oklahoma, but there are others in several western states. There are slightly more Mennonite Brethren in Canada (17,500) than in the United States (17,000). This small church supports the work of 224 missionaries in 16 countries. Their efforts have won twenty thousand adherents in India and eighty-seven hundred in Zaire; home missions serve the American Indians and Mexican Americans in the Southwest.

Most picturesque and traditional of the many Mennonite factions are the Old Order Amish. These eighty thousand Amish impose the strict ban on backsliders, prescribe dress regulations, oppose all education beyond grammar school, worship in homes and barns instead of churches, and speak a dialect known as Pennsylvania Dutch. They do not believe in missions, Sunday schools, or church conferences.

Their communities stretch from Lancaster County through Ohio, Indiana, and Illinois to Iowa, and they own some of the richest farmlands in the nation. The Amish make no compromises with the world or the idea of progress. Their motto is: "The old is the best and the new is of the devil."

Amish parents consider their lives a success if all their children have married Amish, live on farms, and remain within the Amish faith. Young people join the church through baptism in their late teens and subscribe to the Ordnung or rules of their particular branch. In general these rules forbid the use of electricity, telephones, central heating, automobiles, tractors with pneumatic tires, buttons, and higher education. Certain Amish groups add prohibitions against mirrors, high heels, silk clothing, bright colors, photographs, pressed trousers, and the like.

A church that excommunicates anyone who buys an automobile, goes to high school, or marries outside the faith is bound to lose some young people. But because the average Amish family has seven to nine children, the total Amish community grows each year. When one Amish man died in Indiana in 1933, he was said to have 565 living descendants.

Because of the size of their families and the shortage of farmland, most Amish now work in factories rather than in agriculture.

These four major bodies — the Mennonite Church, General Conference Mennonite Church, Mennonite Brethren Church, and Old Order Amish — claim 85 percent of U.S. Mennonites, but there are at least fifteen other branches.

The Amish and other Mennonites invariably win the respect of their neighbors for their honesty, simple living, and industriousness. Their witness for peace is perhaps needed more now than during the past centuries. Yet their doctrinal splits and their traditional way of life have undercut any message they might have for other Americans.

The Reformed

Calvinism took early root in Holland, and Dutch colonists brought their Reformed Church to New Amsterdam. Their Collegiate Church in New York City, organized in 1628, is the oldest Protestant church in the nation with an uninterrupted ministry. Members of this Dutch Calvinist church founded a college at New Brunswick that later became Rutgers.

Church affairs were closely regulated by the Classis of Amsterdam until 1771, when the American branch won the right to train and ordain its own ministers. By 1830 the exclusive use of the Dutch language had ceased. A later Dutch immigration that began in 1847 gave this denomination a sizable Midwest constituency. The present name, which eliminates a national label, was adopted in 1867.

The Reformed Church in America reports 295,000 communicants. Its best-known minister was Dr. Norman Vincent Peale, pastor of Marble Collegiate Church in New York City and author of *The Power of Positive Thinking;* he began his ministerial career as a Methodist. Another prominent minister of this denomination is the Reverend Robert Schuller, TV evangelist and pastor of the huge Garden Grove Community Church in California.

This church is broadly characterized by theological conservatism, a semi-liturgical posture in worship, and a confessional basis summarized in the Heidelberg Catechism, the Belgic Confession, and the Canons of the Synod of Dort.

The Christian Reformed

A protest against laxism in the Dutch Reformed Church led to the formation of the strict Christian Reformed Church in 1857. Ministers of five congregations accused the mother church of diluting Calvinism, slighting the doctrine of predestination, and tolerating Masonry and other secret societies. Within a decade the protesters had won few followers, but immigrants from Holland and anti-Masonic dissenters from the parent body added new strength.

This church supports a seminary in Grand Rapids, Mich., and two colleges, and operates 246 parochial grade schools for parents of 50,000 pupils who wish to educate their children in uncompromising Calvinism.

Since its founding the Christian Reformed Church has held fast to the rigid Calvinism of the Heidelberg, Dordrecht, and Belgic Confessions. This church belongs to neither the National nor World Councils of Churches. It reports 199,000 members. The Christian Reformed Church reflects sixteenth century Geneva Calvinism in twenty-first century America.

The Brethren

To some of the people of Schwarzenau, Germany, in the early years of the eighteenth century, the spiritual level of established Lutheran and Reformed churches was too low for dedicated Christians. Influenced by Anabaptist and Pietist teaching, they formed a new church in 1708 under the leadership of Alexander Mack, Sr. One member of the first congregation of eight baptized Mack by immersing him three times in the name of the Trinity, and Mack in turn baptized the others. The Church of the Brethren was born.

In a few years persecution would drive almost all of the Brethren from their homeland to the New World. Welcomed by William Penn, one group settled at Germantown near Philadelphia in 1719. A second group, led by Mack himself, lived for a few years in Holland and arrived in America in 1729. When a third party left Germany in 1733, the organized life of the Brethren movement came to a close in Europe.

The Brethren also were known by other names. Sometimes they were identified as German Baptists and sometimes as Dunkers from the German word *tunken,* which means to dip or immerse.

Today more than 159,000 members belong to the 1,100 congregations of the Church of the Brethren in the United States. This is the largest of half a dozen churches comprising the Brethren movement. Most Church of the Brethren congregations are found in Pennsylvania, Maryland, Virginia, Ohio, Indiana, and Illinois. Another 19,500 Brethren belong to overseas congregations. Of these there are ten thousand Brethren in Nigeria, nine thousand in India, and small groups in Ecuador and Canada.

In doctrine the Brethren share the basic beliefs of other evangelical Protestants. They belong to the National Council of Churches and World Councils of Churches. Yet the Church of the Brethren observes certain distinctive rites and holds positions not held by mainline Protestants. For example, the Brethren, like the Quakers and Mennonites, belong to one of the historic peace churches. Young men can claim conscientious objector status by simply giving evidence of membership in the Church of the Brethren or other Brethren bodies.

The Brethren observe four ordinances: baptism, the love feast, anointing for healing of the sick, and laying on of hands. The candidate for baptism kneels in the water and is immersed three times in the name of the Father, Son, and Holy Spirit. Infant baptism is rejected as a violation of free choice in religion. Those who may have been baptized by pouring or sprinkling in other denominations and wish to join the Brethren Church need not be rebaptized.

The love feast, observed once or twice a year, takes up the entire evening and includes three parts. In the first part the congregation divides itself into men and women and performs the foot washing ceremony. The entire congregation then enjoys a full meal, regarded as the counterpart of the original Lord's Supper. Finally, the Brethren partake of the bread and wine of the Communion service. The Brethren understand the Eucharist in the memorial sense rather than in terms of a Real Presence. Communion also may be scheduled at other times throughout the year apart from the complete love feast.

Those who are sick or in danger of death may be anointed with oil. This rite is common in Roman Catholicism and Eastern Orthodoxy but rare in Protestantism. Finally, the Brethren employ the laying on of hands in baptism, the installation of deacons, ordination of ministers, commissioning of missionaries, and anointing of the sick.

The Church of the Brethren refuses to accept any creed because it regards the New Testament as its "rule of faith and practice." It rejects the Old Testament as a proper guide for Christians. All other Protestants value both the Old and New Testaments as the Word of God.

The Brethren present the simple life as the ideal. They are asked to avoid all ostentation and extravagance such as jewelry and costly clothes. Brethren are expected to observe total abstinence, avoid secret societies, and refrain from oaths.

Local churches follow a congregational polity. The Annual Conference of representatives has final authority, but this is not necessarily binding on local congregations. Church general offices are in Elgin, Ill.

The Church of the Brethren supports six liberal arts colleges, which enroll about five thousand students, and a graduate school of theology in Chicago. Originally, churches were served by an unsalaried ministry, but full-time ministers now care for most churches.

This church is noted for its relief work overseas and in this country. It organized the Brethren Service Committee after World War II. The Brethren Volunteer Service enrolls young men for one- and two-year tours of service and antedated the Peace Corps. Young men choosing alternative service in lieu of military service also may join the BVS. A Brethren project to send heifers to needy farm families overseas has been supported by many other denominations.

Divisions within the parent church during the past century have given rise to a number of other Brethren bodies. In 1881 a group of about three thousand Brethren objected to what they considered liberalism in the church. Debate raged over the role of revivals, Sunday schools, methods of foot washing, and "worldly" dress. The dissidents formed the Old German Baptist Church, also known as the Old Order Brethren. Most members of the six thousand Old Order Brethren live in Pennsylvania, Ohio, Indiana, Kansas, and California.

In 1882 another group of Brethren withdrew because they thought the church was too conservative; they organized the Brethren Church (Progressive). This church eventually split into two branches. The Grace Brethren, also known as the National Fellowship of Brethren Churches, favor a Calvinist theology and maintain headquarters at Winona Lake, Ind. They report forty-one thousand adherents. The other branch, the Brethren Church, has headquarters in Ashland, Ohio, and has about 13,500 members. Two other tiny Brethren bodies are the Dunkard Brethren Church and the Fundamental Brethren Church.

Other denominations such as the Plymouth Brethren, Moravian Brethren, United Brethren, and River Brethren are identified as "Brethren," but have no connection with the Church of the Brethren.

The Brethren try to live lives of simplicity, peace, temperance, and brotherhood in a world that often prefers sham, war, and dissension.

The Salvationists

In its war against "slumdom, rumdom and bumdom" the Salvation Army adopted a military form of organization that suggests a comparison with a Catholic religious order. Popular opinion often views the Salvation Army as a relief agency with religious undertones. On the contrary, the Army is an evangelical Protestant sect that carries out its religious mission through social service.

Founded by a saintly Methodist minister in England, the "Christian Mission" carried the gospel to the vicious slums of London. But William Booth found his poor converts felt unwelcome in the "respectable" churches, Methodist or Anglican, and he found it necessary to provide separate worship services and church facilities. The name "Salvation Army" and the military organization were adopted in 1878, and Booth became General Booth.

General Booth's devoted wife, the mother of his eight children, died in 1890, but the General continued his tireless efforts for the down and out. He visited America every four years. He was honored by kings and presidents, and received honorary doctorates from Oxford and Brussels Universities. He died blind and penniless at the age of eighty-four.

Clergymen were the officers of this army, with titles from lieutenant to general. Converts became recruits and soldiers and wore a military uniform after they had signed the "Articles of War" against liquor, tobacco, and vice. Orders came from the top and were obeyed by junior officers. The Salvation Army officer wears a uniform at all times, receives "marching orders" to a new post, progresses through a system

162

of ranks, receives a salute, takes his vacation as a "furlough," participates in "knee drills" or prayer meetings, and is lowered into his grave to the sound of taps.

Officers are recruited from the ranks of soldiers and are selected to attend an intensive two-year course at one of the four schools for Officers Training in the United States. Cadets supplement their classroom work with field assignments. They assist in Army centers, practice street-corner preaching, give open-air concerts, and sell copies of the *War Cry*. Upon graduation, they are commissioned lieutenants. Salvation Army officers may perform marriages, preach, christen children, and serve as armed forces chaplains. They agree to marry within the Army family and to serve at their post for life. A wife holds equal rank with her husband.

The Salvation Army can point to a long history of sexual equality in its work. From the beginning the Army ordained both men and women as ministers, and in the mid-nineteenth century the idea of female preachers was far more radical than it is today. The denomination's regulations stipulate "a woman may hold any position of authority or power in the Army from that of local officer to that of general." In fact, Evangeline Booth, the founder's daughter, headed the Salvation Army in the United States for thirty years, and then for five years directed the worldwide organization from its London headquarters. Her father often commented, "My best men are women."

No longer does the Army confine its activities to poor communities. Extensive programs for children and families have been developed. At one time, 80 percent of those who sought help from the Salvation Army had alcohol problems, but now 70 percent have other drug problems. Accordingly the Army has had to change its priorities. The street meeting with brass band and preaching, however, continues to be a basic Army evangelistic technique.

Converts are expected to don the military uniform as soldiers and commit themselves to saving sinners, although they may keep their secular occupations. Many are reluctant to devote their lives to this work and are free to join other churches. About fifty-five hundred officers in the United States supervise the volunteer local officers and soldiers in the Army's widespread activities: citadels (local churches), relief associations, summer camps, hospitals, homes for unmarried mothers, publications, nurseries and day schools, orphanages. No other Protestant church approaches the scope of the Army's welfare work.

Theologically the Salvation Army follows the original Wesleyan emphasis, including belief in the baptism of the Holy Spirit or entire sanctification as preached by the Holiness sects. They uphold man's free will and deny that man's spiritual powers were utterly destroyed by the Fall, contrary to Luther and Calvin. With the Quakers, they reject baptism and the Lord's Supper as unnecessary rituals. Booth debated whether to continue the Lord's Supper, and his decision was based on three factors: the use of wine in the service might tempt his alcoholic converts, the public might object to female officers administering the Communion, and the interpretation of the Eucharist had divided Christians in the past. Referring to sacraments, the Army's *Handbook of Doctrine* says: "As it is the Salvation Army's firm conviction that these ceremonies are not necessary to salvation nor essential to spiritual progress, we do not observe them." The Salvation Army offers classical Methodism without sacraments.

In place of baptism, the Army conducts the Dedication of Children using the following formula: "In the name of the Lord and of the _____ Corps of the Salvation Army, I have taken this child, who has been fully given up by his parents for the salvation of the world. God save, bless, and keep this child. Amen." Other ceremonies in the Army are the swearing in of soldiers, the presentation of colors, covenant services, and marriage. The Army reports 471,000 officers and soldiers in the United States.

Two defections from the Salvation Army led to the organization of groups with similar objectives but more democratic principles. The first, the American Rescue Workers, was begun just two years after the Army invaded this country in 1880. In 1896 General Booth's son and his wife seceded and started the Volunteers of America. This sect now numbers thirty-four thousand members and has done outstanding work among prisoners, parolees, and their families. Unlike the Salvationists, the Rescue Workers and Volunteers observe baptism and the Lord's Supper.

The Covenanters

A protest against the formalism of the state Lutheranism of Sweden began in mission societies within the Lutheran Church and developed into the Evangelical Covenant Church of America.

Transplanted to the United States by Swedish immigrants, the church was formally organized in Chicago in 1885. The majority of Swedes who remained Christian, however, allied themselves with the Swedish Lutheran Church, or Swedish Methodist and Baptist groups. Because each local Covenant church is independent and autonomous, its members are sometimes known as Swedish Congregationalists

This church values the historic Christian confessions, especially the Apostles' Creed, but emphasizes the sovereignty of the Word of God over all creedal interpretations.

A few non-Swedes have affiliated with this church, which seems to be moving further from Lutheran orthodoxy. It supports North Park College and Seminary and reports ninety-six thousand members. For many years it was known as the Mission Covenant Church.

FURTHER READING

Moravians
Gollin, Gillian Lindt, *Moravians in Two Worlds* (New York and London: Columbia University Press, 1967).
Schattschneider, Allen W., *Through Five Hundred Years: A Popular History of the Moravian Church* (Bethlehem, Pa.: Comenius Press, 1956).

Mennonites
Dyck, Cornelius J., ed., *An Introduction to Mennonite History* (Scottsdale, Pa.: Herald Press, 1967).

Hostetler, John A., *Amish Society* (Baltimore: Johns Hopkins Press, 1963).

Mennonite Encyclopedia, 4 vols. ed. by Harold S. Bender and C. Henry Smith (Scottsdale, Pa.: 1955-59).

Smith, C. Henry, *The Story of the Mennonites,* 3rd ed. (Newton, Kansas: Mennonite Publication Office, 1950).

Brethren

Bittinger, Emmett F., *Heritage and Promise: Perspectives on the Church of the Brethren* (Elgin, Ill.: Brethren Press, 1970).

Durnbaugh, Donald F., ed., *The Church of the Brethren: Past and Present* (Elgin, Ill.: Brethren Press, 1971).

Kent, Homer A., *250 Years Conquering Frontiers: A History of the Brethren Church* (Winona Lake, Ind.: Brethren Missionary Herald, 1958).

Mallott, F., *Studies in Brethren History* (Elgin, Ill.: Brethren Publishing House, 1945).

Salvationists

Bishop, Edward, *Blood and Fire* (Chicago: Moody Press, 1964).

Chesham, Sallie, *Born to Battle: The Salvation Army in America* (Chicago: Rand McNally, 1965).

Hattersley, Roy, *Blood and Fire: William and Catherine Booth and Their Salvation Army* (New York: Doubleday, 1999).

Neal, Harry Edward, *The Hallelujah Army* (Philadelphia: Clinton, 1961).

Nygaard, Norman E, *Trumpet of Salvation: The Story of William and Catherine Booth* (Grand Rapids, Mich.: Zondervan, 1961).

CHAPTER 15

The Unitarian Universalists

Religious Liberals Challenge All Dogmas

THOMAS JEFFERSON PREDICTED IN 1822: "I TRUST THAT THERE IS NOT A young man living in the United States who will not die a Unitarian." Our third president further believed that "the present generation will see Unitarianism become the general religion of the United States."

For all his great qualities, Jefferson turned out to be a poor prophet. By 2000 the Unitarians (bolstered by a 1961 merger with the Universalists) claimed only about 155,000 adult members in this country, only a few thousand more than the total reported in 1961.

Yet an impressive case can be made for the proposition that no religious denomination has provided and does provide a greater number of national figures than the Unitarian Universalists. The last Unitarian who ran for the presidency — Adlai Stevenson — lost the election, but five presidents stand in the Unitarian tradition: John Adams, John Quincy Adams, Jefferson, Millard Fillmore, and William Howard Taft.

With a membership of about one-tenth of 1 percent of the U.S. population, the Unitarian Universalists are represented by three members of the current Congress.

This tiny denomination has been the spiritual home of such people as novelist J.P. Marquand, architect Frank Lloyd Wright, diplomat Chester Bowles, composer Bela Bartok, historian Henry Steele Commager, and social theorist David Riesman.

Unitarian figures in American literature include Oliver Wendell Holmes, Henry Wadsworth Longfellow, William Cullen Bryant, Edward Everett Hale, Ralph Waldo Emerson, James Russell Lowell, Nathaniel Hawthorne, Bret Harte, and Louisa May Alcott. Suffragette

Susan B. Anthony, reformer Dorothea Dix, and Horace Mann are claimed by the Unitarians. Of seventy-seven Olympians in the Hall of Fame, seventeen are Unitarians.

Dr. Ellsworth Huntington of Yale studied the listings of people in *Who's Who in America* and concluded, "The productivity of the Unitarians in supplying leaders of the first rank has been 150 times as great as that of the remainder of the population."

Despite the small membership of the denomination, the influence of Unitarian Universalists is a major force in contemporary American life. What is more, millions of Americans hold views similar to Unitarianism but do not belong to a Unitarian Universalist church or fellowship. Some remain in mainline Protestant denominations.

All religious bodies evolve over a period of decades or centuries, but few have changed as radically as Unitarianism and Universalism. Originally, Unitarians affirmed the unity of God in contrast to the orthodox Christian doctrine of the Trinity. They revered Jesus as the unique exemplar of God's revelation, believed in his miracles as well as those of the Old Testament, and relied on the Bible as the Word of God. The Unitarians of the sixteenth century held a heterodox but Christian theological position.

Today the majority of American Unitarians stand in the Humanist tradition; almost all Unitarians in the Midwest and West can be classified as agnostics. Long ago they rejected the orthodox attitudes toward the Bible and miracles, and few today profess belief in a personal God or in immortality. Jesus is considered one of many religious teachers, and the Christian message takes its place alongside the teachings of Buddhism, Hinduism, Islam, and others.

The Unitarian scholar and historian Earl Morse Wilbur has written: "When the Unitarian movement began, the marks of true religion were commonly thought to be belief in the creeds, membership in the church, and participation in its rites and sacraments. To the Unitarian of today the marks of true religion are spiritual freedom, enlightened reason, broad and tolerant sympathy, upright character and unselfish service. These things, which go to the very heart of life, best express the meaning of Unitarian history."

Universalism began with an orthodox position on the Trinity, but a belief that all souls eventually will be reconciled with God. The early Universalists simply denied that God would punish any soul for eternity.

A minority of American Unitarians represented by the Unitarian Christian Fellowship seek to uphold the Christian witness in the denomination, but the odds seem to be against this. The growth of the denomination in recent years has been outside New England, which is where the Christian Unitarians preserve some strength.

Unitarians maintain that primitive Christianity was Unitarian and only gradually changed to belief in the Trinity. At the Council of Nicea in 325 A.D., the Church declared that Jesus was the same essential substance as God the Father; the doctrine of the Trinity was further elaborated at the Council of Constantinople.

Early Unitarians might have been classified as Arians who believed that Jesus was not equal to God but was more than man. Their heroes were Arius, Origen, and Pelagius in early church history.

With the orthodox doctrine of the Trinity firmly held by the Church, little more is heard of Unitarian tendencies until the sixteenth century. About fourteen years after Luther nailed his Ninety-five Theses to the church door, a Spaniard, Michael Servetus, challenged the doctrine of the Trinity. In a tract entitled "On the Errors of the Trinity," he sought to win the Reformers, especially Luther and Calvin, to his theological view. "Your Trinity is the product of subtlety and madness. The Gospel knows nothing of it," wrote the young Spanish rebel.

Far from accepting the anti-Trinitarianism of Servetus, the Reformers recoiled and condemned him as a blasphemer. He lived under an assumed name in France but reopened his correspondence with Calvin. Servetus eventually was arrested as he passed through Geneva, tried, and burned at the stake. Calvin thought this punishment was more than just.

Servetus attracted no followers and held doctrinal positions far from later Unitarianism. Unitarianism took root in two other areas: Transylvania and Poland. Two brothers, Faustus and Lelius Socinus, led the Unitarian movement in Poland. By 1618 there were three hundred congregations of the Minor Reformed Church, the name of the Unitarian church in Poland. During the Counter-Reformation, the Jesuits succeeded in eliminating Unitarianism in that country.

The kingdom of Transylvania maintained its independence from 1543 to 1691; it is now a part of Romania. Here the leader was Francis David, who was protected by the only Unitarian king in history, John Sigismund. By 1600 there were 425 Unitarian churches in the kingdom. Sigismund's successors did not share his religious views and persecuted the Unitarians.

In England the first Unitarian service was held in an auction room in London in 1774. A former Anglican clergyman, Theophilus Lindsey, founded English Unitarianism. He was assisted by Joseph Priestley, best known as the scientist who discovered oxygen.

Although Unitarianism in England was not subjected to the severe persecution it endured on the continent, it did antagonize many orthodox Christians. In 1791 a mob destroyed Priestley's home and laboratory, as well as a Unitarian chapel in Birmingham. The scientist fled to London and a few years later to America. He founded the first church in America to bear the Unitarian name in Northumberland, Pa. James Martineau assumed leadership of the English Unitarians in the early nineteenth century.

In England the denomination suffered a sharp decline after 1900; attendance at Sunday service fell from 42,000 in that year to 13,500 just before World War II. Many Unitarian chapels were destroyed by German bombing during the war.

In America, Unitarianism arose as a schism within New England Congregationalism. Unlike Calvinists, the Unitarians affirmed that human nature was good, not depraved, that man was free rather than predestined, and that Jesus was a great moral teacher but not God. King's Chapel in Boston, the first Episcopal church in New England, adopted Unitarianism in 1787. All references to the Trinity were expunged from the ritual. The Church of the Pilgrims at Plymouth joined the liberal camp in 1800.

The growing controversy between Calvinists and Unitarians was brought to a head by Jedidiah Morse, an orthodox Congregationalist and the father of the inventor of the telegraph. He launched a crusade to smoke out the heretics and found a perfect issue when Harvard chose Henry Ware, a theologian of Arian views, to fill the chair of divinity in 1805. In protest the orthodox founded Andover Theological Seminary. For 128 years, Harvard saw a succession of Unitarian presidents.

The lines now were drawn. Most of the Congregational churches in the Boston area became Unitarian. By 1840, an estimated 135 of 544 Congregational churches had gone over to Unitarianism; many of these were the larger and more affluent parishes.

A group of Boston and New England ministers formed the American Unitarian Association in 1825. (The British association was founded in the same year.) Later, the Western Unitarian Conference was organized to extend the free religion movement to the Midwest and West. Its orientation always has been more Humanistic than that of the New England Unitarians. Western Unitarians were instrumental in the establishment of Washington University in St Louis and Antioch College, but neither institution remained under church control.

Meanwhile, the other partner in the 1961 merger — Universalism — was establishing roots in America. John Murray, a former Methodist, preached the first Universalist sermon in America in 1770. He taught that ultimately all souls would be reconciled to God. Although Universalism as a religious system predated Unitarianism in this country, it did not formally organize until 1866.

Originally Universalism was Trinitarian, but one influential preacher, Hosea Ballou, swung the theological direction of the denomination toward Unitarianism. Ballou served a Boston church from 1817 to 1852.

The Universalists went on record in 1790 as opposing human slavery — the first religious body to take this stand. They also were the first denomination to sponsor women for the ministry. Universalists worked for prison reform and the parole system, and fought capital punishment.

Universalism always found its greatest strength among rural New Englanders. It has not counted the distinguished roster of communicants found in Unitarianism. Yet Benjamin Rush, a Universalist layman and physician, was a signer of the Declaration of Independence, and Clara Barton, founder of the American Red Cross, belonged to the Universalist Church. This church founded Tufts, Akron, and St. Lawrence universities.

Orestes Brownson, one of nineteenth century America's most influential converts to Catholicism, had previously served as a Universalist and later a Unitarian minister. He joined the Church in 1844.

Today the theological battle between theists and Humanists is almost over, and the Humanists must be considered the victors. Here and there you will find individual Unitarians or congregations that still favor the Christian or theistic position, but they are dwindling.

Organized Unitarian Universalist groups can be found in more than one thousand U.S. communities. Most of these are churches with ministers, but several hundred are lay-led fellowships. Every year some fellowships achieve full church status. Some five thousand men and women belong to the Church of the Larger Fellowship, which offers a correspondence-type program for people isolated from a Unitarian congregation.

Ministers usually train at Meadville, affiliated with the University of Chicago, at Harvard Divinity School, or at Starr King School for the Ministry, near the University of California.

Humanitarian activities are carried on throughout the world by the Unitarian Universalist Service Committee. This might take the form of civil rights work in Atlanta, social work training in Korea, community centers in Rhodesia, medical programs in Haiti, or birth control clinics in Nigeria. The committee was organized in 1940 to aid refugees from Nazi tyranny. The committee conducts its projects on a nonsectarian basis.

The Unitarian Universalist Association belongs to the International Association for Liberal Christianity and Religious Freedom, which claims to represent some 1,500,000 Europeans. The American denomination also maintains friendly relations with the Universalist Church of the Philippines, the Philippine Unitarian Church, the Non-Subscribing Presbyterian Church of Ireland, and Unitarian churches in Hungary and Czechoslovakia.

Freedom is the characteristic theme of contemporary Unitarianism. No one in the Unitarian Universalist Church expects any other member to hold any particular belief or subscribe to any creed. A member who believes in the unique mission of Jesus and the inspiration of the Bible may sit beside another Unitarian Universalist who denies the existence of God.

At the same time, it is not difficult to predict Unitarian Universalist positions on given issues. A Unitarian Universalist usually will support civil rights, easier divorce laws, abortion, euthanasia, a strict interpretation of separation of church and state, birth control, sex education programs, prison reform, mental health, the United Nations, cremation or simple burials, and urban renewal. He will oppose capital punishment, censorship, and war.

Sharing many Unitarian Universalist positions are such groups as the Ethical Culture Societies, the American Humanist Association, the Hicksite Quakers, and Reform Jews. The New York Society for Ethical Culture was founded in 1876 by Dr. Felix Adler. The local branches seek "to assert the supreme importance of the ethical factor in all relations of life — personal, social, national and international — apart from any theological or metaphysical considerations." The Fellowship of Religious Humanists, founded in 1963 and affiliated with the American Humanist Association, promotes the cause of Humanistic religious living and ethical religion.

Millions of Americans hold basic Unitarian Universalist positions but do not belong to the denomination. The Unitarian Universalists are making strong efforts to gain converts. The church even has launched an advertising campaign to attract inquiries. But the question is whether liberal religion can appeal to the liberal who works in a factory instead of a university, who reads *Time* instead of *Harper's* or *The Nation,* who holds a high school diploma instead of a college sheepskin or Ph.D.

Unitarian Universalism, freed of all but vestigial Christian traditions, presents itself as a religion that can exert a strong appeal to secular Humanists who do not wish to go it alone. These people can find fellowship, spiritual inspiration, counseling, and organized outlets for humanitarian work through this denomination.

FURTHER READING

Mendolsohn, Jack, *Why I am a Unitarian Universalist* (Boston: Beacon, 1964).

Parke, David B., *The Epic of Unitarianism* (Boston: Starr King Press, 1967).

Robinson, David, *The Unitarians and Universalists* (Westport, Conn.: Greenwood Press, 1985).

Wilbur, Morse, *A History of Unitarianism,* 2 vols. (Cambridge, Mass.: Harvard University Press, 1947).

Wright, Conrad, *The Beginning of Unitarianism in America* (Boston: Beacon, 1955).

CHAPTER 16

The Eastern Orthodox

Churches of East and West Divided Since Eleventh Century

WHEN POPE PAUL VI AND PATRIARCH ATHENAGORAS I, SPIRITUAL leader of the estimated 228 million Eastern Orthodox, lifted the mutual excommunications in 1965 that had precipitated the division of the Christian community into Eastern and Western churches, they took an important step in reconciliation.

Until the demise of the Soviet Union, a majority of Orthodox Christians attempted to preserve their faith despite Communist persecution. Today almost all Greeks and Eastern Slavs who profess Christianity follow the Orthodox way of life. They belong to about fifteen autocephalous (independent) Orthodox churches.

Since 1054 the Roman Catholic and Orthodox churches have gone their separate ways, although several attempts at reunion have been made. Each church recognizes the other's bishops as standing in the apostolic succession, admits the validity of priestly ordinations, confers seven sacraments, venerates the Blessed Virgin and the saints, fosters monasticism, and adheres to basically the same theology. Yet theological and cultural differences have kept the two Churches of the East and the West apart for more than nine hundred years.

Orthodoxy means "right belief" and identifies the various national churches that make up Eastern Orthodoxy. These churches are known as autocephalous; they elect their own bishops, who form a synod and are led by a patriarch, metropolitan, or archbishop.

The ecumenical patriarch of Constantinople holds a primacy of honor among Orthodox prelates. For centuries the number of faithful directly under the ancient patriarchies of Constantinople, Alexandria, Antioch, and Jerusalem has been relatively small.

The ecumenical patriarch and symbolic leader of Eastern Orthodoxy resides in Istanbul (formerly Constantinople) as the spiritual leader of a handful of Greeks in that Turkish city. Even until World War I, more than 1,500,000 Greeks lived in Turkey. The Turkish-Greek War in 1920-22 made their position untenable. Persecution and harassment of this Christian minority drove most Greeks out of the country, so that today only about seven thousand remain.

The Turkish government has closed the Patriarchate's press and seminary, restricted overseas travel of Orthodox clergy, and imposed heavy new taxes on church property. The government even exercises veto power over candidates to fill the highest position in Orthodoxy. This makes it difficult for the Ecumenical Patriarchate to serve as the center of world Orthodoxy.

The strength of Orthodoxy lies in the autocephalous churches of Russia, Greece, Yugoslavia, Bulgaria, Cyprus, Romania, and Georgia. There also are semi-independent churches in such countries as Poland and Finland; Orthodox missionary churches are found in Japan, Uganda, and Tanzania. All legitimate Orthodox bodies acknowledge the jurisdiction of one of the patriarchates or autocephalous churches. In theology, they adhere to the decisions of the seven ecumenical councils held between A.D. 325 and 787.

To Orthodox Christians, their church is the "One, Holy, Catholic, and Apostolic" church that was founded by Jesus Christ and has preserved the faith intact. A contemporary statement of the Greek Orthodox Church in the United States maintains that Orthodoxy is the "authentic and infallible interpreter of the faith in dogmas as contained in the Symbol of Faith (or Nicene Creed) in an unbreakable continuity."

This conviction that Orthodoxy is the one true church has not kept the Orthodox aloof from the ecumenical movement. All the major Orthodox churches belong to the World Council of Churches. Archbishop Iakovos, retired from the Greek Archdiocese of North and South America, has served as one of the five WCC presidents. Most Orthodox churches also hold membership in the National Council of

Churches. Relations between Roman Catholics and Eastern Orthodox have not been more cordial in many centuries.

Another name for the Eastern Orthodox is Greek Orthodox. This does not mean that most Orthodox are Greeks any more than Roman Catholic means most Catholics are Romans. But early Christianity was propagated through the Greek language. The New Testament was written in Greek, as were the works of the Fathers of the Church. Greek was the language even of the Latin Church until the third century.

Christianity naturally took on some of the characteristics of the East and the West as it matured. The first serious trouble took place in 862, when Pope Nicholas refused to recognize the election of Photius as patriarch of Constantinople. This dispute was settled, but the seeds of separation were sown.

When a papal legate excommunicated the patriarch in 1054 and the patriarch excommunicated the pope, the break was complete. The savagery of the crusaders who sacked Constantinople and the Church of Holy Wisdom in 1204 further estranged the Byzantines from Rome.

Meanwhile, the Orthodox brought the Christian gospel to the Slavs and the descendants of Roman settlers known as Romanians. With the baptism of Vladimir, Russia accepted Orthodoxy in 988. After the fall of Constantinople in 1453 to the Ottoman Turks, Russia assumed the leadership of world Orthodoxy.

In 1589 the archbishop of Russia was elevated to the position of patriarch. Church and state were closely allied until the Russian Revolution, when an atheist government sought to eradicate religion from the lives of the people.

The Church of Greece remains the only Orthodox body that is a state church. Until recently, this branch of Orthodoxy had been ultraconservative and looked with disfavor on closer relations with Roman Catholics and Protestants. Such movements as the ZOE brotherhood of theologians and upgrading of seminary training have injected new life into the ten-million-member Church of Greece.

Americans of Greek and Slav descent make up the six million Eastern Orthodox in the United States. Because parish membership is often determined by the number of men older than twenty-one, some Orthodox scholars suggest that the total Orthodox constituency in the United States may be higher. They are concentrated in the larger cities of the East, Midwest, and West Coast.

Eight Russian monks founded a mission on Kodiak Island in 1794 when Alaska was still owned by Russia. Within two years, they had baptized twelve thousand natives. About eighty years later the Russian Orthodox bishop of Alaska moved his see to San Francisco. When Russian immigration began to snowball he moved again to New York City in 1905.

Most Greeks came to these shores after 1880 and built Greek Orthodox churches where they settled. So did Ukrainians, Serbians, Romanians, Bulgarians, and others. Before World War I, the Russian Orthodox diocese and bishops served Orthodox of all nationalities. They encouraged the introduction of English in liturgy and were moving toward formation of an American Orthodox Church. But the events of the Russian Revolution disrupted these plans.

Suspicious of the influence of Communism on Russian church officials, the various national groups organized separate Orthodox bodies in the United States. Recent years have seen a renewed interest in a federation of all Orthodox groups in this country. Orthodox young people seem to prefer an English liturgy and development of a single Orthodox church. Formation of a Standing Committee of Orthodox Bishops in 1960 may speed the day when such unification may become a reality.

The Greek Orthodox Archdiocese of North and South America was organized in 1922 and claims the largest Orthodox membership: about 1,950,000. It maintains 523 churches, 18 parochial schools, and a seminary in Brookline, Mass.

The Orthodox Church in America claims one million adherents under the spiritual rule of nine archbishops and bishops. It was affiliated with the Russian Orthodox Church until 1970. It has set up more than one hundred churches and missions since 1965. Two smaller churches of Russian origin serve about 160,000 members.

A group of immigrants from the mountain region of eastern Czechoslovakia had been members of the Eastern Rite in their homeland; they preserved Byzantine customs and liturgy but recognized the primacy of the pope. Some of these left the Catholic Church and set up the American Carpatho-Russian Orthodox Greek Catholic Church in 1938. They have one hundred thousand members in seventy churches, including a cathedral in Johnstown, Pa. Other national bodies of Orthodox include the Serbians (67,000), Ukrainians (127,000), Bulgarians (86,000), and Romanians (65,000).

In recent years the Orthodox have pressed for recognition as the fourth major faith along with Protestantism, Catholicism, and Judaism. More than half the states have officially granted such recognition. Orthodox prelates offered invocations at several presidential inaugurations. Service personnel can request a dog tag marked "EO" to identify their religious faith. Orthodox priests serve as chaplains in the armed forces. Orthodox students on college campuses join a single Orthodox student foundation. Candidates for the priesthood from the various national churches study at the six Orthodox seminaries; the two main ones are the Greek seminary at Brookline and the Russian Orthodox seminary in Crestwood, N.Y.

The religious life of the Orthodox Christian is sustained by the seven mysteries or sacraments. Infants are baptized by triple immersion. Chrismation or confirmation usually is administered immediately after baptism by the priest. Orthodox are expected to receive Holy Communion at least once a year; the trend is toward more frequent, even weekly, Communion. Communicants receive both bread and wine. Sins are forgiven in the sacrament of repentance and confession.

Orthodoxy considers Christians united in the sacrament of matrimony to be partners in an indissoluble union, but unlike Roman Catholicism, Orthodoxy allows divorce and remarriage in certain situations. For example, the church will grant a divorce for adultery or other immoral conduct, impotence prior to marriage and continuing for two years, desertion for more than two years, apostasy or heresy, or long-term insanity. It strongly discourages mixed marriages. The church equates abortion with murder and generally condemns birth control.

The ministry of the Orthodox Church includes bishops, priests, and deacons. Parish priests are almost always married men, but bishops are chosen from the ranks of celibate monks or widowers. Married men may be ordained priests, but priests may not marry. This means a priest may not remarry if his wife dies.

The seventh sacrament, Holy Unction, is administered for the restoration of health of body and soul. The priest anoints the body with oil and prays for the welfare of the recipient.

The Divine Liturgy or Mass is the highest act of Orthodox worship. The Orthodox tradition has been to celebrate the liturgy in the language of the people, while the Western Church retained Latin until Vatican II. In the United States, the Greek Orthodox allow English only for the sermon but Russian and other Orthodox bodies regularly employ the vernacular in the liturgy. The Divine Liturgy takes from one to three hours and is always sung.

An icon screen or iconostasis divides the worshipers in the nave from the altar in an Orthodox church. Icons are two-dimensional images of Christ, the Blessed Virgin, and the saints and have always been objects of deep devotion in the Eastern Church.

Orthodox monks live according to a rule drawn up by St. Basil in the fourth century. In this respect the Eastern Church differs from the Roman Church, which embraces many different religious orders such as Franciscans, Jesuits, and Dominicans. By far the most famous Orthodox monastery is Mt. Athos, founded in 963. About two thousand monks live in a cluster of twenty separate monasteries on Mount Athos. There are also Orthodox nuns.

Although much closer to Roman Catholicism than is Protestantism, Orthodoxy differs from Rome in several respects. For example, the Orthodox acknowledge the bishop of Rome, the pope, to be the patriarch of the West and will accord him a primacy of honor; they refuse to admit his supreme jurisdiction and infallibility. The Orthodox object to the word "filioque" in the Nicene Creed, believe the Virgin Mary was cleansed from original sin at the Annunciation rather than at her conception, do not define the dogma of the Assumption of Mary, and do not believe in the system of indulgences.

The Eastern Church also differs from the Roman Church in its eschatology. It has no doctrine of purgatory. Orthodox believe each individual undergoes a particular judgment immediately after death. The soul then enters an intermediate state between heaven and hell until the Last Judgment at the Second Coming. Orthodox offer prayers for the dead but do not believe such prayers affect the condition of the dead.

Many Orthodox resent the existence of the Eastern rites of the Roman Catholic Church. About twelve million Catholics, including more than 525,000 in the United States, follow the liturgy and customs of the Eastern Church but acknowledge the primacy of the pope. They are directly subject to Eastern patriarchs in union with Rome.

Another group of Eastern Christians, neither Orthodox nor Catholic, are sometimes collectively known as the Lesser Eastern Christians. They follow a theological system known as Monophysitism, which arose in the fifth century. Monophysitism maintains that Christ's nature remained divine despite his taking on human form. The four main groups number about eight million: the Armenians, the Syrians, the Copts, and the Ethiopians.

Both East and West are attempting to heal the centuries-old separation. The late Ecumenical Patriarch Athenagoras declared: "Christians must realize that they have one church, one cross, one gospel." The Fathers of the Second Vatican Council rejected the idea that the differences between East and West are insurmountable. In the Decree on Ecumenism they declared: "Where the authentic theological traditions of the Eastern Church are concerned, we must recognize the admirable way in which they have their roots in Holy Scripture, and how they are nurtured and given expression in the life of the liturgy. They derive their strength too from the living tradition of the apostles and from the works of the Fathers and spiritual writers of the Eastern Churches. Thus they promote the right ordering of Christian life and, indeed, pave the way to a full vision of Christian truth" (No. 17).

To date the Orthodox bishops have not recognized the ecclesial status of any other church, including the Roman Catholic Church. The latter has invited Eastern Orthodox to receive Communion at its altars, but the Orthodox bishops have not authorized this practice for the faithful.

Signs of improved relationships between the Orthodox and Roman Catholic churches have appeared regularly since the early 1960s. The Ecumenical Patriarch Dimitrios I of Constantinople and the pope announced the formation of a Pan-Orthodox commission in 1975 to conduct reunion talks with Rome.

Pope Paul VI stated: "The Roman Catholic and Orthodox churches are already united in such a deep communion that it lacks very little to reach a fullness allowing the common celebration of the Lord's Eucharist."

Pope John Paul II has made reunion of the Eastern and Western churches a priority of his papacy. He has visited Greece and Ukraine as well as several other predominantly Orthodox countries, but has been met with muted enthusiasm.

FURTHER READING

Benz, Ernest, *The Eastern Orthodox Church* (New York: Doubleday, 1963).

Bratsiotis, Panagiotis, *The Greek Orthodox Church* (Notre Dame, Ind.: University of Notre Dame Press, 1967).

Constantelos, Demetrois J., *The Greek Orthodox Church* (New York: Seabury, 1967).

Meyendorff, John, *The Orthodox Church* (New York: Pantheon, 1962).

Ware, Timothy, *The Orthodox Church* (New York: Penguin, 1967).

CHAPTER 17

The Old Catholics and Polish National Catholics

Conflicts with Rome Led to Separation

Old Catholics

Protests against the definition of papal infallibility at the First Vatican Council in 1869 led to the formation of various Old Catholic churches in Europe.

On November 7, 1966, Bernard Cardinal Alfrink of Utrecht, the Netherlands, and Andreas Rinkel, Old Catholic archbishop of Utrecht, joined in a Eucharistic service in St. Gertrude's Church. Both prelates extended a joint blessing at the common service on the feast of St. Willibrord, first bishop of Utrecht and patron saint of the Netherlands.

During the unprecedented rite, it was revealed that Rome's insistence that Old Catholics assent to the bull *Unigenitus* prior to any theological dialogue had been abandoned. This bull condemned Jansenism in 1713. Rome's new position was clarified in a letter from Augustin Cardinal Bea, president of the Secretariat for Promoting Christian Unity.

Until recently reunion of the Roman Catholic and Old Catholic churches seemed likely, as both bodies acknowledge the validity of the other's orders and apostolic succession. The movement toward reconciliation has stalled, however, since several Old Catholic churches on the continent allowed the ordination of women.

A reunion of the Old Catholics and the Roman Catholics would have affected about 150,000 Old Catholics in Holland, Germany, Austria, Switzerland, Yugoslavia, and Czechoslovakia.

Rome already recognizes as valid the ordination of Old Catholic priests and consecration of Old Catholic bishops. Those who organized the Old Catholic movement in 1870 presented one of their leaders for consecration by the Church of Utrecht, which had been separated from Rome since 1724. The legitimacy of Utrecht's orders has never been questioned by Rome.

The history of Old Catholicism, especially in its American expressions, is complicated and often bewildering. Old Catholicism has harbored both saints and ecclesiastical adventurers. To get some idea of this movement, we will examine three groups of churches that identify themselves as Old Catholic. First are the continental Old Catholic churches, which subscribe to the Declaration of Utrecht of 1899. Second are the numerous small churches and sects, especially in the United States, that have taken the Old Catholic label but enjoy no recognition from the original Old Catholic churches of Europe. Third is the Polish National Catholic Church, whose membership in the United States, Canada, and Poland makes it the largest Old Catholic communion.

During the seventeenth century, a number of Jansenists fled from France to predominantly Protestant Holland. Though they were considered heretics by the Vatican, the Jansenists were received with hospitality by the Dutch Catholics. When the majority of Dutch bishops and priests refused to accept the bull against Jansenism in the early eighteenth century, the Church of Utrecht went into schism.

For many decades this Church of Utrecht continued as a Roman Catholic, but ostracized, Church. The Church dutifully informed the pope when it elected a new bishop, and the popes regularly replied with decrees of excommunication. At the start of the schism three out of five Dutch Catholics sided with the schismatics, but by 1815 the Utrecht Catholics numbered only six thousand, while those in communion with Rome exceeded one million.

Originally the Church of Utrecht had no bishop. A French bishop traveling to his new post in Babylon by way of Amsterdam was prevailed upon to confirm six hundred children at Utrecht. For this and other activities he was suspended by Rome; he settled in Amsterdam. In 1724 he consecrated a priest of the Church of Utrecht, who died the next year. The suspended bishop — Dominicus Marie Varlet —

consecrated three other priests of Utrecht, and it is through one of them — Petrus Johannes Meindaarts — that Utrecht and the Old Catholics trace their orders.

The dogma of papal infallibility proclaimed in 1870 aroused the lively opposition of thousands of Roman Catholics in Germany, Switzerland, and Austria, and pushed many toward Utrecht. Some fourteen hundred Germans alone signed a statement declaring the dogma an innovation. The leader of the resistance, Dr. Ignaz von Dollinger, a professor of theology at Munich, declared: "As a Christian, as a theologian, as a historian, as a citizen, I cannot accept this doctrine."

In 1871 about three hundred delegates met at the first Old Catholic congress in Munich. No Roman Catholic bishops joined the protesters, but a number of priests allied themselves with the Old Catholics. Because the Old Catholics valued the apostolic succession and realized that they would be unable to ordain new priests or administer confirmation without a bishop, they sought consecration from the schismatic Church of Utrecht.

Professor Josef Reinkens of Bonn was elected first bishop of the Old Catholic Church and was consecrated by the bishop of Deventer.

Dollinger himself respected the excommunication of the Roman Catholic Church and ceased to perform spiritual functions as priest. He encouraged the Old Catholic movement but balked at the idea of organizing separate parishes and abolishing clerical celibacy. He died at the age of ninety-one and received the rites of the Old Catholic Church.

In many areas the new Old Catholic churches sided with anticlerical governments and received material support in return. The governments of Prussia, Baden, and Hesse favored the Old Catholics, who also sided with Bismarck in his *Kulturkampf.*

Over the years the Old Catholic churches introduced a number of changes into the religious life their adherents had followed while Roman Catholics. In 1874 fasting and confession were made optional, and the next year the church removed "filioque" from the creed and eliminated the granting of indulgences. The Old Catholics adopted a vernacular liturgy in 1880. Pastors were elected by the people. Clerical celibacy was no longer required in Germany and Switzerland after 1878, although the Dutch Old Catholics insisted on celibacy until 1922.

Except for a small mission in South Africa, the Old Catholics engage in no missionary work. They recognized the validity of Anglican orders in 1925 and signed an agreement in 1931 to enter into intercommunion with the Anglican churches. In 1965 the churches subscribing to the Declaration of Utrecht entered into full sacramental union with the Philippine Independent Church (the Aglipayans), which claims 1,500,000 members.

A representative of the Old Catholic churches attended the sessions of Vatican II, and a Vatican observer attended the 19th International Congress of Old Catholics in 1965. This meeting, held in Vienna, brought together four hundred Old Catholic delegates from seventeen countries and included twenty-two bishops. Two Old Catholic bishops from Poland were denied travel permits.

At the present time there are about 40,000 Old Catholics in Germany, 40,000 in Austria, 28,000 in Switzerland, 12,000 in Holland, 5,000 in Czechoslovakia, and small communities in Poland and Yugoslavia.

No one would suggest that after almost a century of existence the Old Catholic churches have achieved the membership or influence their founders anticipated. At the same time, we can see certain changes in Roman Catholicism in such areas as the vernacular liturgy and the married diaconate that were foreshadowed by the Old Catholics.

The irrelevancy of the Jansenist controversy in the modern world, the willingness of Old Catholics to reexamine the role of the papacy and the concept of collegiality, and the renewal of Roman Catholicism have combined to encourage the Old Catholics and the Roman Catholics to investigate reunion possibilities. But the decision by some Old Catholic bodies to ordain women will no doubt dampen reunion prospects.

Old Catholic Churches in the United States

Churches in the United States that use "Old Catholic" in their titles derive their orders from questionable sources and stand outside the fellowship of the legitimate Old Catholic churches of Europe. Only the Polish National Catholic Church is recognized by the Europeans and holds valid orders.

The chronicler of these independent Old Catholic churches, Peter Anson, estimates there are more than one hundred fifty such bodies in the United States, England, Australia, and other countries. His definitive 593-page study of these fascinating sects, *Bishops at Large*, describes most of them in detail.

These sects aspire to some degree of legitimacy only because the Roman Catholic Church follows the Augustinian theory of orders. This theory states that a validly consecrated bishop retains the power to transmit valid but irregular orders even though he separates himself from the rest of the Church. In practice, however, the Roman Church ignores the orders received by apostates from schismatic bishops. If such individuals return to the Catholic Church, they may not say Mass nor are they bound to celibacy or to recitation of the Divine Office.

The establishment of these wildcat churches follows a familiar pattern. Someone, possibly a former Roman Catholic or Anglican priest, obtains what he believes to be valid consecration as a bishop. He founds his own "Old Catholic" church or outmaneuvers rival bishops in his home church. These bishops regularly excommunicate each other, make up, start new churches, return to Rome, or construct elaborate paper churches with few or no members.

These "Old Catholic" prelates put primary emphasis on valid orders and often tolerate the oddest theological teaching, even theosophy. They enjoy the ritual of Catholicism and the titles they assume: Catholicos, Hierarch, Mar, Metropolitan, Monsignor, Pontifex, Primate, Patriarch, and so forth. It seems the smaller the church following, the more grandiose the titles and the larger the hierarchy. A tiny band of such "Old Catholics" may be served by a metropolitan, a couple of archbishops, and a group of bishops.

These assorted "Old Catholic" churches attract disaffected Roman Catholics and Anglicans. Some make frankly nationalistic appeals to Poles, Italians, and others who are dissatisfied with Roman Catholicism as they experience it in the United States. While these U.S. "Old Catholic" groups claim thousands of members, their rolls often number in the hundreds.

Two former Roman Catholics provided orders to most of the groups in the United States and England claiming to be Old Catholic. One of these — Joseph René Vilatte — was ordained by an Old Catholic bishop in Switzerland but was consecrated a bishop by a Jacobite bishop in Ceylon, an island off South India. The other — Arnold Harris Mathew — was ordained a Roman Catholic priest and consecrated by the Dutch Old Catholic bishops. About twenty churches each trace their orders to the Vilatte and Mathew successions.

The dozens of groups in the United States that purport to be Old Catholics trace their apostolic succession through questionable sources. These bodies include the American Catholic Church, Christ Catholic Church, the North American Old Catholic Church, and many others — some of which report their membership in the hundreds.

Polish National Catholics

The largest single component of worldwide Old Catholicism is the Polish National Catholic Church. This church also represents the only serious schism in the history of American Catholicism. The Polish National Catholic Church does not furnish current statistics. In 1980 it reported 280,000 members in 110 parishes, with additional congregations in Canada.

In externals a Polish National Catholic church looks much like a Roman Catholic church, with altar, tabernacle, statues, stations of the cross, sanctuary lamp, holy water fonts, and other such items. At Mass, Polish National Catholic priests wear vestments identical to those of the Latin rite.

In addition to most of the holy days observed by the Roman Catholic Church, the Polish National Catholic Church has added a number of unique feast days, such as the feasts of the Poor Shepherd, the Remembrance of the Dear Polish Fatherland, Brotherly Love, and the Christian Family. The church also holds special commemorations for

Polish patriots and for heroes and reformers such as John Huss, Savonarola, and Peter Waldo.

Although the Polish National Catholics believe in seven sacraments, they have added a new sacrament, the Word of God; they combine baptism and confirmation into one sacrament. The faithful receive the sacrament of the Word of God by hearing the reading of the Scriptures. Young people must go to a priest for confession, but after age twenty they may receive absolution in a general public confession at Mass that does not involve an enumeration of specific sins. If they wish, older members also may continue to avail themselves of private confession.

The sacramentals of the Polish National Catholic Church would be familiar to Roman Catholics: the sign of the cross, the Angelus, holy oils, holy water, candles, ashes, palms, incense, crucifixes, and images. Devotions to the Blessed Virgin play an important part in the religious life of Polish National Catholics.

Despite its strongly nationalistic appeal, it has been able to attract only about one out of thirty Polish Americans. The faithfulness of the Polish people to the Roman Catholic Church in this country as well as in Poland is well-known. Probably no ethnic group has a smaller percentage of defections from the Church.

Sts. Cyril and Methodius brought the gospel to the Slavic people in the ninth century. In 965 the Poles accepted Catholicism. They rejected the new religious doctrines of the Hussites and Lutherans during the Reformation period and have remained stalwart defenders of the faith to the present day.

Hundreds of thousands of Poles emigrated to the United States before World War I and brought with them their Catholic faith and ethnic customs. The parish served as a family and community center for these new Americans. They preserved their Polish Christmas carols, the *Kolenda,* and the *Gorzkie Zale* lamentations in memory of the passion of Christ.

The Polish immigrants soon discovered, however, that the Church in the United States was not governed by Polish bishops but by bishops of Irish and German descent. Even though these bishops helped establish more than eight hundred fifty predominantly Polish parishes, some Polish nationalists objected to their treatment at the hands of non-Polish prelates. Sometimes it became necessary to appoint non-Polish priests as pastors of Polish parishes. These priests were usually unable to speak and preach in Polish, and their appointments sometimes aroused hostile feelings.

Several groups of separated Poles emerged to form the present Polish National Catholic Church. In 1895 a curate in Chicago, the Reverend Anton Koslowski, organized an independent parish, All Saints, for a group of Poles who objected to the way they were treated by the hierarchy. He was consecrated by a bishop of the Old Catholic Church in Switzerland in 1897 and proceeded to organize parishes in what he called the Polish Old Catholic Church. By the time of his death in 1907, he had started twenty-three such parishes.

A dispute over control of church property led to the formation in 1895 of an independent parish in Buffalo called Our Lady of the Rosary. The pastor, the Reverend Stanislaus Kaminski, was consecrated a bishop by an Old Catholic bishop in 1898. Bishop Kaminski died in 1911, and several years later his followers joined the previously organized Polish National Catholic Church.

Meanwhile in Pennsylvania a group of Poles, mainly miners and factory workers, demanded greater control of the parish affairs of Sacred Heart parish in Scranton. They were admonished by their bishop, and the controversy continued until it resulted in a fistfight in front of the church for which twenty participants were arrested. The dissidents appealed for support to a former Scranton priest who had become pastor of a church in nearby Nanticoke. He was the Reverend Francis Hodur, a thirty-year-old priest who had been born and ordained in Poland.

Father Hodur agreed to lead the two hundred fifty families, who built a new church and named it St. Stanislaus. Their new pastor traveled to Rome to plead their case and saw two cardinals, but obtained no satisfaction.

Hodur began publishing a weekly newspaper, *The Sentinel*, in which he outlined the three major principles of the new independence movement. These were: control by the Polish people of all churches built and maintained by them; the right of Polish Catholics to administer their own church property through a parish committee; and the right to choose their own pastors. These demands conflicted with the established forms of church property control drawn up by the Council of Baltimore.

Hodur was excommunicated in 1898; he burned the document of excommunication in the presence of his congregation. He celebrated the first Mass in the Polish language on Christmas Eve in 1900.

Other independent congregations joined the Hodur group in the following years. A synod was held in Scranton in 1904 representing about sixteen thousand dissident Poles. The delegates elected Father Hodur to be their bishop, but the Old Catholics hesitated to consecrate him as long as Bishop Koslowski was living. When he died in 1907, the Old Catholics consecrated Hodur a bishop in St. Gertrude Church in Utrecht.

The 1904 synod also acted to translate all Latin service books into Polish, cooperate with Protestant denominations, and repudiate the claims of the Roman Catholic Church to be the one true church.

The Polish National Catholics set up the Polish National Union in America to provide insurance benefits for members who had left Roman Catholic fraternal societies. They established their own cemeteries when their deceased members were denied burial in Catholic cemeteries. Further changes were authorized in a synod in 1921. Over some opposition by lay delegates, the synod approved marriage of the clergy. Bishop Hodur never married, but most bishops and priests in recent years have been married; newly ordained priests must wait two years before marriage. The 1921 synod also authorized a mission to Poland and elected four more bishops, who were consecrated in 1925 by Bishop Hodur.

Hodur guided the destiny of the new church from 1897 until his death in 1953. He made fourteen trips to Poland. In many ways Hodur's theological views on such questions as original sin, eternal punishment and the unique role of Christ were unorthodox. This does not mean all of his views have become normative. Since his death the Polish

National Catholic Church seems to have drawn closer to traditional Christian positions. A visit by the Old Catholic archbishop of Utrecht also has helped steer the Polish National Catholic Church away from Unitarianism.

Bishop Hodur emphatically denied the doctrine of eternal punishment. He declared it would show a lack of confidence in the justice and mercy of God to believe in an eternal hell. "He would not deliver His creatures into the power of evil spirits, for them to torment or destroy," he wrote. A man's conduct on Earth somehow determines his status after death, but eventually all men will attain the goal of union with God, Hodur believed. He taught that the soul may undergo purification or cleansing after death but will never be lost.

He claimed to place a high value on apostolic succession and membership in the holy Catholic Church, which, he said, was composed of all baptized Christians. At the same time he would declare: "The leaders of the Polish National Catholic Church are of the opinion that before God and before America all beliefs, all sects, are equal. If God did not wish a certain sect to exist, He would not give it the necessary powers to exist and develop."

The Polish National Catholic Church recognizes only the first four ecumenical councils and its General Synods as authoritative. In contrast, the Eastern Orthodox acknowledge the authority of the first seven councils, and the Catholic Church has held its twenty-first ecumenical council. The Prime Bishop consecrates other bishops, examines candidates for the priesthood, directs Savonarola Seminary and other church institutions, and controls the church's publications program.

The Polish National Catholic Church forbids divorce and remarriage, although the Prime Bishop may grant annulments. The church has taken no stand on artificial contraception; it leaves the use of various forms of birth control methods to the wishes of the couple.

Authority in faith, morals, and discipline resides with the Prime Bishop and clergy, while authority in social and economic matters is shared by the laity. The top administrative body is the General Synod; each parish is entitled to send one delegate for each fifty active members.

The church sent a bishop to Poland in 1925 to supervise missionary work in the homeland. He consecrated a native Polish bishop in 1930, but when the latter began to remarry divorced people contrary to church law, he was deposed by Hodur. Another Polish bishop was consecrated in 1936; he survived the war but was imprisoned by the Communists and died in prison in 1951. The Polish National Catholic Church in Poland enrolls about sixty thousand adherents.

Fruitful dialogues were initiated by the Roman Catholic and Polish National Catholic churches in 1984 and have continued since. An historic service of healing took place in the St. Stanislaus Cathedral of the Polish National Catholic Church in 1992. Cardinal Edward Cassidy, head of the Pontifical Council for Promoting Christian Unity, led the Roman Catholic delegation and read a letter from Pope John Paul II that stated "new hopes are raised that the events which some decades ago led to a break in the ecclesial unity which we had previously enjoyed can be put behind us, and that one day full communion in the one apostolic faith, sacramental life and mission, to which Christ calls us, can be restored."

When the Episcopal Church authorized the ordination of women, the Polish National Catholic Church severed its relations. The Polish National Catholic Church took similar action when several Old Catholic churches in Europe ordained women.

The great majority of Polish Americans have remained loyal Roman Catholics. The fires of intense nationalism have banked in recent years, affecting the Polish American community as well as other ethnic groups. Fewer Americans become fluent in a language other than English, limit marriage to members of their own ethnic group, and see themselves primarily as members of an ethnic minority.

The election of a Polish cardinal as Pope John Paul II practically rejected the argument that Polish Americans must join a schismatic church to win recognition of their ethnic heritage.

Because of recent developments, reunion of the continental Old Catholic bodies and the Roman Catholic Church is now doubtful, but the prospect of such a reunion with the Polish National Catholic Church has never been brighter.

FURTHER READING

Andrews, Theodore, *The Polish National Catholic Church in America and Poland* (London: S.P.C.K., 1953).

Anson, Peter, *Bishops at Large* (London: Faber and Faber, 1964).

Fox, Paul, *The Polish National Catholic Church* (Scranton, Pa.: School of Christian Living, n.d.).

Moss, C.B., *The Old Catholic Movement* (London: S.P.C.K., 1948).

Piepkorn, Arthur C., *Profiles in Belief,* Vol. 1 (New York: Harper & Row, 1977).

CHAPTER 18

The Cultists

Many Travel Side Streets on America's Religious Map

Aᴌᴛʜᴏᴜɢʜ ᴛʜᴇ ᴛᴇʀᴍ "ᴄᴜʟᴛ" ᴄᴀɴ ʜᴀᴠᴇ ᴀɴ ᴜɴꜰᴏʀᴛᴜɴᴀᴛᴇ ᴘᴇᴊᴏʀᴀᴛɪᴠᴇ connotation, it simply describes a minority religious body whose teachings are considered unorthodox or spurious by members of the majority faiths. This chapter examines a number of the smaller cults active in the United States, while the following chapters consider Mormonism, Christian Science, and Jehovah's Witnesses.

In general, the cults appeal to a special revelation such as that claimed by Emanuel Swedenborg or Joseph Smith, Jr., or they revere certain scriptures such as *Science and Health With Key to the Scriptures*, whose divine inspiration is denied by mainline denominations. If Christians see cultists as standing outside the central Christian tradition, some cultists are just as confident that they alone constitute the true church and all others give allegiance to apostate churches. The Mormons and Jehovah's Witnesses hold this view.

Some groups are classified as cults by certain scholars, and as nothing more than smaller denominations by other scholars. For example, the prophetic role of Mrs. Ellen G. White in Seventh-day Adventism leads such Protestant writers as Professor Anthony Hoekema and J.K. Van Baalen to group the Adventists with other cultists.

The cults we will describe do not belong to the National or World Councils of Churches and seldom participate in even local church associations. Cultists may be popularly known as Protestants and may be included in Protestant membership statistics, but fundamentally they are no more Protestant than Catholic. The fact that these cults have arisen in Western societies since the Reformation is no reason to classify them as Protestant. Typically they deny basic Protestant positions on the sole sufficiency of the Bible, the priesthood of all believers, and the like.

The Swedenborgians

After a distinguished scientific career, a latter-day Leonardo da Vinci by the name of Emanuel Swedenborg turned to religion. A Ph.D. at the age of twenty-one, he had mastered the mathematics, anatomy, and science of his day, traveled throughout Europe, and written sixty books and pamphlets when, at age fifty-five, he announced he had received the power to live in two worlds, the material and the spiritual.

This respected Swedish scientist abandoned science to produce twenty-nine volumes in Latin that described the spirit world in detail and presented his own version of the gospel. He recounted his spirit conversations with St. Paul, Luther, infidels, angels, popes, and Muslims. He had earlier rejected the doctrine of justification by faith alone as had his father, a Lutheran bishop. Now he discounted the Trinity and other traditional Christian beliefs. He claimed to have witnessed the Last Judgment, which took place in 1757.

Swedenborg devised an allegorical interpretation of the Bible in which stones always represented truth, houses meant intelligence, snakes were carnality, cities were religious systems, and so on.

At death, Swedenborg explained, man awakens in the spirit world and continues a life quite similar to his earthly existence. Eventually each man goes to the realm in which he will feel most at home: heaven, the spirit world (similar to purgatory), or hell. Bachelor Swedenborg revealed that marriage continues in the next world as an eternal relationship, although there may be some reshuffling of partners. He carefully described the flora and fauna of heaven, as well as the appearance of the inhabitants of other planets such as Mercury, Jupiter, Mars, and the moon.

Despite these bizarre revelations, Swedenborg continued to enjoy the respect of his fellow Swedes. He seldom attended the state Lutheran Church because, he complained, spirits kept interrupting the sermons and contradicting the minister. He also won a reputation as a seer by disclosing a number of secrets and reporting events at a distance, such as the details of a Stockholm fire some three hundred miles from his home.

He did not found a church. An English printer and some Anglican clergymen initiated the Swedenborg movement in 1783, eleven years after the seer's death in London. Lancashire became the main center for the Church of the New Jerusalem. The original American branch was founded in Baltimore in 1792, and a secession produced a second, smaller body in 1890. Together the Americans make up about half of the world's twelve thousand Swedenborgians.

The larger body, the General Convention, maintains a theological seminary at Cambridge, Mass., and most of its members may be found on the Atlantic seaboard. Swedenborg's works are offered in inexpensive editions and a modest advertising program has been launched, but few express particular interest in the Swedish seer. Clarence Walker Barron, the financial expert, and Helen Keller are probably the best-known Swedenborgians. The father of William and Henry James was a Swedenborgian.

Nevertheless, Swedenborg exerted an influence on modern Spiritualism by claiming immediate contact with the spirit world. His view on eternal marriage was elaborated upon by the Mormons. The Swedenborgian cult, however, now is stagnant and declining in membership.

To devout New Churchmen, Emanuel Swedenborg was a "divinely illuminated seer and revelator." To the founder of Methodism, John Wesley, he was "one of the most ingenious, lively, entertaining madmen that ever set pen to paper." To most Christians, he remains unknown.

The Spiritualists

Attempts to pierce the veil of death and communicate with the spirits of the departed are recorded in man's earliest history. But modern Spiritualism began with the Fox sisters in Hydesville, N.Y., and March 31, 1848, is usually given as the founding date.

The Fox family, which included two little girls, Kate and Margaret, occupied a cottage known by their neighbors to be haunted. Strange nocturnal rappings and noises had been heard in the house for some time and on March 31, little Kate addressed the noisemaker: "Here, Mr. Splitfoot, do as I do." The spirit responded and a rapping code was devised.

The two sisters, exploited by older sister Leah, went on tour and staged public demonstrations of the mysterious rappings in many American cities. The new religion attracted hundreds of thousands of enthusiasts and gave rise to a flood of Spiritualist publications. Horace Greeley of the *New York Tribune* contributed many newspaper columns to publicity of the Fox exhibitions.

Margaret eventually entered a common-law marriage, gave birth to a son, turned to drink, and finally startled the Spiritualist world by announcing her conversion to Catholicism. She admitted the whole thing was a hoax and demonstrated how she and her sister Kate had produced the loud rappings by snapping their toes. "I know that every so-called manifestation produced through me in London or anywhere else was a fraud," she confessed. Her exposé failed to shake the faith of the hard-core believers, and Margaret herself eventually recanted and returned to Spiritualism to eke out a living.

Meanwhile Andrew Jackson Davis, the Poughkeepsie seer, provided a systematic Spiritualist theology and terminology in thirty-three volumes supposedly written with spirit aid. He, rather than the discredited Fox sisters, is considered by many devotees to be the real founder of the religion, but the Fox sisters are esteemed by most Spiritualists, and the Hydesville cottage has become a shrine.

Spiritualism reached its membership peak within five years after its dramatic arrival on the American scene. By the first part of the twentieth century it had all but disappeared, only to be revived after World War I. American Spiritualism never achieved the respectability of English Spiritualism, which counted A. Conan Doyle (and presumably Sherlock Holmes) and Sir Oliver Lodge among its propagandists. Exposures and fraud have harried the Spiritualist cause in the United States. The enthusiasm of Episcopal Bishop James A. Pike and the resurgence of interest in the occult in the 1970s have given American Spiritualism a boost.

Spiritualist mediums use various physical devices to prove their powers of spirit communication. These include the time-tested rappings, the Ouija board, slate writing, spirit photography, levitation, telekinesis (moving heavy objects without visible means), clairvoyance, knowledge of foreign tongues, and automatic writing. In a typical séance, the medium sits with a circle of devotees and attempts to establish contact by rappings or voice with the deceased. At times a go-between or "control" relays messages from the deceased to the medium. Healing services also are conducted by some Spiritualists.

Harry Houdini, the magician, claimed he could duplicate any Spiritualistic phenomena by legerdemain. He exposed dozens of mediums and published his findings after twenty-five years' study in *A Magician Among the Spirits*. A number of Societies for Psychical Research have studied alleged Spiritualistic phenomena in the United States and Europe.

Spiritualists ignore most Christian doctrines, although they sometimes seek incorporation as a Christian church. They usually refer to Christ as an exceptionally able medium and adduce the annunciation, transfiguration, and resurrection as spirit phenomena. The theology of Spiritualism pays little attention to God and ends up as a base ancestor worship. The highest ideal is to be assured that one's loved ones are happy and contented in the spirit world. Spiritualism is singularly free of ethical or social content.

Spiritualists describe seven levels of life after death and claim that most begin their upward evolution in the third, or Summerland, sphere. The religion is Universalist, and no one ends up in hell. The first of the seven levels is thought to start about three hundred miles above the Earth's surface, and the seventh heaven begins at eighteen thousand miles. Life in Summerland seems to resemble life on Earth except sorrow and evil are missing. The dead marry their soul mates, live in houses, wear clothes, and keep pets. The trite and contradictory messages received from the "other side" disappoint many who investigate Spiritualism from a religious motive.

Women dominate the movement, but men usually hold the top national offices. About five hundred local congregations are grouped in a dozen denominations. The oldest (1893) and largest is the National Spiritualist Association of Churches, which prescribes rituals for worship, baptisms, and funerals, and ordains clergymen, licentiates, and mediums. Congregations are likely to meet in private homes or hotel rooms rather than church buildings. Other national organizations are the National Christian Spiritual Alliance and the International General Assembly of Spiritualists. About 180,000 Americans are affiliated with recognized Spiritualist churches.

All Spiritualist spokesmen admit that fraudulent mediums abound in the movement, but they insist there remains a core of sincere devoted mediums. Some associations seek to raise the educational requirements for Spiritualist clergymen, and a seminary in Wisconsin, the Morris Pratt Institute, offers a course for would-be mediums.

Spiritualism may attract some bereaved Christians by offering an assurance from the other world that the departed loved one is safe and happy. For others it supposedly offers tangible evidence of a hereafter, which some Protestant churches seldom mention. Many people dabble in Spiritualism and drift in and out of the movement. Spiritualism's religious impulse is slight. Not worship of God but chats with the dead are its motivation.

The Unity School of Christianity

Unity School of Christianity, which grew out of New England transcendentalism and New Thought, propagates its religion of optimism and healthy mindedness from a thirteen-hundred-acre farm and headquarters near Kansas City. Unity is often confused with Christian Science. Unlike it, however, Unity acknowledges the reality of sin, sickness, and death, but teaches that God works through man's right thinking to overcome these difficulties.

Each year millions of copies of a half-dozen attractive periodicals and pamphlets are mailed from the one-hundred-man printing plant at Lee's Summit, Mo. These include *Unity, Weekly Unity, Daily Word,* and *Wee Wisdom.* Many Protestants and Catholics read Unity literature without ever bothering to investigate Unity's philosophy and religious basis.

Myrtle and Charles Fillmore were debt-ridden and sickly before discovering the transforming principles of Unity. Both had studied many of the New Thought ideas, including Christian Science, and the new religion they taught after 1889 was based on Myrtle Fillmore's healing. She experienced a change in her bodily condition as she believed, "I am a child of God and therefore I do not inherit sickness."

Devotees were encouraged to think good thoughts, dismissing the delusion that sickness and death had any power over them. From the beginning, the Fillmores used the U.S. mail as their pulpit and relied wholly on voluntary contributions. Unlike Christian Science practitioners, they made no charge for their healings, which were published as testimonials in their magazines.

The Fillmores established Silent Unity, which offers around-the-clock prayer for all who phone, wire, or write for such help. A corps of Unity employees is on duty at all times to answer these appeals for prayers and to accept love offerings. An average week brings twenty thousand appeals.

Myrtle and Charles Fillmore are both dead, but their sons carried on the work. Unity moved to its new headquarters, eighteen miles from downtown Kansas City, in 1949. The property now includes an administration building, a 170-foot tower, a 22-acre artificial lake, a training school, Unity Inn (with vegetarian menu), the printing plant, a swimming pool, a golf course, picnic areas, and an amphitheater. More than 425 Unity workers are employed at the facility in Lee's Summit.

People of widely varying religions subscribe to their literature, listen to the radio programs, watch the TV series called "Daily Word," and write to Silent Unity. There is a ministerial school that offers a three-year resident program and a summer school for teachers and counselors. These departments train leadership to serve some two hundred local congregations, known as Unity centers or churches, which sponsor worship services, healing services, and Sunday schools, and offer classwork in counseling.

Unity converts are not required to sever connections with their former churches as is demanded of Christian Scientists. Many find the

Christianity of their own churches prosaic compared with the esoteric teachings of Unity; they are likely to rely more and more on Unity centers and Unity ministers for their spiritual needs.

Unity students interpret much of the Bible and many of the Christian doctrines allegorically or "metaphysically," as they would prefer to call it. A Hindu or Jew would find little to upset his religious sensibilities in Unity literature. In fact, the Hindu might feel more at home perusing Unity books than the Christian, as the sect teaches that the soul passes through various reincarnations "till we all come into Unity." Unity sponsors no social welfare programs, hospitals, orphanages, or homes for the aged.

For all practical purposes Unity has become another sect, and its claims to be nothing but a school of Christianity and nonsectarian are misleading. Its well-printed publications no doubt offer some comfort and inspiration to many millions who do not care about the cult's basic philosophy. Certainly, few Unity readers subscribe to Unity's belief in reincarnation. Were they to dig deeper into Unity, they would find a school not of practical but of Gnostic Christianity.

The New Thoughters

A variety of religious groups carry on the work begun in the mid-nineteenth century by Portland, Maine, healer Phineas P. Quimby. Some are tiny fellowships meeting in rented hotel rooms or private homes, while others such as the Church of Divine Science and the Church of Religious Science have become substantial denominations with scores of local congregations.

New Thought covers a wide spectrum, but all groups identified by this term insist that man need not believe in sickness, evil, or poverty. They prefer not to draw a sharp line between God and man, and their philosophies often verge on pantheism. New Thought teaches that man can always apply a spiritual solution to his problems; in this way he can achieve health, wealth, and happiness.

Most but not all such groups belong to the International New Thought Alliance; one of the larger holdouts is the Unity School. The

Yearbook of American Churches fails to catalog most New Thought churches, even though they influence millions of people through their publications and lectures. A metropolitan telephone book would list many New Thought groups.

Phineas P. Quimby, born in New Hampshire in 1802, treated patients for many years before opening an office in Portland in 1859. He himself said he had been cured of tuberculosis. At one stage in his healing career he practiced hypnotism, but later he relied exclusively on mental healing. Quimby was critical of orthodox Christianity but nevertheless believed Jesus had discovered the principles of spiritual healing. Among his many clients was a Mrs. Patterson — known later as Mary Baker Eddy, founder of Christian Science.

Horatio Dresser edited Quimby's voluminous writings in 1921; the original manuscript in the Library of Congress runs to twenty-one hundred pages in twelve journals. Charles Braden declares: "Carefully dated, they revealed beyond question to any but the most convinced Eddy disciples that Quimby had held the basic ideas of mental healing years before Mrs. Eddy sought healing at his hands in 1862" *(Spirits in Rebellion,* p. 57).

Warren Felt Evans left the Methodist ministry to become a Swedenborgian and later gave Quimby's ideas literary form. Quimby and the New Thoughters drew upon transcendentalism, Swedenborgianism, Mesmerism, Hinduism, Spiritualism, and other systems. New Thought rejected the Calvinism of American Protestantism and proposed an optimistic, empirical faith.

Most New Thoughters believe in the divinity of man and the impersonality of God. They admire the moral teachings of Jesus but repudiate the dogmas of orthodox Christianity such as those of original sin, the Trinity, and the atonement.

Quimby died in 1866 and founded no church. New Thought groups began to be organized in the 1890s and often gained initial strength by absorbing disaffected Christian Scientists. New Thought is more syncretic, less authoritarian, and less monolithic than Christian Science. The cultists prefer spiritual healing, but express less opposition to medicine than do the followers of Eddy. Unlike Christian Science, the New Thought cults do not insist devotees cut all ties with other, more traditional churches.

New Thought ideas have been popularized by such authors as Ralph Waldo Trine, whose *In Tune With the Infinite* has sold more than a million copies. The books of Emmet Fox, a former Roman Catholic, have introduced thousands of Americans to New Thought. For years Dr. Fox preached to the largest congregation in New York City, first in the Hippodrome and then in Carnegie Hall.

Four ladies participated in the founding of the Church of Divine Science in Denver in 1898. This church teaches that God is Spirit, Mind, Principle, Love, Truth, Substance, Soul, Intelligence, Being, Omniscience, Omnipotence, and Omnipresence. Ministers trained at the College of Divine Science staff several dozen autonomous churches.

Dr. Ernest Holmes started the Church of Religious Science in 1952; previously he had founded the Institute of Religious Science and Philosophy in 1927. He wrote the textbook of the movement: *Science of Mind.* This movement has split into two branches: About thirty churches form the International Association of Religious Science Churches, and seventy belong to the Affiliated Churches of the Church of Religious Science. More than half of these congregations are found in California.

Other groups that fall into the New Thought category usually can be identified by such names as Metaphysical Science, Mental Science, Home of Truth. The importance of New Thought lies not in the number of adherents, although membership is in the tens of thousands, but in its influence on those who never set foot in a New Thought church. William James once wrote that New Thought, "together with Christian Science, constitutes a spiritual movement as significant for our day as the Reformation was for its time."

The Worldwide Church of God

Shortly after the death of its founder in 1986, the Worldwide Church of God lost half its members, saw its annual income fall from

$200 million to $50 million, and heard its new head declare that the founder had been fundamentally wrong on many theological positions.

The original church was established in 1943 as the Radio Church of God by Herbert W. Armstrong. He told his followers true Christianity disappeared in A.D. 69 and was revived only through his ministry.

Members of the renamed Worldwide Church of God were told to observe the Sabbath on Saturday rather than Sunday, contribute as much as 30 percent of their income to the church, stop observing Christmas, Easter, and birthdays, and follow the dietary laws of the Old Testament. The church denied the Trinity and the personality of the Holy Spirit.

At its peak, the church operated three universities, distributed millions of free copies of its magazine *Plain Truth*, and reached millions through programs on four hundred radio and ninety-nine television stations. Under Armstrong's successor, Joseph Tkash, Sr., the church sold its universities and its Pasadena, Calif, headquarters. The circulation of its magazine fell to 125,000 paid subscribers.

Born in 1892 and raised in an Iowa Quaker home, Armstrong pursued several careers in advertising and business before turning to religion. He and his Methodist wife joined a tiny sect in Oregon that advocated the Saturday Sabbath. Armstrong was ordained a minister in the group but broke away and began a religious broadcast on a 100-watt station in Eugene, Oregon. Eventually he moved his base to California.

Armstrongism has been characterized as an amalgam of Adventism, Mormonism, Judaism, Russellism, Fundamentalism, and British-Israelism. The last-mentioned movement spins prophecies around the theory that the lost tribes of Israel migrated to northern Europe and became the ancestors of the British people.

Armstrong promised his followers they will become part of God's family, which now includes two personages: God the Father and Jesus Christ. He denied that man has an immortal soul, but said God will raise up the faithful who have observed the laws of the Old and New Testaments.

Congregations usually meet in rented halls and schools and do not welcome visitors or advertise their services. They had to give full allegiance to Armstrong, observe the seven Old Testament feasts, and attend the eight-day summer meetings held around the country. They were forbidden to smoke or seek medical treatment. Like Jehovah's Witnesses, Worldwide Church of God members do not vote or serve in the armed forces and generally stand apart from secular society.

Discontent in the Armstrong empire began to surface in the 1970s. Armstrong was drawing a $200,000-a-year salary, living in a mansion, and flying around the world in church-owned jet planes. The cost of the auditorium on the opulent Pasadena campus exceeded $11 million.

In 1972 the elder Armstrong stripped his son, Garner Ted, of all church authority because of alleged improprieties. When his son repented and was reinstated, some thirty-five ministers of the sect rebelled and formed a rival Associated Churches of God. Those who joined the new sect need not pay a triple tithe to remain in good standing.

Another falling out between father and son occurred in 1978, and this time Garner Ted Armstrong set up his own Church of God International. He told the press that members of his father's church lived in fear, and that the church was facing severe financial difficulties. He said he could not communicate with his father, who had been widowed for many years but married a 39-year-old divorcee and moved to Tucson, Ariz.

Joseph Tkash, Jr., assumed the leadership of the original Worldwide Church of God when his father died in 1995. By this time, at least three other splinter groups had attracted former church adherents: the Global Church of God, the United Church of God, and the Philadelphia Church of God.

The Hare Krishnas

Strolling down the street of a major city, you have no way of telling a Lutheran from a Catholic or a Methodist from a Mormon. You would most likely not mistake a devotee of the International Society of Krishna

Consciousness, however. The young men wear saffron robes and sandals; their heads are shaved except for a pigtail. Women wear saris and special marks on their foreheads. Hands upraised and bodies twisting, they chant the Hare Krishna mantra over and over:

Hare Krishna hare Krishna
Krishna Krishna hare hare
Hare Rama hare Rama
Rama Rama hare hare.

The Hare Krishnas follow a strict Hindu sect that has been around since the late fifteenth century but was imported to the United States in recent years. In New York, San Francisco, Los Angeles and a score of other American cities, the inner core of devotees live in communes and practice an asceticism far removed from the drug culture that once enmeshed many: no drugs, alcohol, tobacco, meat, fish, eggs, illicit sex, gambling, coffee, or tea. Married members limit sexual relations to once a month at the time most favorable to conception.

Hundreds live on a Hare Krishna farm in West Virginia, and at the Los Angeles center. Worldwide the sect supports ninety temples in such places as London, Montreal, Singapore, and Amsterdam.

The swami who introduced the sect to this country in 1965 was born in Calcutta in 1896. Known as His Divine Grace A.C. Bhaktivedanta Swami Prabhujada, he engaged in business before meeting his guru in 1922 and adopting the beliefs of this branch of Hinduism. Lord Krishna is believed to be one of the eight incarnations of the Hindu deity Vishnu. The sect seeks spiritual enlightenment by chanting the name of this god.

Other Hindu gurus had sought converts in the West, but most of them worked out various adaptations to American culture. Swami Prabhujada refused to compromise. His converts, mostly middle-class Americans from Protestant homes, assume a Hindu name after a six-month novitiate. They get up at about 4 a.m. to begin a day in a Hare Krishna temple, which includes worship, chanting, cleaning, work, reading, vegetarian meals, and two daily showers. The group's unusual garb and its practice of frequenting city streets, airports, and shopping centers tend to give an exaggerated impression of its size. Current worldwide membership is about ten thousand, half of whom are Americans. Only the fully committed followers live in communes; others may visit temples to worship and contribute to the cause.

The Scientologists

L. Ron Hubbard, a prolific science-fiction writer, launched a self-help fad in 1950 with the publication of his book *Dianetics.* Four years later, he founded a religion called the Church of Scientology based on the superstructure of Dianetics with additional religious concepts.

Hubbard was born in 1911, attended George Washington University for a while, and served as a navy officer during World War II. He unveiled his first concepts of Dianetics in the pages of *Astounding Science Fiction.* He died in 1986.

Hubbard refers to two compartments of the mind: the analytic and the reactive. The analytic corresponds to the conscious mind and is rational and, in fact, infallible. The reactive mind, however, stores up unpleasant memories and traumas known as engrams. These engrams might be recorded in childhood, in the womb, or even in previous lives.

The goal of the process of auditing in Scientology is to bring these engrams to light and thereby erase them. As the engrams disappear, the analytic mind assumes complete control over the reactive mind and the subject's troubles go away.

In Scientology the newcomer is called a preclear. By confessing details of their past lives to an auditor (a minister of the Church of Scientology), preclears rid themselves of their engrams, which have been causing their problems and hang-ups.

During the auditing sessions the preclear holds two tin cans attached to the E-meter, a primitive type of lie detector. The auditor asks the same question until satisfied that the truth has been told, and the particular engram eliminated. Hubbard explains: "The E-meter is never wrong. It sees all; it knows all. It tells everything."

As a religious organization, Scientology has sought tax exemption and freedom from what it considers government harassment. In 1963 the Food and Drug Administration seized a supply of E-meters, declaring them misbranded as useful in the cure and treatment of disease; a federal judge later reversed the ruling. The Internal Revenue Service hesitated to grant tax exemption status to many Scientology churches because of a suspicion that Hubbard himself benefited from the income of the church.

In the 1960s the governments of Australia and England called Scientology a danger to mental health. Sensitive to any criticism and quick to resort to litigation, the Scientologists have filed dozens of lawsuits against various newspapers, the American Medical Association, ABC-TV, government agencies, and ex-members. For years the church has engaged in running battles with the IRS, the psychiatric profession, and the FBI. In 1978 more than one hundred thirty FBI agents raided Scientology headquarters in Washington, D.C., and Los Angeles and carted away thousands of documents. Later a grand jury charged eleven top Scientologists, including Hubbard's third wife, with burglary, wiretapping, obstruction of justice, and conspiracy.

An introductory course in Scientology costs only $15 or so, but a devotee can easily spend as much as $5,000 for the necessary auditing sessions that lead to "Clear" status. The cult claims a membership in the millions but actually lists only twenty-four U.S. churches and twice that number in other countries. Perhaps a reasonable U.S. active membership might be thirty thousand, although many others dabble in Scientology and purchase Hubbard's books. Scientology makes a special effort to win converts among motion-picture celebrities.

The Moonies

Few Asian cults have won many converts or headlines in the United States. One exception is the Holy Spirit Association for the Unification of World Christianity, the creation of the Korean evangelist the Reverend Sun Myung Moon. His church is popularly known as the Unification Church, and his followers as Moonies.

The estimated five thousand committed Moonies in this country work full time at their religion. From dawn to dusk they sell peanuts, flowers, and incense to support the Reverend Moon and the church's ambitious programs. Perhaps twice that number of Americans have some interest in the Unification church.

The church has invested heavily in real estate, such as the forty-two-story New Yorker hotel, the former Columbia University Club, and the Tiffany building in New York City. Ninety miles away, the church operates its seminary in a former Christian Brothers house of studies.

Moon usually lives in a $625,000 mansion in Tarrytown, N.Y., with his second wife and some of his nine children. A multimillion-aire, he owns factories in South Korea that manufacture air rifles, pharmaceuticals, titanium, and other products.

Sun Myung Moon was born in what is now North Korea in 1920. He joined the Presbyterian Church with the rest of his family, but claims that at the age of sixteen he was visited by Jesus and given a new revelation. This and later such revelations would be compiled in the cult's basic text, *Divine Principle.*

Moon studied engineering for a time in Japan. Returning to his native Korea, he began his religious preaching and ran afoul of the Communist government. He was twice sentenced to prison, but was freed by United Nations forces in 1950. Four years later he launched his church.

The first Unification missionary to the United States started to seek converts on the West Coast in 1959. Jesus told Moon himself to go to America in 1972, even though he knew little English. Meanwhile, in 1960 Moon remarried after divorcing his first wife.

Reverend Moon believes the Bible is written in code and he is God's chief cryptographer. He tells his followers that his theological ideas do not come from study of the Bible but from direct revelation from Jesus and other spirits.

Basic to Unification theology is the concept of the three Adams. The first Adam was supposed to marry Eve and become the father of the perfect human family. Instead, the serpent (Satan) seduced Eve. She in turn thought she could remove the stigma of this offense by having sexual relations with Adam without waiting to get God's approval. As a result, the pair was driven out of the Garden of Eden and the original divine plan was frustrated.

Jesus, the second Adam, was supposed to marry and beget children according to the divine plan. The Unification Church believes he was a perfect man with a messianic mission, but no more. The Jews, however, rejected the Messiah, and the crucifixion aborted God's second attempt to establish the perfect human family. The Unification Church is the only so-called Christian body to declare that Jesus failed in his mission.

A third Adam must marry and start the long-delayed perfect family that will usher in the kingdom. According to *Divine Principle,* the new Messiah will have been born in Korea between 1917 and 1930, will have married in 1960, and will live in America. Reverend Moon makes no public claims that he is the Messiah. but understandably many of his followers make that assumption.

The Unification Church has no ordained ministers or sacraments; baptism and the Lord's Supper are identified with the failed mission of Jesus. The closest thing to a sacrament might be the mass marriages arranged for Moonies by the Reverend Moon and the church hierarchy. Moon presided over one such ceremony that united eighteen hundred couples in Seoul in 1975.

Worldwide, the Unification movement may enroll as many as five hundred thousand people, mostly in South Korea and Japan. All members are expected to give up alcohol, drugs, tobacco, and illicit sex.

American converts, mostly in their twenties, often leave comfortable middle-class homes to spend their days peddling on the streets or seeking followers on college campuses. Distraught parents have engaged professional deprogrammers, who kidnap the young men and women and attempt to get them to recant. What one side calls religious conversion, the other side labels brainwashing.

Reverend Moon has written: "God is now throwing Christianity away and is now establishing a new religion and this new religion is Unification church." He predicts: "All the Christians in the world are destined to be absorbed by our movement."

The National Council of Churches commissioned a theological study of the teachings of *Divine Principle* and the Unification Church. Sr. Agnes Cunningham of Mundelein College headed the study group, which included a number of Protestant scholars. The report they prepared concluded: "The Unification Church is not a Christian Church." Specifically, the theologians criticized Moon's ideas of the nature of God, his Christology, and his teachings on salvation, and the means of grace.

FURTHER READING

General

Ellwood, Robert S., *Religious and Spiritual Groups in Modern America* (Englewood Cliffs, N.J.: Prentice-Hall, 1973).

Lewis, James R., *Cults in America* (Santa Barbara, Calif.: ABC-CLIO, 1998).

_____, ed., *Odd Gods: New Religious and the Cult Controversy* (New York: Promeseus Books, 2001).

Martin, Walter, *The Kingdom of the Cults*, rev. ed. (Minneapolis: Bethany House, 1997).

Needleman, Jacob and George Baker, *Understanding the New Religions* (New York: Seabury Press, 1978).

Whalen, William J., *Strange Gods: Contemporary Religious Cults in America* (Huntington, Ind.: Our Sunday Visitor, 1981).

Swedenborgians

Swedenborg, Emanuel, *The True Christian Religion* (New York: E. P. Dutton, 1936).

Trowbridge, George, *Swedenborg: Life and Teaching* (New York: Swedenborg Foundation, 1944).

Spiritualists

Barbanell, Maurice, *Spiritualism Today* (London: Herbert Jenkins, 1969).

Brown, Slater, *The Heyday of Spiritualism* (New York: Hawthorn, 1970).

Ford, Arthur, *Unknown but Known* (London: Psychic Press, 1969).

Pike, James, *The Other Side* (Garden City, N.Y.: Doubleday, 1968).

Thurston, Herbert, *The Church and Spiritualism* (Milwaukee: Bruce, 1933).

Unity School of Christianity

Bach, Marcus, *The Unity of Life* (Englewood Cliffs, N.J.: Prentice Hall, 1962).

Cady, H. Emilie, *Lessons in Truth* (Lee's Summit, Mo.: Unity School of Christianity, 1954).

D'Andrade, Hugh, *Charles Fillmore* (New York: Harper & Row, 1974).

Freeman, James Dillet, *The Story of Unity* (Lee's Summit, Mo.: Unity School of Christianity, 1954).

New Thoughters

Braden, Charles S., *Spirits in Rebellion* (Dallas: Southern Methodist University Press, 1963).

Judah, J. Stillson, *The History and Philosophy of the Metaphysical Movements in America* (Philadelphia: Westminster, 1967).

Worldwide Church of God

Chambers, Roger R., *The Plain Truth About Armstrongism* (Grand Rapids, Mich.: Baker, 1972).

Hopkins, Joseph, *The Armstrong Empire* (Grand Rapids, Mich.: Eerdmans, 1974).

Scientologists

Cooper, Paulette, *The Scandal of Scientology* (New York: Tower, 1971).

Corydon, Bent and L. Ron Hubbard, Jr., *L. Ron Hubbard: Messiah or Madman?* (Secaucus, N.J.: Lyle Stuart, 1987).

Hubbard, L. Ron, *Dianetics: The Modern Science of Mental Health* (New York: Hermitage House, 1950).

Malko, George, *Scientology: The Now Religion* (New York: Delacorte, 1970).

Moonies

Bjornstad, James, *The Moon is Not the Son* (Minneapolis, Dimension Books, 1976).

Divine Principle (Washington, D.C.: The Holy Spirit Association for the Unification of World Christianity, 1973).

Horowitz, Irving Louis, ed., *Science, Sin, and Scholarship: The Politics of Reverend Moon and the Unification Church* (Cambridge, Mass.: M.I.T. Press, 1978).

Kim, Young Ong, *Unification Theology and Christian Thought* (New York: Golden Gate, 1975).

Sontag, Frederick, *Sun Myung Moon and the Unification Church* (Nashville: Abingdon, 1977).

Yamamoto, J. Isamu, *The Puppet Master* (Downers Grove, Ill.: InterVarsity Press, 1977).

CHAPTER 19

The Mormons

'What Man Is Now, God Once Was; What God Is Now,
Man May Become'

MORE THAN ELEVEN MILLION PEOPLE, INCLUDING FIVE MILLION Americans, who claim the name Christian believe:

- That Christ preached to the American Indians after His ascension and founded a church among them for the Western Hemisphere;
- That an angel revealed the history of these people on golden plates to a young man in New York in 1827 and furnished magic spectacles to enable him to translate the record;
- That this youth reestablished the church of Christ, which had been wiped out in the Americas and had apostatized elsewhere;
- That there is not one God but many gods for many worlds;
- That man lived with God in a previous existence, and that after death he may become a god for his own planet;
- That polygamy is the divine pattern of marriage.

These people are "Mormons" or, properly speaking, members of the Church of Jesus Christ of Latter-day Saints. Preponderant in Utah and strong in Idaho, Arizona, California, and other western states, Mormonism has grown tenfold since World War II. An unusually high birth rate, low death rate, and an aggressive missionary program account for the growth of Mormonism into one of the largest denominations in the United States.

Fifteen Mormon senators and representatives serve in the U.S Congress. About 74 percent of the population of Utah belongs to this church. With current assets of at least $30 billion, the church owns farms, insurance companies, a department store, a daily newspaper, and radio stations. It operates a 312,000-acre cattle and citrus ranch near Orlando, Fla.

The church reports 847,000 members in Mexico and about 2,500,000 in South America. Once confined mainly to the intermountain states, the Latter-day Saints Church is busy establishing new wards (parishes) in Eastern, Midwestern, and Southern states.

The church operates what has become the largest church-related university in the nation: Brigham Young University in Provo, Utah. It enrolls three times as many students as Notre Dame, and 97 percent of its students are Latter-day Saints. The Mormon Church also claims to enroll a higher percentage of its young people in colleges and universities than any other major denomination.

Things have changed for the Mormon Church, whose members were once massacred and driven out of Missouri and whose founder and first prophet was murdered in the Carthage, Ill., jail by an enraged mob. Now noted for their sobriety, honesty, and industriousness, the Mormons once were branded from pulpits and political platforms as barbarians and lechers. After the Civil War, the federal government turned from the fight against slavery to the fight against polygamy and eventually forced the Mormon Church to suspend the practice of plural marriage.

A federal army once entered Utah and threatened to depose Brigham Young, but the Mormons vowed to burn their cities to the ground if the troops entered Salt Lake City. A compromise prevented a tragedy comparable to the burning of Moscow before Napoleon. For years American audiences were regaled by the stories of Mormon polygamy and alleged treason; one of the most popular lecturers was Young's twenty-seventh wife, who had divorced him and joined forces with Gentile critics.

One basic reason for this persecution was the Mormon insistence that it was not just *a* Christian Church but *the* one and only Christian Church. This claim infuriated frontier Protestants. The Mormon position has not changed much today. Mormonism teaches that all other

Christian bodies lack any authority from God to teach or baptize; this includes all Catholic, Protestant, and Orthodox churches. Without exception these churches are considered apostate and counterfeit.

Mormonism claims to be a restored rather than a reformed church. Founder Joseph Smith maintained that the Christian Church fell into apostasy shortly after the death of the last apostle. But he maintained that God the Father and Jesus Christ had appeared to him in person and restored the true church and the authority of the priesthood in 1829. Acceptance of the claims of Smith and of the authenticity of the *Book of Mormon* and other Mormon scriptures is demanded of all members.

Mormondom is split into two main branches and a handful of tiny schismatic bodies. The main branch in Utah represents the majority of early Saints who followed Brigham Young westward after the Prophet's assassination. The other significant body of Mormons, the Reorganized Church of Jesus Christ of Latter Day Saints, objected to Young's leadership and eventually rallied around Joseph Smith's son. Its 140,000 U.S. members look to Independence, Mo., as their Mecca. Except where noted, our comments will apply to the larger Utah or Brighamite group rather than the so-called Josephites. (In 2001 the Reorganized Latter Day Saints Church changed its name to the Community of Christ.)

Smith, a Vermonter by birth, was a visionary, good-natured young blood who passed his time hunting buried treasure by means of "peep stones." According to his own account and official Mormon history, he was visited by a number of angels from the time he reached fourteen. One such angel, Moroni, informed him that all existing churches were in error, corrupt and apostate. His mission was to reestablish the true church and priesthood. Finally, the angel gave him permission to dig near the top of the Hill Cumorah, near Palmyra, N.Y. There he unearthed a box of golden plates inscribed in "Reformed Egyptian." The obliging angel also supplied him with a pair of magic spectacles called the Urim and Thummim, which enabled him to decipher the hieroglyphics.

The twenty-two-year-old Smith employed various amanuenses, including Oliver Cowdery, an unemployed schoolteacher. Sitting behind a blanket, he dictated the *Book of Mormon*, the supposed history of the original inhabitants of this continent from 600 B.C. to A.D. 421.

According to this book, North and South America were peopled by Jews who came by ship from Palestine. Two nations arose, the Lamanites and the Nephites. Essentially Mormonism is based on a version of the lost-tribes-of-Israel legend; Cotton Mather, Roger Williams, and William Penn also speculated that the American Indians were Jews. Other variations of the lost-tribes legend place the Israelites in Ireland, Japan, England (Anglo-Israel cult), and the lost continent of Atlantis.

The Mormon Bible relates that Christ appeared among the Nephites, chose twelve Indian apostles and set up a church, which was a counterpart of the church he had established in Jerusalem. Eventually the dissolute Lamanites destroyed the virtuous Nephites in a battle near Palmyra in A.D. 421. Moroni, son of the vanquished Nephite general Mormon, buried the golden plates that recounted the history of his race. The plates also recorded the history of the Jaredites, who were supposed to have come to America after the Tower of Babel.

After translating the Reformed Egyptian, Smith delivered the plates and goggles to the angel and they have not been seen since. Linguists know nothing about a language called Reformed Egyptian, and some of Smith's early disciples urged him to submit a specimen to a scholar to confound the skeptics. He copied down what he called some "caractors" and presented them to Professor Charles Anthon of Columbia College. Anthon declared the sample consisted of "all kinds of crooked characters, disposed in columns . . . evidently prepared by some person who had before him at the time a book containing various alphabets." He repeatedly denied the Mormon claim that had declared the markings to be genuine "Reformed Egyptian."

The original edition listed Joseph Smith, Jr., as "Author and Proprietor." Of the eleven witnesses who testified to having seen the plates, none ever admitted he had been duped or had perjured himself. Martin Harris, a farmer who mortgaged his land to pay the printer, testified in court years later that he had seen the plates "with the eyes of faith . . . though at the time they were covered over with a cloth." Five of the witnesses were Whitmers and three were Smiths, including the Prophet's father. Harris, Cowdery, and David Whitmer eventually apostatized; the latter pair were driven out of Missouri by eighty Mormons who signed a complaint that they were thieves and counterfeiters.

Lengthy passages from the New Testament were included verbatim in the *Book of Mormon*, and the entire book, supposedly written before A.D. 421, is phrased in King James idioms. It abounds in anachronisms, contradictions, and Campbellite answers to the theological questions of the early nineteenth century. At times its hindsight prophecy becomes entangled in such statements as "the Son of God shall be born of Mary at *Jerusalem.*"

Smith relates that John the Baptist appeared to Cowdery and himself in 1829 and ordained them into the Aaronic priesthood. The two baptized each other in the Susquehanna River. Later the Apostles Peter, James, and John conferred the higher priesthood of Melchizedek.

The small church, organized at Fayette, N.Y., the next year, moved to Kirtland, Ohio, where Sidney Rigdon was pastor of a church. Here the group found a ready welcome, built their first temple, chose twelve apostles to assist President Smith, and attempted to establish a communist order. Another band of Mormons continued to Missouri, and the two Mormon settlements continued for some years one thousand miles apart.

Smith went to Missouri on a scouting expedition in 1831 and dedicated sixty-three acres in Jackson County, which was proclaimed the exact site of the Temple of Zion where Christ would live and rule after His Second Coming. Today a tiny splinter group of Mormons owns the holy ground but has no funds to build the temple. The schismatics say they have refused an offer of $5 million from the Utah Mormons for the property.

With the failure of a wildcat bank and an impending indictment, Smith and Rigdon fled Kirtland by night and headed for the Missouri colony. Here the strange beliefs of the Mormon settlers and their suspected anti-slavery attitudes had antagonized the Missourians. Riots and incessant squabbles between Saints and Gentiles prompted the governor to call out the militia, and the Mormons were expelled from the state in midwinter 1838-1839. Smith had been imprisoned for four-and-a-half months as a hostage; when he escaped he rejoined the Saints in neighboring Illinois.

Purchasing swampland on the Mississippi River, the Saints began to build their city of Nauvoo, which Smith maintained was a Hebrew word meaning "the beautiful." Its twenty thousand residents made it the largest city in the state, and it received a liberal municipal charter. Thousands of English converts followed the exhortations of the Mormon missionaries to gather in Zion. To this day both Utah and Missouri Mormons look for the establishment of Zion at the Second Coming at Independence, Mo., (also reputed to be the site of the Garden of Eden).

The industrious Saints built a handsome temple at Nauvoo, laid out broad streets, and built substantial homes and factories. Smith recruited a private army, the Nauvoo Legion, and designated himself lieutenant general.

Rumors of polygamy, envy of Mormon prosperity, and fear of the Saints' political power and dominance stirred the Gentiles to provocative actions. Smith contributed to the unrest when he announced himself a candidate for the presidency of the United States on a three-plank platform of abolition, nationalization of the banks, and prison reform. Rigdon ran for vice-president, and Mormon missionaries were pressed into service as campaign spokesmen.

Disgruntled ex-Saints attempted to publish an anti-Smith newspaper in Nauvoo, but Smith ordered his henchmen to pi the type and smash the presses. When the governor of Illinois promised Smith protection and safe conduct, he agreed to appear in Carthage to face charges of immorality, counterfeiting, sheltering criminals, and treason. But a mob of two hundred men with blackened faces stormed the Carthage jail and shot the Prophet and his brother Hyrum to death. The Mormon prophet was dead at thirty-nine.

In stricken Nauvoo, rivals vied for positions of leadership. The murder of Smith and his brother, the heir apparent, left the community in an unforeseen quandary. When Brigham Young returned from a mission in New England, he managed to win the confidence of most of the bewildered Saints. Rigdon was banished. Many abandoned the Prophetless church; a minority who insisted the leader should be a lineal descendant of the Prophet formed the nucleus of the Reorganized faction. Smith's widow Emma married a Nauvoo tavernkeeper, raised her family in the deserted city of Nauvoo, and eventually joined the Reorganized Church.

The demoralized Saints found an outstanding leader in Young. An ex-Methodist and fellow Vermonter, Young had joined the Prophet in Kirtland and never seemed to doubt Smith's claims. Although he had the benefit of only eleven days of formal schooling, this determined carpenter would build a theocratic empire in the West.

Realizing the precarious situation of the Saints in Nauvoo, Brigham Young set about organizing the epic march to the West. To all who asked why he was leading the Saints out of Illinois he had one answer: "To get away from Christians and out of the United States." The first party left the state in the middle of the winter of 1846. By April, the last of the Saints had bidden farewell to their homes, factories, fields, and temple in Nauvoo. Thousands would never reach their destination.

"This is the place," declared Young on July 24, 1847, when his advance party reached the valley of the Great Salt Lake, then a part of Mexico. The Mormons made the desert bloom. They irrigated, built homes, and started work on a new temple.

After the Mexican War, the Saints found themselves subject to the same United States government from which they had fled. Congress turned down their petition for statehood for the "State of Deseret," but Young was appointed first governor of the Utah territory.

After 1853 polygamy was openly practiced and defended. The Utah Mormons claim Smith received the revelation on plural marriage at Nauvoo in 1843, but the controversial doctrine was not published until the Saints were safely entrenched in their intermountain sanctuary. Obviously polygamy was an afterthought, as the *Book of Mormon* plainly states: "Wherefore, my brethren, hear me, and hearken to the word of the Lord: For there shall not any man among you save it be one wife; and concubines he shall have none" (Jacob 2:26). In other passages in the Mormon scriptures polygamy is called an "abomination before the Lord," and in *Doctrine and Covenants*, published in 1835, we read: "Inasmuch as this Church of Christ has been reproached with the crime of fornication and polygamy, we declare that we believe that one man should have one wife, and one woman one husband, except in case of death, when either is at liberty to marry again" (Section 101).

Nevertheless, the revelation to the Prophet no longer speaks of the "crime" of polygamy: "If any man espouse a virgin, and desire to espouse another, and the first give her consent; and if he espouse the second, and they are virgins, and have vowed to no other man, then he is justified; he cannot commit adultery with that that belongeth unto him and to no one else. And if he have ten virgins given unto him by this law, he cannot commit adultery, for they belong to him, and they are given unto him, therefore he is justified" (Section 132).

Not all Saints welcomed this innovation, and four thousand English converts who balked at polygamy were summarily excommunicated. In Utah the leaders of the priesthood advised the wealthier Saints to take a second or additional wife. The cult found itself with a surplus of female Saints, a theology that deprecated celibacy, and a desert that needed people. When Young died in 1877, he left his $2,000,000 fortune to twelve widows (other wives had preceded him in death) and forty-seven children. Another leader of the Mormon hierarchy, Heber Kimball, supported forty-five wives.

The church has never renounced its belief in polygamy, which Mormons believe was revealed by God Himself. It has become a "suspended" doctrine since 1890, when President Woodruff yielded to federal law and declared: "Inasmuch as laws have been enacted by Congress, which laws have been pronounced constitutional by the court of last resort, I hereby declare my intention to submit to these laws, and to use my influence with the members of the church over which I preside to have them do likewise. And now I publicly declare that my advice to the Latter-day Saints is to refrain from contracting any marriage forbidden by the law of the land."

Opposition by the federal government to the practice of polygamy was registered as early as 1862, when President Lincoln signed a bill condemning polygamy in the territories of the United States. In his inaugural address President Garfield stated: "The Mormon Church not only offends the moral sense of mankind by sanctioning polygamy, but prevents the administration of justice through the ordinary instrumentalities of law." Finally, in 1890 the Supreme Court upheld the constitutionality of the Edmunds Law of 1882, which disfranchised any person who practiced plural marriage. Polygamy was traded for statehood in 1896 when Utah became the forty-fifth state in the union.

If the federal government were to withdraw its opposition to plural marriages, the Saints probably would resume the practice. They always have considered the laws against polygamy to be unjust and an infringement of religious freedom. Scores of Saints went into exile in Mexico or served prison sentences rather than submit to the federal government. Several Utah congressmen were denied seats because they had more than one wife. A number of polygamist sects flourish in Utah, Arizona, Idaho, California, and other western states. Estimates of the number of people in polygamous families run from twenty thousand to fifty thousand. All hold the Mormon Church in contempt for bowing to political pressure and abandoning plural marriages. Several times state officials have raided a settlement of Mormon fundamentalists in Arizona who were following Joseph Smith's revelation on polygamy.

Mormons accept four sources of doctrine: the Bible "insofar as correctly translated," *The Book of Mormon, Doctrine and Covenants,* and *The Pearl of Great Price.* Smith labored for months over his own translation of the Bible, but the Utah Mormons continue to use the King James Version.

Doctrine and Covenants is a collection of dated revelations from God to the Prophet and a single revelation to his successor, Young. One such divine revelation set the price of the *Book of Mormon* at $1.25 and another presented the godhead's advice on the financing of a boarding house at Nauvoo: "And they shall not receive less than fifty dollars for a share of stock in that house, and they shall be permitted to receive fifteen thousand dollars from any one man for stock in that house." This book also includes the Word of Wisdom forbidding alcohol, tobacco, and hot drinks, which the Saints have taken to mean coffee and tea.

The Pearl of Great Price is a slim volume of three sections: the so-called Book of Moses in which certain visions are described, the Book of Abraham, and a potpourri entitled the "Writings of Joseph Smith." The Book of Moses discloses that Satan originated Freemasonry to ensnare mankind.

The background of the Book of Abraham is instructive. At Kirtland, a traveling carnival owner invited Smith to examine the papyrus accompanying his circus mummy. The Prophet solemnly declared the hieroglyphics to be the writings of Abraham and Joseph and proceeded to produce a translation. Egyptologists realized the hieroglyphics were part of the well-known Book of the Dead and bore no similarity to Smith's efforts.

Mormon theology teaches that the god of this world is a man (probably Adam), a physical being, a polygamist. God did not create matter, which existed eternally (he "organized" it), but he did create a tremendous number of spirits or souls. All humans have entered a pact with the god of this world to erase the memory of their former existence if he would send them to Earth. If they faithfully follow Mormon precepts and obey the priesthood, they may be given charge of a planet of their own after death. Their leading theologian states simply, "All men are potential gods," and Young himself phrased the Mormon aphorism, "What God was once, we are now; what God is now, we shall be."

They believe in a practical universalism. Of the billions of souls who have inhabited the Earth, only murderers and apostates, sons of perdition, will go to hell. The afterlife for all others will be spent in a graded heaven: the celestial, terrestrial, and telestial. The celestial is reserved for Mormons who are married in the mystic temple rites.

Lower-grade Mormons and exceptional Gentiles may attain the terrestrial heaven, which is presided over by Christ. Run-of-the-mill Gentiles may expect to spend eternity in the telestial plane and fraternize neither with God nor Christ but with angels. Their conception of heaven comes closer to the Muslim paradise than the Christian beatific vision.

The distinctive Protestant doctrine of justification by faith alone receives a thoroughgoing criticism by the cult, which demands ethical, ceremonial, and moral works besides faith. Of course, the sole sufficiency of the Bible, another Reformation principle, is automatically denied.

The dead may receive Mormon baptism by proxy, which enables them to advance to a higher plane in the afterlife. A Saint may be baptized for his ancestors as many as thirty times in an afternoon; President Woodruff was baptized for the signers of the Declaration of Independence, John Wesley, and others. The Saints specialize in genealogical studies so they can trace their ancestors. Some Mormons claim to be able to identify members of their family tree to A.D. 500. These proxy baptisms for the dead are performed only in the temples. Ordinarily Mormons are baptized by immersion at age eight.

Until 1978 black members were denied ordination to the Mormon priesthood; they could belong to the church but could not participate in temple rites such as baptism for the dead. Brigham Young explained, "Why are so many inhabitants of the earth cursed with a skin of blackness? It comes in consequence of their fathers rejecting the power of the Holy Priesthood, and the Law of God." The cult considers all black individuals to be descendants of Cain, cursed by a dark skin or, as the *Book of Mormon* puts, "the Lord did cause a skin of blackness to come upon them." At another time Young told Horace Greeley, "We consider slavery of divine institution and not to be abolished until the curse pronounced on Ham shall have been removed from his descendants."

Finally, President Spencer Kimball announced a revelation that henceforth "all worthy male members of the church may be ordained to the priesthood without regard for race or color." This change in a 148-year policy of excluding black individuals from full membership removed a great embarrassment for the church. It should encourage missionary efforts in black communities in the United States and Africa.

The hierarchy that controls the church consists of a "President, Prophet, Seer, Revelator, and Trustee in Trust," a First and Second Counselor, and the twelve apostles, a self-perpetuating body that selects the president for a life term.

A bishop and two counselors supervise the ward, which corresponds to a parish. The wards are gathered into stakes of Zion similar to dioceses. All but a few dozen of the church's personnel serve without pay and carry on daytime secular occupations.

A Mormon lad advances in the lesser Aaronic priesthood from deacon to teacher to priest. As a priest he may baptize, administer the sacrament, and ordain other priests. A priest enters the Melchizedek priesthood and may continue his advance as an elder, Seventy, high priest, patriarch (hereditary in the Smith family), apostle, and president.

The cult places importance on sex and the family. Celibacy is regarded as an inferior state, and virgins have no chance of attaining the celestial plane in heaven. To remain single is considered contrary to the Word of God, and those who do not marry at a fairly early age are urged to do so by the priesthood.

Large families are encouraged; birth control is condemned; family solidarity is fostered by the regular recreational "Home Evening"; divorces in temple marriages are rare. Recently church leaders have spoken out against abortion, homosexuality, pornography, and extramarital sex.

Mormon temples are closed to Gentiles and to Mormons who do not tithe, observe the Word of Wisdom, and attend church regularly. Visitors may enter the eight thousand-seat Salt Lake City Tabernacle and attend services at ward chapels. Three main rites are performed in Mormon temples: proxy baptism of the dead, marriage for time and eternity, and the endowment.

Mormons classify marriages as those for time and those for time and eternity. The latter can be solemnized only in one of the temples. Christians usually marry with the formula "until death do us part," but

Mormons consider marriage an eternal contract if performed by two Mormons in the temple rites. Saints who are unable to travel to a temple, who contract a marriage with a Gentile or who fail to meet temple entrance requirements are married "for time" in a ward chapel. Later they may undergo a second ceremony of "sealing" in the temple — if their circumstances change. Children born in a temporal marriage may be sealed to parents in the temple.

In the daylong endowment rites, young Mormons are initiated into the esoteric aspects of the cult. The endowment ceremony usually precedes the marriage rites. Participants enter the temple with their temple vestments of white shirt and trousers, white robe and girdle, cloth cap, moccasins, and a Masonic-type green apron with fig leaf design.

They first bathe and are anointed with oil. After this they don their long white underwear (LDS Approved Garments, as they are known in Utah), which they will wear throughout life as believing Mormons. Three symbols stitched in the garment signify that if the initiate should reveal temple secrets, he will allow his legs to be amputated, his intestines disemboweled, and his heart cut out. Mormons are buried in their endowment garb.

The initiates then receive secret names and secret grips. They pass from one room to another to watch a continuing playlet that includes scenes wherein Catholic and Protestant clergymen are ridiculed for their inadequate religious beliefs. The Five Rooms of the temple are called the Creation Room, Garden of Eden, World Room, Terrestrial Kingdom, and Celestial Kingdom.

Masonic influence is apparent in Mormon temple rites, which is not surprising as both Smith and Young were Freemasons in Illinois but expelled from the lodge. Utah Mormons are forbidden to join the Masonic lodge.

In 1990 the church revised parts of the endowment ceremony and diminished elements of the rites obviously lifted from Freemasonry. It also deleted the scene in which Satan hires non-Mormon clergy to deceive Christians and altered the section in which wives were asked to pledge obedience to their husbands.

The regular Sunday afternoon worship service includes a simple observance of the Lord's Supper. Water is used in place of wine lest the Word of Wisdom be violated. The Saints believe their church possesses all spiritual gifts such as healing, speaking in tongues, communication with spirits, and prophecy.

At one time the doctrine of blood atonement embarrassed Mormon proponents, but this vicious doctrine gradually has been forgotten by Gentile critics and young Mormons alike. Early Mormon theologians argued that some sins could only be forgiven by the shedding of the sinner's blood. As Young explained: "Cutting people off from this earth . . . is to save them, not to destroy them." The Danites were a band of avenging Saints who liquidated apostates and Gentiles for their own good.

The greatest scandal in Latter-day Saint history is the famous Mountain Meadow massacre of 1857. A party of one hundred twenty people on their way to the California gold fields passed through Utah and were promised safe passage and protection from the Indians if they would surrender their weapons to Mormon Bishop John D. Lee and his men. They agreed to this arrangement, but at a signal from Bishop Lee ("Do your duty, men!") the Mormons murdered the men, hacked the women to death, and kidnapped the children. Twenty years later, Lee, a Catholic in his youth, was convicted and executed; the role of Young in this affair has never been ascertained. That this was a case of blood atonement rather than simple cold-blooded murder has been suggested by some Gentile historians.

Mormonism is the largest sect in the country to insist on tithing. A member who does not contribute 10 percent of his income to the church does not qualify as a Mormon in good standing. This source of income provides the cult with huge sums for missionary activities, relief, educational programs, building, and other enterprises. The canny Mormon businessmen undertake their major church construction projects during economic depressions, getting materials at lower prices and providing work for unemployed church members. Mormons also refrain from two meals on the first Sunday of each month and donate the proceeds to church welfare funds. The church maintains more than seventy warehouses for food and clothing for those in need.

All young men are expected to spend a year or two as unpaid missionaries. At present about sixty thousand young men are spreading the message of the Prophet around the globe. All are members of the priesthood and graduates of a short course in missiology. They average twenty-one years of age and have memorized a sales talk, Bible proof texts, and stock answers to Gentile objections. They direct their efforts at members of other denominations rather than the unchurched and in a recent year claimed three hundred thousand baptized converts. Augmenting door-to-door missionary work, the Mormon Church uses ads in *Reader's Digest,* radio and TV programs, exhibits at fairs, open houses, genealogy classes, and even bumper stickers to seek converts. Strangely the Mormon Church has had little success in converting Gentiles in predominantly Mormon communities. One analyst of Mormonism's success in winning converts attributes this to their promise of "instant community." New members are welcomed into a supportive group that emphasizes clean living, patriotism, hard work, cooperation, and a strong family life. A Mormon in need can get free food and clothing through the church welfare plan.

Rather than operate its own high schools as it once did, the church supports seminaries in forty-nine states that supplement the high school curriculum with Mormon theology. Institutes of Religion provide a similar service for Mormon students on college campuses. Besides Brigham Young University, the church operates colleges in Idaho and Hawaii.

Somewhat closer to traditional Christianity, the Reorganized Church denies polygamy, blood atonement, temple worship, baptism of the dead, and the Adam-god doctrine of their Utah cousins. They flatly deny Young's assertion: "When our father Adam came into the Garden of Eden, he came into it with a celestial body, and brought Eve, one of his wives with him. . . . He is our father and our God, and the only God with whom we have to do." This branch of Mormondom was organized at Beloit, Wis., in 1852 and was headed by Joseph Smith III from 1860 to 1914.

Smaller groups that accept the authenticity of the *Book of Mormon* and the prophetic role of Joseph Smith include the Church of Christ (Temple Lot), the Church of Jesus Christ or Bickertonites, and the Church of the First Born of the Fullness of Time, which reportedly tolerates polygamy.

The high birth rate and successful missionary programs seem to guarantee continued growth of this American-born religion that proclaims itself the only true Christian Church on Earth.

FURTHER READING

Allen, James B. and Glen M. Leonard, *The Story of the Latter-day Saints* (Salt Lake City: Deseret, 1976).

Arrington, Leonard J. and Davis Bitton, *The Mormon Experience: A History of the Latter-day Saints* (New York: Knopf, 1979).

Beck with, Francis J., Carl Mosser, and Paul Owen, eds., *The New Mormon Challenge* (Grand Rapids, Mich.: Zondervan, 2002).

Brodie, Fawn M., *No Man Knows My History* (New York: Knopf, 1945).

Hirshon, Stanley P., *The Lion of the Lord, A Biography of Brigham Young* (New York: Knopf, 1969).

Mullen, Robert, *The Latter-day Saints: The Mormons Yesterday and Today* (Garden City, N.Y.: Doubleday, 1966).

Shipps, Jan, *Mormonism: The Story of a New Religious Tradition* (Urbana and Chicago: University of Illinois Press, 1985).

Tanner, Jerald and Sandra, *Mormonism: Shadow or Reality?* (Salt Lake City: Modern Microfilm, 1964).

Turner, Wallace, *The Mormon Establishment* (Boston: Houghton Mifflin, 1966).

Whalen, William J., *The Latter-day Saints in the Modern Day World*, rev. ed. (Notre Dame, Ind.: University of Notre Dame Press, 1967).

CHAPTER 20

The Jehovah's Witnesses

They Expect Final Battle of Armageddon to Start Any Day

EVERY WEEK MILLIONS OF HOUSEHOLDERS AROUND THE WORLD FIND A pair of Jehovah's Witnesses on their doorstep. They are invited to buy a copy of the *Watchtower* magazine and to agree to home Bible study. Most people decline the offer, but enough accept to give the Witnesses a 5 percent annual growth rate since World War II. They rank among the fastest growing religions.

Currently the Witnesses count 6 million members, of which 1,040,000 — 1 of 6 — live in the United States. They meet several times a week in eleven thousand Kingdom Halls, which sponsor new halls when membership exceeds two hundred.

A public relations face-lifting, a series of successful legal battles, and shrewd leadership have pushed this fanatical eschatological sect into the forefront of modern religious movements.

Compared with Jehovah's Witnesses, Calvin Coolidge's minister who declared himself against sin was a piker. The Witnesses oppose blood transfusions, business, Catholics, Christmas trees, communism, civic enterprises, the doctrines of hell and immortality, evolution, flag saluting, higher education, liquor, lodges, Protestants, priests, the pope, public office, military service, movies, Mother's Day, religion, Sunday schools, the Trinity, tobacco, the United Nations, voting, the YMCA, Wall Street, and women's rights. This list does not pretend to be complete.

The Witnesses want no inactive or "associate" members. Everyone save the lame and the blind is expected to devote many hours a month to door-to-door preaching.

A growing full-time body of Pioneers works one hundred fifty hours a month supervising congregations, handling administrative details, and distributing publications. All contributions for books and magazines are forwarded to Brooklyn headquarters, while the Pioneer lives on a small expense account and boards with sect members.

Charles Taze Russell, son of a Pennsylvania haberdasher, adopted Adventist views after a Congregational boyhood and temporary loss of faith. He became distressed at the thought of hell, and his Bible searching convinced him that the Hebrew word *sheol* should invariably be translated "grave" instead of "hell." He began his preaching activities in 1872, and many people found comfort in his flat denial of everlasting punishment.

Russell toured the nation preaching his novel biblical interpretations an average of six to eight hours a day. But two scandals rocked his new movement. His wife sued him for divorce. charging him with infidelity and cruelty. The court declared that "his course of conduct toward his wife evidences such insistent egotism and extravagant self-praise that it would be manifest to the jury that it would necessarily render the life of any sensitive Christian woman an intolerable burden." Russell contested the divorce five times without success and eventually attempted to avoid alimony payments by transferring his property to corporations he controlled. The cult leader's involvement in a phony $60-a-bushel Miracle Wheat disillusioned other converts. He also promoted a "cancer cure," which consisted of a caustic paste of chloride of zinc, a wonderful Millennial Bean, and a fantastic cotton seed.

Russell died in 1916 on a Santa Fe Pullman after requesting an associate to fashion him a Roman toga, whereupon he "drew up his feet like Jacob of old" and passed away. His successor, Joseph F. Rutherford, was a small-town Missouri lawyer who preferred writing to preaching. He consolidated Russellism, quietly supplanting the founder in the memory of the devotees. His scripture-heavy polemics soon formed the bulk of the sect's printed propaganda. Later he recorded the short talks Witnesses played for householders on their portable phonographs.

He also shrugged off Russell's pyramidism, a system by which the founder claimed to be able to foretell history by measuring the rooms of the Great Pyramid in Egypt. Several schisms erupted when old-timers objected to the mild debunking of the late "Pastor" Russell.

During World War I, Rutherford and other officers of the cult were imprisoned for nine months on charges of sedition. Shortly after his release from an Atlanta federal prison, the "Judge" coined the slogan "Millions Now Living Will Never Die," which expressed the urgently Adventist hopes of the movement and soon blossomed on road signs, handbills, and posters.

Rutherford's followers were known variously as Russellites, International Bible Students, Millennial Dawnists, Rutherfordites, Watchtower Bible and Tract People. This untidy situation was cleared up in 1931 when Rutherford disclosed that their new name would be "Jehovah's Witnesses." This proved a happy choice because any mention of "witness" in the Old or New Testament could now be adduced as evidence of the antiquity of the cult.

When not at his Brooklyn Vatican, "Judge" Rutherford resided in a mansion near San Diego, Calif., whose deed was made out to Abel, Noah, and Abraham. This estate was kept in readiness for any Old Testament princes who returned to life before the Battle of Armageddon. Meanwhile, it served as western headquarters. The "Judge" was not among the millions now living who will never die. He died in 1942 after dictating the affairs of the cult for more than twenty-five years.

The self-perpetuating hierarchy chose Nathan Knorr to succeed Rutherford. He had left the Reformed Church while in high school to join the Witnesses and worked his way up the ladder at Brooklyn headquarters. When Knorr died in 1977, the Society elected Frederick Franz, eighty-three. He was the first head of the Watchtower Society to have gone beyond high school; he completed two years at the University of Cincinnati.

Many basic teachings of Jehovah's Witnesses resemble those of Seventh-day Adventism, through whom Russell was introduced to millennial doctrines. Mankind lives in the latter days. The great battle between Satan and Christ, Armageddon, may occur any day now. Prepare. The Witnesses have learned by experience not to specify dates, but all members confidently expect to see these events in their lifetimes.

Satan was cast out of heaven and now rules the world; however, Jesus Christ returned to Earth invisibly in 1914. We have already entered the early days of the millennium that will terminate in A.D. 2914, but only a few people recognize the theocracy. These few include Jehovah's Witnesses.

Satan is marshaling his forces for the battle of Armageddon. He finds his principal allies in an evil triumvirate: organized religion, the commercial world, and political organizations. During the course of the battle, the faithful few will sit on a mountainside and watch Jesus and His angels defeat Satan and his cohorts. After the great battle Satan will be bound and cast into an abyss. The righteous survivors will marry and repopulate the Earth during the remainder of the thousand-year reign. The dead will remain in their graves until the resurrection, but the wicked will be annihilated. Those who have died without a chance to know the Lord will be resurrected and given a second chance. If they persist in their disbelief, they, too, will be totally destroyed.

At the end of the one thousand years Satan will be loosed, and he will try one last time to seduce mankind. A few men will succumb to his temptations and with Satan will be annihilated. The billions who have repopulated the Earth and been resurrected from the dead will continue to dwell on Earth forever.

Only a fraction of Jehovah's Witnesses can be members of the invisible church, because they believe its number has been set at 144,000, no more, no less. This quota has been filling up since Pentecost, and few places remain. Only these few can entertain hopes of reaching heaven. They are the only ones who partake of the annual spring observance of the Lord's Supper in local Kingdom Halls.

The best that other Witnesses can hope for is to be counted among the Jonadabs or "other sheep," who will protect and assist the "bride's class" from their earthly habitation. To summarize the final disposition of mankind according to Russell-Rutherford-and-Knorr: 144,000 will attain heaven and reign with Christ, the wicked will be annihilated, and the righteous will live on Earth forever.

Witnesses reject many fundamental Christian beliefs such as original sin, the divinity of Christ, His resurrection, immortality, and the Trinity. Christ was originally Michael the Archangel, lived and died a man, and is now an exalted being. He was not God. And besides, say the Witnesses, he was born on October 1, 2 B.C., rather than December 25, which just goes to show how heathenish Christendom has become. The authoritative text *Let God Be True* explains the Jehovah's Witness views on Christ:

> "Prior to coming to earth, this only-begotten Son of God did not think himself to be co-equal with Jehovah God; he did not view himself as 'equal in power and glory' with Almighty God; he did not follow the course of the Devil and plot and scheme to make himself like or equal to the Most High God and to rob God or usurp God's place. On the contrary, he showed his subjection to God as his Superior by humbling himself under God's almighty hand, even to the most extreme degree, which means to a most disgraceful death on a torture stake" (*Let God Be True,* 2nd. ed., p. 34).

They agree with the Seventh-day Adventists on immortality: "Immortality is a reward for faithfulness. It does not come automatically to a human at birth" (*Let God Be True,* 2nd. ed., p. 74).

They ridicule the doctrine of the Trinity: "When the clergy are asked by their followers as to how such a combination of three in one can possibly exist, they are obliged to answer, 'That is a mystery.' Some will try to illustrate it by using triangle, trefoils, or images with three heads on one neck. Nevertheless, sincere persons who want to know the true God and serve him find it a bit difficult to love and worship a complicated, freakish-looking, three-headed God. The clergy who inject such ideas will contradict themselves in the very next breath by stating that God made man in his own image; for certainly no one has ever seen a three-headed human creature" (*Let God Be True,* 2nd. ed., p. 102).

The Witnesses consider all religious bodies, Catholic and Protestant, to be tools of Satan and deceivers, but they reserve a special hatred for Roman Catholicism. During the 1930s, Rutherford instructed his followers to picket Catholic churches on Sunday mornings with signs reading "Religion is a Snare and a Racket." Their literature offers kind words for Arius, a presbyter of Alexandria; Peter Waldo; John Wycliffe; John Huss; and the early Anabaptists, but they lament that the Reformation never really got off the ground.

Some Protestant churches ask no more of a prospective member than that he sign the register, attend church with some regularity, promise to read the Bible, and contribute to the support of the church. Not so with Jehovah's Witnesses. Anyone who conscientiously meets the demands of the cult finds little time for anything else. A convert completes courses in the Bible, speech, salesmanship, and missionary techniques before being assigned to ring doorbells with an experienced Witness. Most members hold regular jobs and attempt to get in their required hours evenings and weekends.

A Witness will avoid active participation in a labor union and will stay away from civic associations, lodges, and secular organizations. He is encouraged to live and eat decently but invited to turn over any surplus wealth or income to the cult. Witnesses neither tithe their incomes (like Mormons and Adventists) nor pass the collection plate; members drop their contributions in a box at the rear of each local Kingdom Hall.

Witnesses may be disfellowshipped for a variety of reasons, such as heresy, habitual smoking, and talking with ex-members. Parents and siblings may not even converse with a family member who has been disfellowshipped.

Mass baptisms by immersion are scheduled at the conventions; more than four thousand converts were baptized at one time at a New York meeting. The baptism service, like the Lord's Supper, is more of a dedicatory than a sacramental rite.

Witnesses do not vote in local or national elections, hold public office, salute the flag, or enter military service, as they consider the

United States government and every other government an instrument of the devil. On this score one government is about as wicked as another, be it democratic, fascist, or communist. To cast a vote or accept a public office would be supporting Satan's political ally. But they have never objected to paying taxes. At one time the sect discouraged marriage and the begetting of children because the theocracy was just around the corner, but this prohibition has been relaxed.

Some fourteen hundred Witnesses live a community life at Bethel House, a nine-story apartment building in Brooklyn. These members run the presses, set the type, bind the books, handle the mail and other chores at national headquarters. The Bethel residents eat in a common refectory whose food is supplied by several Witness-operated farms. Bells arouse the workers at 7 a.m. and signal lights-out at 10:30 p.m.

The local congregation or "company" meets in a Kingdom Hall, usually a rented store or small building. Congregations are grouped in circuits; a circuit servant visits each company once every six months. Sunday and Thursday evening meetings resemble discussion groups more than worship services. Prayer, study of scripture and Watchtower publications, reports of activities, and business comprise the meetings. Hymn singing has been considered a waste of time and music has played a minor role in Witness assemblies.

In recent years Witnesses have learned how to smile, to treat householders with some courtesy and tact, to inquire about the children and pet the dog. The old-fashioned belligerency and "hear me or be damned" approach antagonized most prospects. To many bibliolaters the scriptural gymnastics of a trained Witness are a sure sign of godliness. What matter if this "minister" never finished high school, knows no biblical languages, or chooses to quote out of context? As a matter of fact, anyone who itches to engage an experienced Witness in a biblical duel had better make sure he has spent as much time memorizing proof passages and persuading doubters as his opponent.

A center in rural New York state trains hundreds of Pioneers and missionaries. It includes 624 apartments and a dining facility that can seat 1,600.

The Watchtower Society has no interest in health or social service agencies. Because the end is imminent, they operate no hospitals or clinics, orphanages, homes for the aged, or the like.

Outside the United States, some of the largest groups of Witnesses are found in Nigeria, Brazil, Germany, Mexico, the British Isles, and the Philippines. Persecution in Nazi Germany cost the Society half its twenty-five thousand members, and an estimated twelve hundred died in concentration camps.

Few college graduates join the movement. Younger members in the cult are not encouraged to extend their formal education beyond high school. The main appeal has been to the socially, economically, and intellectually disinherited. The sect promises that the rich and powerful soon will get their comeuppance. About 20 percent are black members, and the sect makes a special effort to win Puerto Ricans and Mexican-Americans. Racial equality has been one of the longtime policies of the cult, but no black has held a top administrative office. Naturally the sect counts no representatives of the commercial, military, political, or academic worlds.

Evidently to many people the advantages of cult membership outweigh the burdens. Without spending years in college and seminary they can become "ministers." They can sit in other people's living rooms and command respect as they spin their doctrines and impress their listeners with heavy doses of proof texts. As "ministers" they can claim exemption from the draft, preach, and baptize.

Witnesses have been stoned, imprisoned, fined, sent to concentration camps, tarred and feathered. They have become involved in dozens of lawsuits over their refusal to salute the flag, their peddling books without a license, their slandering of religious groups, and their denial of blood transfusions to their sick children. Between 1940 and 1945 almost four thousand were sent to federal prisons as draft dodgers, although all claimed to be ministers of the gospel. They have won about two-thirds of the forty cases that have reached the Supreme Court. In most instances they were supported by the American Civil Liberties Union, and in return they have branded the ACLU an agent of the devil.

A passage in Leviticus condemning the eating of blood is taken to refer to blood transfusions, although the practice condemned was obviously a primitive tribal rite rather than a medical technique. Christmas trees are pagan-inspired because the Witnesses quote Jeremiah 10:3-4: "The customs of the people are vain; for one cutteth a tree out of the forest, the work of the hands of the workman with the axe. They deck it with silver and with gold."

Only unsigned articles now appear in their two magazines: *Watchtower* and *Awake!* The latter is published semimonthly in eighty-eight languages and has reached a circulation of nineteen million. A thirteen-story magazine publishing plant has been built to supplement the Brooklyn factory. All books are now published anonymously and neither Russell's nor Rutherford's works are being reprinted. Even correspondence from the Society is anonymous and signed with a rubber stamp.

Already we can observe the beginning of a transition from sect to church. The full-time Pioneers are assuming more of the duties ordinarily assigned to ministers and priests. Witnesses encourage their children to enter Pioneer work as a career. Kingdom Halls move from rented quarters to modest Witness-owned buildings. Publications have dropped their lurid illustrations and Rutherford-era vilification, and a new look tempers their attitude toward the public. Anonymous leadership replaces the colorful Russell and the brooding Rutherford. The democratic congregational organization of the local company has been replaced since 1938 by the autocratic theocracy.

The October 1966 issue of *Awake!* announced that Armageddon would begin in the fall of 1975. The Watchtower Society had previously predicted the end times for 1914, 1918, 1925 and 1941. When 1975 came and went without incident, hundreds of thousands of Witnesses were said to have left the movement. The Witnesses still believe that the millennial kingdom will be established before the last generation of people alive in 1914 have passed away, but they have given up naming the date. This avoids future embarrassments, but also forfeits the sense of urgency that propelled many into the Society in years past.

FURTHER READING

Beckford, James A., *The Trumpet of Prophecy* (Oxford: Basil Blackwell, 1975).

Gruss, Edmond Charles, *Apostles of Denial* (Nutley, N.J.: Presbyterian and Reformed Publishing Co., 1970).

Harrison, Barbara Grizzuti, *Visions of Glory: A History and Memory of the Jehovah's Witnesses* (New York: Simon & Schuster, 1978).

Let God Be True, 2nd ed. (Brooklyn: Watch Tower Bible and Tract Society, 1946).

Martin, Walter R., and Norman H. Klann, *Jehovah of the Watch Tower,* 6th rev. ed. (Grand Rapids, Mich.: Zondervan, 1963).

Pike, Royston, *Jehovah's Witnesses* (New York: Philosophical Library, 1954).

Sterling, Chandler W., *The Witnesses* (Chicago: Regnery, 1975).

Stevenson, W.C., *The Inside Story of Jehovah's Witnesses* (New York: Hart, 1967).

Whalen, William J., *Armageddon Around the Corner* (New York: John Day, 1962).

CHAPTER 21

The Christian Scientists

'Man Is Incapable of Sin, Sickness and Death' —
Mary Baker Eddy

IN THIS AGE OF ANTIBIOTICS, REVOLUTIONARY SURGICAL TECHNIQUES, the X-ray, and vaccinations for smallpox, diphtheria, and polio, we may forget that for religious reasons a substantial minority deprive themselves and their children of the benefits of medical science. They are following the teachings of an elderly New England matron, Mrs. Mary Baker Glover Patterson Eddy, discoverer of Christian Science.

For some one hundred twenty years her loyal devotees have not only denied the reality of disease, but also the reality of matter, of evil, and of death itself. Our Christian Science neighbors constitute a group of citizens of greater wealth and higher social standing and better education than most. Their ranks include college professors, an astronaut, a U.S. senator, movie stars, scientists, editors, financiers, lawyers, and artists.

Membership has declined for decades. The U.S. Census Bureau estimated Christian Science adherents at 269,000 in 1936. The present total is perhaps half that number. (The church refuses to tabulate members.)

With Mormonism and Jehovah's Witnesses, Christian Science stands as one of the three successful homegrown religions. Excepting Madame Blavatsky's Theosophy, it remains the only religion of consequence founded by a woman. Denying every fundamental Christian dogma, it presents itself to the public as a Christian denomination and appropriates a Christian vocabulary.

How a penniless woman of fifty carried through her plans to build a church to perpetuate her beliefs makes a fascinating story. She compiled a book that, doctored and edited, has been given a place next to the Bible in many cultured homes.

Born Mary Baker on a New Hampshire farm in 1821, she spent a childhood plagued by sickness and "fits." In the space of a few decades, early nineteenth-century New England would witness such enthusiasms as Shakerism, Mormonism, Spirtualism, and transcendentalism. Mary Baker had to miss most formal schooling because of her delicate health. At the age of seventeen she joined the Congregational Church, of which she remained a nominal member for forty years.

At twenty-two she married George Washington Glover, a bricklayer and small-time contractor. The newlyweds set up housekeeping in South Carolina, but in six months Glover was dead of yellow fever. His young widow returned home and gave birth to her only child.

The tragedy aggravated her hysterical attacks, and she dabbled in poetry, Mesmerism, and Spiritualism for some years. Eventually she married an itinerant dentist and philanderer by the name of Daniel Patterson. Her four-year-old son had been taken to Minnesota to be raised by foster parents, and she would not see him again until he was thirty-four. Dr. Patterson had the misfortune to visit a Civil War battlefield as an observer. He mistakenly crossed into Confederate territory and spent the duration of the war in a southern prison.

Neither morphine nor Mesmerism seemed to help Mrs. Patterson's numerous physical complaints. But she happened to hear of a marvelous healer in Portland, Maine. To this day the healer with the Dickensian name of "Dr." Phineas P. Quimby remains the skeleton in Christian Science's closet.

Mrs. Patterson visited Quimby as a patient and student for three weeks in 1862 and again for three months in 1864. She received a copy of Quimby's writings on healing entitled *Questions and Answers* and expressed her appreciation for his help through letters to the press and quaint versicular testimonials. She would later explain these embarrassing tributes by commenting, "I might have written them twenty or thirty years ago, for I was under the Mesmeric treatment of Dr. Quimby from 1862 until his death" *(Boston Post, 1883)*.

At any rate his death in 1866 evoked a eulogy by Mrs. Patterson entitled "Lines on the Death of Dr. P. P. Quimby, Who Healed With the Truth That Christ Taught in Contradistinction to All Isms." The founder and her followers have since sought to ignore or minimize Quimby's contribution and to defend the complete originality of Mrs. Eddy's system.

Her P.O.W. husband, meanwhile, had returned, promptly announced he had had enough and left home. She eventually obtained a divorce in 1873 on grounds of desertion. He left his profession, died a hermit in 1897, and was buried in a potter's field. The wife he abandoned left a fortune estimated at $3,000,000.

"The Fall at Lynn" is considered the first authentic Christian Science healing. Mrs. Glover (she had assumed her first husband's name) relates that she slipped on the ice returning from a ladies' aid meeting and suffered injuries that she (but not her doctor) pronounced incurable.

She could not appeal to the dead Quimby, although she had dipped into Spiritualism. At this crisis she claims to have rediscovered the laws of healing, which Christ had demonstrated in the New Testament and which had been lost through apostasy by the primitive Church. She began to read her Bible and came across the passage in St. Matthew in which Christ addressed the man sick with palsy: "Arise, take up thy bed." She now realized that death and sickness were illusions, and within a few days she was walking around to the amazement of her few friends.

Her physician later signed an affidavit in which he declared, "I did not at any time declare, or believe, that there was no hope for Mrs. Patterson's recovery, or that she was in critical condition."

Between the fall in 1866 and 1870 she labored on her "textbook." Of *Science and Health With Key to the Scriptures,* Mark Twain wrote, "Of all the strange and frantic and incomprehensible and uninterpretable books which the imagination of man has created, surely this one is the prize sample." Despite the best efforts of editors and proofreaders, *Science and Health* scares off most inquirers by its inconsistency, awkwardness, and abstruseness. The author shrugged off all criticisms and pointed out that "Learning was so illumined that grammar was eclipsed."

Christian Scientists considered the work inspired. "I should blush to write a *Science and Health With Key to the Scriptures* as I have, were it of human origin, and I, apart from God, its author; but as I was only a scribe echoing the harmonies of heaven in divine metaphysics, I cannot be super-modest in my estimate of the Christian Science textbook," declared Mrs. Eddy.

The first edition carried the following verse on the fly leaf *a la* Gertrude Stein:

I, I, I, I, itself, I.
The inside and the outside, the what and the why
The when and the where, the low and the high.
All I, I, I, I, I, itself, I.

This has since been deleted.

Revised and expanded many times, the book now includes chapters on Christian Science versus Spiritualism, Animal Magnetism Unmasked, Marriage, Physiology, and more. The Key to the Scriptures section was added in 1884 and consists of an allegorical interpretation of Genesis and the Apocalypse. The final edition concludes with a glossary and pages of "fruitage," or healing testimonials.

The book sold for $3 a copy when first offered in 1875; this was mostly profit in those days. The original edition was advertised as "a book that affords an opportunity to acquire a profession by which you can accumulate a fortune." Church members and practitioners were forced to buy each new edition during the author's lifetime, although the changes sometimes amounted to nothing more than a few words.

Shunted from one rooming house to another for nine years, the destitute grass widow decided to team up with Richard Kennedy. Like the late Quimby, he called himself "Dr." and advertised himself as a faith healer. Mrs. Eddy offered a series of lectures on her healing method, Christian Science. This series, originally twelve and then seven lectures, cost $300. She admits she hesitated to ask such a sum, half a year's wages for the Lynn, Mass., shoe workers who comprised her early disciples, but a voice from heaven commanded it.

She taught a garbled pantheism that denies the reality of matter, evil, sickness, and death. These were not created by God and therefore constituted simply errors of mortal mind. Remove the erroneous conceptions and you remove the suffering and defeat the grave. Man's purpose in life is to free himself from these errors of mortal mind through application of the laws she had discovered. Once freed, he would find himself healthy, sinless, and immortal.

Her mechanical application of these mysterious laws forced her to conclude that if they could be employed to produce health, they could be perverted to inflict sickness and death. This Yankee voodooism, a revival of New England witchcraft, she termed Malicious Animal Magnetism. In her later years she lived in terror of MAM, tormented by the malevolent forces of her enemies and critics. As protection she surrounded herself with a corps of devoted followers whose task was to ward off evil thoughts and forces. Christian Scientists who had been hexed told their troubles in a MAM column in the *Christian Science Journal.* Today this black magic aspect of the cult shares the closet with Phineas P. Quimby.

Her third venture into matrimony involved Asa Gilbert Eddy, a sewing machine agent whose name she would perpetuate. A few years later neither her healing laws nor the medical doctor's could prevent his death. She disagreed with the postmortem (postmortems were later forbidden in her *Church Manual)* and maintained that her spouse had died of "arsenic mentally administered." She added emphatically: "My husband's death was caused by malicious animal magnetism. . . . I know it was poison that killed him, not material poison but mesmeric poison." Now she had all the more reason to dread the devils of MAM she had unleashed.

Kennedy was the first of a succession of co-workers and students who left to found cults of their own or who refused to turn over royalties to Mrs. Eddy for the use of her healing techniques. All were violently denounced; all were sinisterly accused of employing MAM to destroy the frail high priestess. She became embroiled in innumerable lawsuits to collect her 10 percent royalty on students' healing fees.

A revolt of her students at Lynn finished her career in that community, and at sixty-one she transferred her activities to Boston. Here she founded the First Church of Christ, Scientist. She had obtained a charter for the Massachusetts Metaphysical College, of which she was the sole instructor.

Between 1881 and its discontinuance in 1889, four thousand students each paid $300 tuition for the course. Later three advanced options were added, including Metaphysical Obstetrics. Anyone taking the full course paid Mrs. Eddy $800. She probably collected $1,200,000 in the eight years the school functioned. Some charity cases were admitted.

In Lynn she had preached her new religion to factory workers. In Boston she managed to interest the wealthier classes for whom the cult would exert a perennial appeal. By now she had ordained herself and assumed the title "Reverend." Her organization prospered with practitioners, former students, and branch societies in the East and Midwest. She hired a retired minister to polish her textbook, and by 1891 she had sold 150,000 copies.

A forty-one-year-old physician, Dr. Foster, joined the college staff as instructor in obstetrics. At the age of sixty-eight Mrs. Eddy legally adopted the doctor, who changed his name to Ebenezer J. Foster Eddy. He played the role of crown prince in the cult until a falling out with his "mother" and subsequent exile.

Despite her successes, Mrs. Eddy was restless. MAM dogged her day and night; she knew her enemies were trying to poison her just as they had murdered her husband. She decided to leave Boston, close her profitable college, disband her present church structure.

A shrewd woman, Mrs. Eddy saw the need to forge stronger bonds between herself and her church. Defections and schisms were no novelty to her. A strong Boston organization with decentralized and wholly dependent branch churches seemed the answer. Now an elderly woman, she undertook a series of bold steps to insure her complete control of Christian Science not only during her lifetime but after her death.

She set up a single Christian Science church, the Mother Church in Boston. All others were and are simply branch churches of this one church — buildings where nonresident members of the Boston congregation and neophytes could meet to study, sing hymns, and deliver testimonials. Only members of the Mother Church could teach Christian Science, receive the degrees C.S.B. and C.S.D., and serve as Readers in branch churches. Only Mother Church members could qualify as practitioners. Those holding only branch membership had little standing in the cult.

District organizations and conferences were forbidden, which frustrated attempts at organized revolt. Mrs. Eddy deposed all pastors and substituted her textbook and the Bible as "pastors." First and Second Readers conducted the worship services, but their terms were limited to five years. They were not allowed to elaborate on the *Science and Health* and Bible passages selected by Boston.

Mrs. Eddy encouraged each branch to sponsor an open lecture annually, but all lecturers had to be approved by Boston. All lectures were submitted for censorship and no questions from the audience were tolerated. Only the Bible, the works of Mary Baker Eddy, and church periodicals could be sold in reading rooms operated by the branch societies.

A Committee on Publications set about correcting criticisms and misstatements about the cult in the press. Its boycott of the debunking Edwin Dakin book some thirty-five years later in 1929 backfired and turned *Mrs. Eddy, the Biography of a Virginal Mind,* into a best seller. In recent years the committee's methods of boycott and intimidation have managed to stifle nearly all published criticism of the cult.

After her reorganization of her church, all decisions and power rested in Boston and Mrs. Eddy controlled Boston. She lived at her Concord estate seventy miles away. The Mother Church, dedicated in 1895, featured The Mother's Room. Pastor Emeritus Eddy is said to have spent one night in the shrine. A light has since burned before her portrait in the room.

The faithful undertook pilgrimages to Concord to get a glimpse of their Leader (a title that replaced Mother). Many vied for a chance to serve in her household. She fussed with her textbook, collecting royalties of $50,000 to $100,000 a year. She accused her foster son of practicing MAM and disowned another devotee who claimed to have experienced a virgin birth.

The old lady's health was failing, but her followers could not be disillusioned. If the discoverer and founder of Christian Science could not apply its laws and defeat sickness and death, who could?

After 1900 her health declined rapidly. She had worn glasses and visited dentists for years. Now a doctor was called to administer regular doses of morphine. She was too ill to attend the ceremonies for the $2,000,000 addition to the Mother Church, which was completed in 1906. Some thirty thousand people jammed the edifice during six identical dedication services; retouched photographs of the Leader were distributed.

Her natural son reappeared but withdrew his suit to declare his wealthy mother mentally incompetent; he received $250,000 and Dr. Foster Eddy $50,000. When she excommunicated the popular Mrs. Augusta Stetson of the New York City branch, she eliminated her last rival.

Two years before her death she founded the daily *Christian Science Monitor*. The *Monitor* ranks high in any appraisal of American journalism, and its sponsorship by the cult has brought Christian Science considerable prestige. It has won sixty awards for excellence in journalism since 1915 and now reports 72,000 subscribers throughout the nation. Nevertheless the newspaper is said to be a financial drain on the church, losing several million dollars a year. It avoids sensationalism and observes the expected taboos on news of deaths, tragedies, epidemics. No advertisements are accepted for coffee, tombstones, cemeteries, undertakers, dentists, oculists, or hearing aids. It never uses the word death but prefers the euphemism "passed away." The *Monitor* news story about the World War I battlefield littered with "passed on mules" is probably apocryphal. The official publication of the church, the *Christian Science Journal,* has been published since 1883. The Christian Science Publishing Society also publishes Mrs. Eddy's works and the three other official periodicals: *Christian Science Sentinel, Herald of Christian Science,* and *Christian Science Quarterly.* Authors must be members of the Mother Church.

Mrs. Eddy could make no real provision for her impending death without compromising her religious principles. "Matter and death are mortal illusions," declares her textbook. Her associates grew alarmed, but she was confident she had bequeathed a workable polity in her *Church Manual.*

Mary Baker Eddy died of pneumonia December 3, 1910, at the age of eighty-nine. Most of her fortune went to her church. Her cult had no provision for funeral rites. Probably one hundred thousand people called her Mother or Leader at the time of her final succumbing to error of mortal mind.

A self-perpetuating five-member Board of Governors ruled the church after her death. An article of her *Church Manual* asserts that nothing can be adopted, amended, or annulled without the written consent of the Leader, which has been an impossibility since 1910.

Another tenet forbids the tabulation of membership, so we can only guess at the present strength of the movement. The two thousand or so branches of the Mother Church in the United States enroll an average of perhaps seventy members. Only sixteen are needed to found a branch society. One sign of the church's decline has been the drop in practitioners in the United States from ninety-six hundred in 1946 to fewer than sixteen hundred. In recent years dozens of branch churches have closed their doors for lack of members or severed ties with the Mother Church.

Perhaps three out of four Scientists are women. The church is strongest in California, Illinois, New York, Ohio, and Massachusetts.

A true Christian Scientist will take no medicine, consult no physician. Yet she will employ the services of an obstetrician, dentist, oculist, bonesetter, and mortician. She will wear glasses and dentures but will vigorously oppose public health measures, compulsory vaccination, X-ray examinations, or flouridation of water supplies. Assured by her religion that matter is unreal, she ordinarily evinces the same interest in food, property, success, a home, and security as her Christian neighbors.

In many cases Christian Science seems to produce happy, serene, optimistic individuals. Perhaps some adjust to a world that knows no sin or death. The cult stresses self-mastery and Stoic courage.

Does Christian Science cure? Certainly. Recent research in psychosomatic medicine confirms the belief in the close interaction of mind and body. "A merry heart doeth good like a medicine" (Prov. 17:22). Any medical physician will testify that mental disturbances lie behind a large percentage of his patients' ills. Recognizing the role of mind in sickness and health is not the same thing as denying all sickness, sin, and death.

Christian Scientists are encouraged to treat themselves, but a class of professional healers, practitioners, tackles stubborn cases. Like doctors and dentists these practitioners hold regular office hours, and bill their clients for their services (payments are deductible for income tax purposes). They attempt to convince the sufferer, who may or may not be a Christian Scientist, that she is in error in thinking she is sick or dying. They read from the Bible and textbook in the office or at the bedside. Authorized teachers of Christian Science are limited to thirty students a year.

The Christian Science Church does not baptize members and observes only two spiritual communions a year; at these communion services there is no bread or wine, but the worshipers spend a few moments in silent prayer. Mrs. Eddy prepared no ritual for marriage in her church; Christian Scientists seek the services of Protestant ministers or civil officials when they wish to be married. Of course, the church prescribes no burial ritual as this would imply the possibility of death.

Christian Scientists are urged to overcome any "depraved appetite" for alcoholic drinks, tobacco, tea, coffee, and opium.

The standardized Sunday morning service (identical in all branch churches) consists of Mrs. Eddy's version of the Lord's Prayer, alternate reading of the Bible, the Lesson-Sermon prepared by a committee in Boston, the collection, and the recital of the "scientific statement of being." Mrs. Eddy may have borrowed her term "Father-Mother God" from the Shakers, a defunct religious cult also founded by a woman, Ann Lee. The Shakers also called their main church the Mother Church.

Traditional Christian holidays such as Christmas and Easter are ignored, but special services are held on Thanksgiving Day. Wednesday evening is devoted to oral testimonials of healing.

Scientists allot large sums for the erection of temples. Of course, they operate no hospitals, clinics, welfare agencies, or orphanages, as this would entail coddling error. The Principia, a small Illinois college, is Christian Scientist in faculty and student body but is not owned by the church.

Practically all basic Christian beliefs, Catholic and Protestant, are disavowed by Christian Science. It rejects the idea of a personal God, the Trinity, original and actual sin, the devil, the atonement, the resurrection, the divinity of Christ, judgment, heaven, and hell. Casual inquirers must be warned, however, not to assume that the use of common Christian terms in Christian Science literature supposes common meanings and interpretations.

Considering perhaps only one American out of five hundred adheres to Mrs. Eddy's teachings, Christian Scientists held enormous power during the Nixon administration. They included H.R. Haldeman, chief of staff; John Ehrlichman, domestic affairs adviser; and Egil Krogh, deputy assistant to the president for domestic affairs. Senator Charles Percy of Illinois also belonged to the church. During the late 1970s, practicing Christian Scientists headed both the FBI and CIA.

The church inculcates an attitude toward life that nonmembers find impossibly inconsistent. In this it shares the difficulties of all systems of absolute idealism. The demands of faith it imposes on its members are enormous. Christian Science claims to offer much more than health to its faithful. It is advertised as the key to success in business, marriage, and financial undertakings. The writer once heard a Scientist testify at a Wednesday meeting that he attributed his success in obtaining travel and hotel reservations to his application of Christian Science.

Mrs. Eddy was a shrewd, tenacious, and courageous woman. She seemed an utter failure before she discovered Christian Science in 1866; she died a millionairess.

Although Christian Science is only one of some forty sects that feature faith healing, it has achieved a respectability, membership, and power most have lacked. Its period of greatest growth may be seen between 1906 and 1926, and it seems to have reached its zenith.

Four main agencies are employed in its widespread proselytizing program: the open lectures, the reading rooms maintained by each branch society, the *Monitor* and other church periodicals, and radio and TV programs. In each medium, the healing testimonial is the basic selling point.

Its wealthy and educated devotees, impressive temples, and dignified publications make a good impression on the public. The Committee on Publications silences adverse publicity. But a taste of *Science and Health* disenchants many inquirers. Few can dissuade themselves from the commonsense view of life and the world around them. The facts of measles and murder and mortuaries appear self-evident to most of mankind.

In the late 1980s, a number of court cases charged Christian Science parents with denying their children medical care that might have saved their lives. They had turned to prayer instead of medical treatment. Most convictions were reversed, and no new cases have been filed since 1992.

Unhappy Christian Scientists sued the Mother Church in the 1980s for squandering church assets. Church leaders dipped into financial reserves and pension funds to launch a cable TV network, a radio network, and an expensive new magazine. All these projects failed; the cost to the church has been estimated at $300 million.

Millions of Americans have turned to alternative medicine and New Age therapies in recent years, but few have sought answers to their health concerns in Christian Science. With a dwindling and graying membership, legal battles, and financial crises, the Christian Science Church faces an uncertain future.

FURTHER READING

Braden, Charles S., *Christian Science Today* (Dallas: Southern Methodist University Press, 1958).

Dakin, Edwin Franden, *Mrs. Eddy* (New York: Charles Scribner's Sons, 1929).

Eddy, Mary Baker, *Science and Health With Key to the Scriptures* (Boston: Christian Science Publishing Society).

Gottschalk, Stephen, *The Emergence of Christian Science in American Religious Life* (Berkeley: University of California Press, 1973).

Peel, Robert, *Mary Baker Eddy: The Years of Discovery* (New York: Holt, Rinehart and Winston, 1966).

_____, *Mary Baker Eddy: The Years of Authority* (New York: Holt, Rinehart and Winston, 1977).

The Christian Science Way of Life (Englewood Cliffs, N.J.: Prentice-Hall, 1962).

CHAPTER 22

The Jews

God's Mystery People

WE CAN HARDLY IMAGINE WHAT THE WORLD WOULD BE LIKE IF IT HAD not been decisively influenced by descendants of a small Semitic tribe that took form more than three thousand years ago. From this people came the chief Western religions of Judaism, Christianity, and Islam. From them came such figures as Moses, Jesus, Karl Marx, Sigmund Freud, and Albert Einstein, who reshaped human history. In a world of six billion Gentiles, the fourteen million Jews continue to uphold ancient beliefs and traditions.

Common sense would tell us that the Jews should have disappeared centuries ago. In the year 70 the Romans destroyed the Temple in Jerusalem and scattered the Jews throughout the world. Christians and Muslims tried to convert the Jews; many did accept the newer faiths but millions kept their Jewish identity. Hitler murdered millions of Jews in what the Nazis called the "final solution" to the Jewish problem, but the Jews remain.

Most Jews are Caucasians, but there are also Chinese, black, and Indian Jews. If not by blood then by conversion all Jews claim to be children of Abraham. He was a nomad who traveled from Chaldea to the land of Canaan now known as Israel. His vision of God as one, loving, and merciful was passed on to his son, Isaac, and his grandson, Jacob. Jacob led the tribe to Egypt to escape a severe famine, but there they were enslaved. Still they held fast to their belief in the one God and were led out of bondage by Moses about 1280 B.C. En route to their ancient homeland, Moses underwent a transforming experience on Mount Sinai that led to the proclamation of the Ten Commandments.

Through a long history of prosperity and disaster, freedom and bondage, apostasy and religious fervor, the Jews were called back to their simple creed: "Hear, O Israel, the Lord our God, the Lord is One." Calling the Jews back to their spiritual heritage and ideals were the prophets: Isaiah, Jeremiah, Ezekiel, and others.

In their darkest hours the Jews looked for a Messiah who would usher in a new age for mankind. Almost two thousand years ago a rabbi called Jesus proclaimed himself that Messiah, gathered a band of followers, and was crucified. Most Jews rejected Jesus as the long-awaited Messiah, but his disciples established a sect within Judaism. For a while the Christians continued to attend the synagogue, follow the Jewish laws, and submit to circumcision, but they finally broke away from Judaism and carried the Christian message to the Gentiles. Paul became known as the apostle to the Gentiles. The Christians accepted Jesus not only as the Messiah but as God incarnate, the second person of a Trinity. They continued to use the Jewish Scriptures but added a New Testament.

Six centuries later an Arabian teacher, Mohammed, also accepted the Old Testament and acknowledged the prophethood of Jesus but declared that Allah is God and Mohammed was his prophet. He founded Islam, which became one of the major religions of Africa and Asia. Through Christianity and Islam, the Jewish beliefs in monotheism, in revelation, and in the commandments would be carried to billions of Gentiles.

The first Jews to come to the New World came from Spain and Portugal. For centuries the Jews had lived in relative peace under the Moorish rulers of Iberia. Some Jews, the Marranos, accepted Christian baptism under duress but continued Jewish practices within the family. The Inquisition saw no possibility of uniting Spain unless the Jews were driven out. Ferdinand and Isabella signed the expulsion order in 1492, and many Jews eventually looked for haven in South America.

A party of twenty-three Jews came from Brazil to New Amsterdam in 1654. For a brief period they had enjoyed freedom in Brazil under the Dutch, but faced renewed persecution when the Portuguese returned to power. If not welcomed by the Dutch, they were at least tolerated. These Portuguese founded the first congregation in North America, Shearith Israel in New York City. Another group of Jews settled in Newport, R.I., and dedicated Touro synagogue in 1763; this building still stands and has been designated a national shrine. Another Jewish settlement was made in Savannah, Ga.

Forbidden to own land in the Old World, the Jews in the colonies tended to settle in the cities, where they became merchants and traders. By the time of the American Revolution, their number had risen to about two thousand. Almost all had come from Spain or Portugal. Jews served under Washington in the Revolution and favored the cause of the colonists.

After the defeat of Napoleon and again after the failure of the 1848 rebellion, thousands of Jews from the ghettos of Germany came to the United States. Jewish peddlers carried goods from city to city and started many of America's department stores.

One Jew, Judah P. Benjamin, represented Louisiana in the U.S. Senate. At the outbreak of the Civil War he became Attorney General in the Confederate cabinet, and then Secretary of War and Secretary of State. After the South's defeat, Benjamin fled to England.

Starting in 1881 waves of Russian and Eastern European Jews sought refuge from the czar's pogroms in America. For centuries the rulers of Russia had forbidden Jews to live in that country. But in 1654 the czar took the Ukraine and inherited the Jews living there; later when Poland was partitioned, the czar gained an additional one million Jewish subjects. By law these Russian Jews were confined to shabby villages along the western border. The fierce persecutions directed by Alexander III drove the Jews to seek safety elsewhere. Between 1881 and 1924, more than two million came to this country.

The tenements of the Lower East Side of New York City absorbed many of these immigrants. Like other Jews they brought not only their religious faith but their love of learning. They spoke Yiddish, the daily language of East European Jewry; it was a German dialect written with Hebrew characters. Many Jews entered the garment industry and worked long hours in the sweatshops. Jews entered the labor movement and organized unions such as the International Ladies Garment Workers Union. Samuel Gompers became one of the founders of the American Federation of Labor and served as its president for almost forty years.

Several factors helped the Jews achieve success in American society. They found a freedom denied them in the ghettos of Europe. They worked hard, provided the best possible education for their children, seldom wasted money on liquor or gambling, maintained a stable family life, and helped one another. Today the Jewish community provides a disproportionate number of the nation's scientists, physicians, lawyers, writers, musicians, entertainers, college professors, and artists.

Because of the virtual extinction of the European Jewish community, the Jews in the United States have become the largest and most influential section of world Jewry.

The pious Jew follows the Torah, the Talmud, and the Prayer Book. The Torah consists of the first five books of the Bible (Genesis, Exodus, Leviticus, Numbers, and Deuteronomy). The Talmud provides the rabbinical commentary on the Torah. Strictly speaking an orthodox Jew must keep the six hundred thirteen rules of Halakah, but many of these are obsolete laws involving agriculture or property.

Observance of the Sabbath is basic to Jewish life. From sunset Friday to sunset Saturday, the devout Jew leaves the things of the secular world and enters a world of prayer and family celebrations. Orthodox Jews will not travel, cook, write, use electrical appliances, buy or sell, light fires, or smoke on the Sabbath. The begins when the mother lights the candles at the festive table twenty minutes before sunset and the father says the prayer over the wine.

Throughout the year, Judaism marks the seasons and the religious events of her history with festivals. There is Passover in spring, Shavuous in summer, and Sukkos in the fall. The minor feast of Hanukkah has assumed increasing importance in recent years as a sort of Jewish counterpart of Christmas. Even Jews who seldom attend a synagogue or temple during the year will try to observe the High Holy Days in the fall. Ten days after Rosh Hashanah, the Jewish New Year, comes Yom Kippur or the Day of Atonement. Many Jews observe a twenty-four-hour fast from food and drink and spend all day in the synagogue. This is the day on which man makes peace with his God.

A traditional Jew follows a regimen of daily prayers. During morning prayer he wears a shawl called a tallis and a head covering, usually a skull cap called a yarmulka. He affixes phylacteries or tefillin to his forehead and left arm. These are black leather boxes containing small scrolls.

Orthodox and Conservative Jews observe dietary laws that continually remind them of the covenant between God and Israel. These laws demand that a Jew will eat no flesh cut from a living creature, will drink no blood, will not mix milk and meat at the same meal, and will not eat certain fats such as suet. Certain foods such as ham, pork, lobster, and shrimp are forbidden. Animals must be slaughtered in a ritual way to qualify as kosher.

The infant male is circumcised eight days after birth. Of course, circumcision has recently become a common practice among Gentiles as well. The young Jew of thirteen becomes a full member of the congregation at his bar mitzvah. After years of study under a rabbi, he reads the Scriptures in Hebrew and perhaps delivers a short sermon. A similar rite called the bas mitzvah has been introduced into many congregations for girls of twelve-and-a-half years.

The Torah allows polygamy, but this has not been practiced in Judaism for one thousand years. Bride and groom in a Jewish wedding are married under a canopy, receive seven blessings, and break a wine glass. Married couples in the Orthodox branch follow a sexual code that traditionally forbids marital relations during the menstrual period and for seven days thereafter. Judaism upholds the permanence of the marriage bond; the Jewish divorce rate is low, but the religion allows numerous grounds for divorce.

Traditionally the dead are buried as soon as possible in a shroud and wooden coffin. Embalming is forbidden unless required by law. The mourners recite the Kaddish at the fresh grave and during the eleven months of mourning.

Almost all Jews believe in an afterlife, but Judaism discourages speculation on the nature of the immortality of the soul. Judaism rejects the concept of original sin and the Christian idea of salvation. It also rejects the idea of eternal punishment or hell.

Because of the influence of the Enlightenment and the liberation of the Jews from the restrictions of the ghetto, many Jews in the early nineteenth century were shedding Judaism and becoming Christians or agnostics. The Reform movement in Germany sought to adapt Judaism to modern life by denying the normative value of many laws and traditions. The Reform leaders preferred a religion of ethics to one of laws. They changed the liturgical language from Hebrew to the vernacular, introduced organ music, allowed men and women to sit together, abandoned the dietary laws, and prescribed daily prayers. Instead of a personal Messiah, the Reform Jews spoke about a Messianic age for mankind. Isaac Mayer Wise became the leading Reform spokesman in the United States; Cincinnati became the center of Reform Judaism. Contemporary Reform has reintroduced some Hebrew and some of the older traditions.

To Jews uneasy with the radical nature of Reform, the abandonment of traditional elements had gone too far. They formed the Conservative movement, which seeks to occupy a middle ground between Orthodoxy and Reform. Conservatives keep the dietary laws and Hebrew liturgy but allow mixed seating and some vernacular. Conservatism owes a deep debt to Solomon Schechter, who came to the United States from Cambridge University to head the Jewish Theological Seminary (founded in 1886). About six hundred Jewish congregations can be identified as Conservative, which is approximately the strength of Reform Judaism.

Within Orthodoxy, various sects interpret the Torah and Talmud in their own ways. For example, the Hasidic movement begun in the Polish ghettos by Baal Shem (1700-1760) combines Judaism with the magic and folklore of the Cabala. The Cabala is the expression of Jewish mysticism that corresponds to Gnosticism in Christianity; it concerns itself with numerology and angelology, which hold little interest for most Jews. The Hasidim attach themselves to a Rebbe, or wonder worker, and remain suspicious of secular education. Yet the movement has had a considerable influence on Martin Buber, religious philosopher, biblical translator and interpreter. The Hasidim can be identified by their long earlocks, fur hats, and beards. They live in certain neighborhoods in Brooklyn and other cities.

Jewish grade and high schools have blossomed in this country. In 1945 there were only thirty such schools, but the number has risen to several hundred. American Jewry has founded two institutions of higher education outside of rabbinical seminaries. These are the Yeshiva University in New York City, which includes the Albert Einstein College of Medicine, and Brandeis University in Waltham, Mass. The Hillel foundations serve Jewish students and scholars on many campuses.

The number of Jewish organizations devoted to charity, culture, Zionism, and other causes runs into the hundreds. Twelve Jews founded the B'nai B'rith mutual aid society in 1843, which supports Hillel groups and the Anti-Defamation League. Others established the Young Men's Hebrew Association, the Jewish counterpart of the YMCA. All three of the major Jewish denominations support these organizations. At least two hundred periodicals are published in the United States in English, Yiddish, and Hebrew.

Judaism is a family-centered religion, but the synagogue or temple also serves the community. Each synagogue is an independent body, although it may belong to larger associations. The congregation hires and fires the rabbi and sets the pattern of religious observances.

At least ten male Jews are needed to offer public worship; even nine rabbis could not offer such worship. The service consists of prayers, the chanting of psalms, and the reading of the Torah. A rabbi (literally a teacher) has no powers that any Jewish male does not have; his role in worship can be assumed by any man in the congregation. Of course, a rabbi is trained in rabbinical school and is expected to strive for holiness and scholarship, but he receives no special spiritual authority as does, say, a Catholic or Eastern Orthodox priest. The rabbi preaches and teaches, marries and grants divorces, and conducts funerals and other ceremonies.

In a thousand ways American Jews have enriched the nation's culture. For example, the field of music includes George Gershwin, Nathan Milstein, Mischa Elman, Benny Goodman, Jascha Heifetz, Leonard

Bernstein, Jerome Kern, Irving Berlin, Richard Rodgers, Arthur Rubenstein, Yehidi Menuhin, and Aaron Copland.

The Supreme Court of the United States has been served by Louis D. Brandeis, Benjamin Cardozo, Felix Frankfurter, Abe Fortas, and Arthur Goldberg. Jews have been governors, senators, congressmen. The names of Herbert Lehman, former senator and New York governor; Jacob Javits, former senator from New York; and Connecticut Senator Joseph Lieberman come to mind. Barry Goldwater, whose grandfather was a Jewish peddler, was an Episcopalian.

Americans sew dresses on a machine invented by Singer. Their children are protected from the ravages of polio by a vaccine bearing the name Salk. They read the Jewish-owned *New York Times.* They enjoy the plays of Arthur Miller.

Despite the prosperity of American Jews and the lessening of anti-Semitism, Judaism faces serious problems. In 1947 about 5 percent of the population identified themselves as Jews; at the start of the twenty-first century this had dropped to 2 percent. Of the 5,500,000 Jews in the United States, fewer than half belong to a synagogue or temple.

Not many decades ago only a handful of Jews married Gentiles, but the intermarriage rate has risen to 57 percent. One in twenty spouses in such marriages converts to Judaism, and studies indicate only 28 percent of the children of these marriages are raised as Jews.

Except for the ultraorthodox Hasidic Jews, who average six children per couple, the great majority of Jewish couples have birth rates lower than the general population.

All of these factors — assimilation and intermarriage, a low birth rate, and a paucity of converts — lead some scholars to predict the virtual disappearance of U.S. Judaism in this century. The surviving Jews may be the Hasidim.

FURTHER READING

Bermant, Chaim, *The Jews* (New York: Times Books, 1977).

Epstein, Isidore, *Judaism, a Historical Presentation* (New York: Pelikan, 1959).

Trapp, Leo, *Eternal Faith, Eternal People* (Englewood Cliffs, N.J.: Prentice-Hall, 1962).

Yaffe, James, *The American Jews* (New York: Random House, 1968).

CHAPTER 23

The Muslims

Youngest of World's Major Religions Gains
Millions of American Believers

Many Americans go through life without ever meeting a Muslim, although the religion of the Muslims — Islam — rivals Christianity in size and influence on the world scene. In the Arab countries North Africa, Pakistan, and Indonesia, the estimated one billion Muslims constitute the dominant faith and way of life.

The religion started in Arabia in the seventh century when a religious genius known as Mohammed proclaimed that God (Allah) is one and that he (Mohammed) is His prophet. Influenced by Judaism and Christianity, Mohammed acknowledged that Abraham, Moses, and Jesus also were prophets, but that Mohammed was the final revelator of God's will.

Mohammed (probably born in A.D. 570) lived in Mecca, a trading center also known for its religious shrine, the Kaaba. This was a huge, cube-shaped structure full of idols and a black meteorite. Some Jews and a few Christians lived in Mecca, but most of the residents were polytheists.

Mohammed worked as a shepherd, camel driver, and merchant and finally married a widow some fifteen years his elder. He cultivated a deep interest in religion and meditation but despised the idolatry of most of his fellow Meccans. As he later recounted, the Angel Gabriel appeared to him during one of his periods of meditation and began to dictate the words of what became the Muslim Bible, the Qua'ran. These revelations from the angel and from Allah continued for twenty years.

At first Mohammed's converts consisted of his wife and a few friends, who formed what was almost a secret society in Mecca. As their views became known, the townspeople who profited from the pagan pilgrimages turned against them. Mohammed fled to the city of Yathrib (renamed Medina) in 622, which became the year 1 of the Islamic calendar.

Far more successful in winning converts in Medina, Mohammed led his forces in an attack on Mecca and entered his hometown in triumph in 630. He destroyed the idols in the Kaaba, but retained the black stone as the object of veneration and promised the city fathers to continue the pilgrimages. Before his death in 632 the prophet had unified most of central and southern Arabia. In a few decades his followers, sometimes through the Holy War or Jihad, had won over most of the Middle East and North Africa. The Muslims swept into Spain, Portugal, and France but were defeated by the Franks at the battle of Tours in 732. Almost all the Christian communities of Africa disappeared in the Muslim advance.

Islam means "to submit" to the will of God; Muslims object to being identified as Mohammedans because they insist they follow God (Allah) rather than any man. Mohammed is revered as the greatest prophet but in no sense a divine person or messiah. He never distinguished himself as a miracle worker or ascetic.

Muslims believe God's final word to mankind is given in the two-thousand-word Qua'ran. The book is mainly a series of maxims grouped in one hundred fourteen chapters or *suras*. It expresses the simple theology of Islam, that God is one and that Mohammed is His prophet. The anthropomorphic character of Islam startles some Christian observers. For example, the afterlife is described in very human terms. Hell is described in terms of intense heat, scalding water, and hot winds. But the faithful Muslims can anticipate a heaven of gardens, wine, and abundant sexual opportunities.

Islam rejects polytheism as well as the Christian doctrine of the Trinity. The religion honors Jesus as one of the messengers of Allah but in no sense a divine person. Islam pays particular respect to Mary as the Mother of Jesus; she is mentioned thirty-four times in the Qua'ran and is honored above Mohammed's favorite wife and his daughter

Fatima. Mohammed taught that Mary and her mother, Anne, were the only women not touched by the power of Satan.

The religious life of the Muslim demands daily prayers, recited at daybreak, noon, midafternoon, sunset, and early evening. The strict fast of Ramadan is imposed on all believers except the sick, aged, very young, and pregnant women. During this lunar month, Muslims must not eat, drink, take medicine, or engage in sexual intercourse between sunrise and sunset. Each Muslim is expected to make at least one pilgrimage to Mecca during his lifetime. All pilgrims wear the identical seamless white robe; they walk seven times around the Kaaba, run seven times between two hills in Mecca, and make a journey to the Mount of Mercy about twenty-five miles away. Unbelievers are forbidden to enter either Mecca or Medina. Other religious requirements of Islam include the declaration of faith (the *shahada*) and almsgiving.

Islamic culture flourished in the ninth, tenth, and eleventh centuries, when the Muslims invented algebra, pioneered in medicine, and made important contributions in art, poetry, and philosophy. The schisms and sects within Islam weakened its impact, but the imposition of colonial rule did more to limit its influence. As foreign rule ended, Islam grew strong in more than a score of independent African and Asian nations.

Islam has had notable success in winning adherents in black Africa. In contrast to Christian missionaries, the Muslims offer a simple theology, easy initiation, no objection to polygamy. Islam has no sacraments or prescribed ritual, no images. Although the Muslims once prospered as slave traders, they do not bear the colonial stigma that handicaps many Christian missionaries in Africa and Asia.

Islamic society is strongly patriarchal. The role of women has been far more subservient than in Judaism or Christianity. Traditionally the Muslims have kept their women in seclusion and heavily veiled; this custom is still strictly observed in a country such as Saudi Arabia, but is ignored in modern Turkey. The Arabs of Mohammed's day practiced unlimited polygamy. The prophet revealed: "Of women who seem good in your eyes, marry but two, or three, or four; and if ye still fear ye shall not act equitably, then one only." The devout Muslim will never have more than four legal wives at one time, although divorce is a simple procedure. Economic reasons and the rise of women's rights movements have discouraged polygamy in most Islamic societies. Mohammed himself had fourteen wives and three concubines.

Like Christianity, Islam has not escaped fragmentation. Besides the majority Sunnites there are the Shi'ites, who predominate in Iran and have constituencies in India and Indonesia. The Kharijites form a Puritan elite, and the Wahhabites seek to reform Islam from the taint of liberal tendencies.

The Arab-Israeli war intensified hatreds between these two Semitic people, but both share a number of beliefs and customs. For example, Muslims honor the Old Testament prophets, circumcise boys, forbid pork, worship one God. Muslims, despite the memories of the Crusades, display less animosity toward Christianity.

The Declaration on the Relationship of the Church to Non-Christian Religions of Vatican II looks on the Muslims with esteem:

"They worship God, who is one, living and subsistent, merciful and almighty, the Creator of heaven and earth, who has also spoken to men. They strive to submit themselves without reservation to the hidden decrees of God, just as Abraham submitted himself to God's plan, to whose faith Muslims eagerly link their own. Although not acknowledging him as God, they venerate Jesus as a prophet, his virgin Mother they also honor, and even at times devoutly invoke. Further, they await the day of judgment and the reward of God following the resurrection of the dead. For this reason they highly esteem an upright life and worship God, especially by way of prayer, alms-deeds and fasting.

"Over the centuries many quarrels and dissentions have arisen between Christians and Muslims. The sacred Council now pleads with all to forget the past, and urges that a sincere effort be made to achieve mutual understanding; for the ben-

266

efit of all men, let them together preserve and promote peace, liberty, social justice and moral values."

During his 2001 visit to Syria, John Paul II became the first pope to enter a mosque.

Islam has experienced rapid growth in the United States in recent decades. About two million American Muslims belong to the twelve hundred mosques around the country. Another estimated four million follow the faith of Islam without a formal affiliation. This means Muslims probably outnumber Jews to form the second largest faith community in the country.

Large concentrations of Muslims can be found in California, New York, Illinois, and some major cities. About 42 percent of converts come from African-American backgrounds, and 24 percent have immigrated from such South Asian nations as Pakistan and India. Others have come from Syria, Lebanon, Egypt, Iran, Turkey, Africa, and Eastern Europe.

Elijah Muhammad founded the Nation of Islam, which gained thousands of converts but was marked by anti-white, anti-Jewish, and anti-Christian rhetoric. After his death, his son brought the group closer to orthodox Islam. As many as five hundred thousand African-Americans belong to this branch of Islam. Perhaps twenty thousand to fifty thousand follow the leadership of Louis Farrakhan, who revived Elijah Muhammad's original positions.

As American Muslims advance in education, wealth, and political power, they will form an increasingly influential segment of society.

FURTHER READING

Armstrong, Karen, *Islam* (New York: Modern Library, 2000).

Brockelmann, Carl, *History of the Islamic Peoples* (New York: Putnam, 1947).

Cragg, Kenneth, *The Call of the Minaret* (New York: Oxford University Press, 1964).

Lincoln, C. Eric, *The Black Muslims in America* (Boston: Beacon, 1961).
Smith, Jane I., *Islam in America* (New York, Columbia University Press, 1999).

CHAPTER 24

The Buddhists

Worldwide Buddhism Embraced by 325 Million People

THE RELIGION THAT DOMINATES THE SPIRITUAL LIFE OF ASIA, EXCEPT for India, has become a growing presence in the United States. Large-scale immigration has led to an estimated eight hundred thousand Buddhists in this country; this figure may be much higher. The dozens of Buddhist sects reflect the origins of its practitioners: Japan, Cambodia, China, Vietnam, Thailand, Tibet, Korea, and other countries.

Buddhism began as a heresy within Hinduism in the sixth century before Christ. Hinduism taught the transmigration of souls; man is reincarnated in a series of lives. Many Hindu sects attempted to instruct devotees on how to escape this chain of incarnations. Originally Buddhism was one of these sects.

Buddhists venerate an Indian sage who showed the path to emancipation. He was known as Siddartha Gautama (born about 560 B.C.) or simply the Buddha, which means the Enlightened One. He was born a member of the warrior caste and was apparently shielded from most of the harsher aspects of life as a young man. One legend tells that his father provided him with three palaces and forty thousand dancing girls for his pleasure.

He eventually married and had a son. But the Gautama renounced his family and began a search for the answer to the problem of suffering. His decision may have been brought about by contact for the first time with the facts of sickness, old age, and death. The search lasted five or six years. He tried yoga and asceticism, but these led to no satisfactory answers. One day while he was sitting under a Bo-tree, the true path was revealed to him; he spent the rest of his life spreading this teaching.

Buddha proclaimed "Four Noble Truths." These are that existence involves suffering, suffering is caused by desire, the way to escape suffering and existence is to eliminate desire, and to eliminate desire man should follow the eightfold path. This eightfold path asked that man pursue right views, right intentions, right speech, right action, right livelihood, right effort, right mindfulness, and right concentration.

Essentially Buddhism offers a way by which man can escape suffering. This is accomplished by extinguishing the three main desires: for pleasure, for prosperity, and for continued existence. Buddhism neither affirms nor denies the existence of God but adopts an agnostic position.

This effort to escape suffering may take many lifetimes, but finally a man should be able to achieve Nirvana — the extinction of all desire, hatred, and ignorance. Buddha declared: "One thing only I teach. Sorrow, the cause of sorrow, the cessation of sorrow, and the path which leads to the cessation of sorrow."

Within the Buddhist world there developed two main schools: the Mahayana, or Greater Vehicle of China, Japan, Korea, and Vietnam; and the Hinayana, or Lesser Vehicle of Thailand, Burma, Ceylon, Cambodia, India, and Indonesia. In Tibet, Buddhism blended with magic and demon worship in a form known as Lamaism. Since the Communist takeover of Tibet, the Dalai Lama has lived in India and much of the property of the Tibetan monasteries has been expropriated.

Monasticism plays a part in almost all Buddhist sects. A man who enters a Buddhist monastery shaves his head, wears a yellow or orange robe, gets a new name, and agrees to follow the two hundred twenty rules of Buddhist monasticism. The monks beg for a living and carry with them only three robes, a needle, water strainer, begging bowl, and razor. They may leave the order when they wish as they take no vows; older men often enter a monastery after raising a family. Buddhism also includes religious orders of nuns.

A Japanese group founded the first Buddhist church in the United States in 1905; in 1942 the Buddhist Churches of America was incorporated. A bishop heads the church, which reports 140 churches and branches, and about 180,000 members. These congregations hold weekly services and often sponsor Japanese language instruction. Most of the adherents are found in California, Utah, Arizona, Washington, Oregon, and Hawaii.

Zen Buddhism, a monastic form of Buddhism originating in Japan, has attracted both Western intellectuals and hippies. A former Episcopal minister, Alan Watts, popularized this form of Buddhism in books and lectures. Many people study Zen more as a philosophy than a religion.

FURTHER READING

Dumoulin, Henrich, *Buddhism in the Modern World* (New York: Macmillan, 1977).

Layman, Emma McCloy, *Buddhism In America* (New York: Nelson-Hall, 1976).

Prebish, Charles, ed., *Buddhism: A Modern Perspective* (University Park, Pa.: Pennsylvania State University Press, 1977).

Seager, Richard Hughes, *Buddhism in America* (New York: Columbia University Press, 2000).

GENERAL BIBLIOGRAPHY

Ahlstrom, Sydney E., *A Religious History of the American People* (New Haven: Yale University Press, 1972).

Attwater, Donald, *The Christian Churches of the East*, 2 vols., rev. eds. (Milwaukee: Bruce, 1961, 1962).

Backman, Milton V., *Christian Churches of America* (Provo, Utah: Brigham Young University Press, 1976).

Bouyer, Louis, *The Spirit and Forms of Protestantism* (Westminster, Md.: Newman, 1956).

Braden, Charles S., *These Also Believe* (New York: Macmillan, 1953).

Campbell, Robert, *Spectrum of Protestant Beliefs* (Milwaukee: Bruce, 1968).

Clark, Elmer, *The Small Sects in America* (Nashville: Abingdon, 1949).

Daniel-Rops., H., *Our Brothers in Christ* (New York: E.P. Dutton, 1967).

Davidson, James D., et al., *The Search for Common Ground* (Huntington, Ind.: Our Sunday Visitor, 1997).

Davies, Horton, *The Challenge of the Sects* (Philadelphia: Westminster, 1961).

Dowley, Tim, *The History of Christianity* (Grand Rapids, Mich.: Wm. B. Eerdmans, 1977).

Dustan, J. Leslie, *Protestantism* (New York: Washington Square Press, 1962).

Eck, Diana L., *A New Religious America* (New York: HarperCollins, 2001).

Ferm, Vergilius, *The American Church of the Protestant Heritage* (New York: Philosophical Library, 1953).

Finke, Roger and Rodney Stark, *The Churching of America, 1776-1990* (New Brunswick, N.J.: Rutgers University Press, 1992).

Gaustad, Edwin Scott, *Historical Atlas of Religion in America* (New York: Harper & Row, 1962).

_____, *A Religious History of America* (New York: Harper & Row, 1964).

Gillis, Chester, *Roman Catholicism* (New York: Columbia University Press, 1999).

Handy, Robert T., *A History of the Churches in the United States and Canada* (New York: Oxford University Press, 1977).

Hardon, John, *The Protestant Churches of America* (Westminster, Md.: Newman, 1956).

_____, *Religions of the* World (Westminster, Md.: Newman, 1963).

Hoekema, Anthony, *The Four Major Cults* (Grand Rapids, Mich.: Eerdmans, 1963).

Landis, Benson Y., *Religion in the United States* (New York: Barnes and Noble, 1965).

Littell, Franklin Hamlin, *From State Church to Pluralism* (Garden City, N.Y.: Doubleday, 1962).

Marty, Martin E., *Protestantism* (New York: Holt, Rinehart and Winston, 1972).

Mayer, F.E., *The Religious Bodies of America* (St. Louis: Concordia, 1954).

Mead, Frank and Samuel S. Hill, *Handbook of Denominations in the United States*, 10th ed. (Nashville: Abingdon, 1995).

Melton, J. Gordon, *Encyclopedia of American Religions*, 3 vols. (Tarrytown, N.Y.: Triumph Books, 1989).

Morris, Charles R., *American Catholics,* (New York: Times Books, 1997).

O'Brien, Thomas C., ed., *Corpus Dictionary of Western Churches* (Washington, D.C.: Corpus Books, 1970).

Piepkorn, Arthur C., *Profiles in Belief* Vol. 1 (New York: Harper & Row, 1977).

Roof, Wade Clark and William McKinney, *American Mainline Religions* (New Brunswick, N.J.: Rutgers University Press, 1987).

Rosten, Leo, *Religion in America* (New York, Simon & Schuster, 1975).

Smith, Huston, *Illustrated World's Religions: A Guide to Our Wisdom Traditions* (San Francisco: HarperSanFrancisco, 1995).

Spence, Hartzell, *The Story of America's Religions* (Nashville: Abingdon-Apex Books, 1962).

Van de Pol, W.H., *World Protestantism* (New York: Herder and Herder, 1964).

Williams, J. Paul, *What Americans Believe and How They Worship* (New York: Harper, 1962).

Williamson, William B., *An Encyclopedia of Religions in the United States* (New York: Crossroad, 1992).

Yearbook of American and Canadian Churches (New York, National Council of Churches of Christ in the U.S.A., published annually).

Zaretsy, Irving I. and Mark P. Leone, *Religious Movements in Contemporary America* (Princeton, N.J.: Princeton University Press, 1972).

GENEALOGY OF MAJOR CHRISTIAN CHURCHES, SECTS, AND CULTS IN THE UNITED STATES

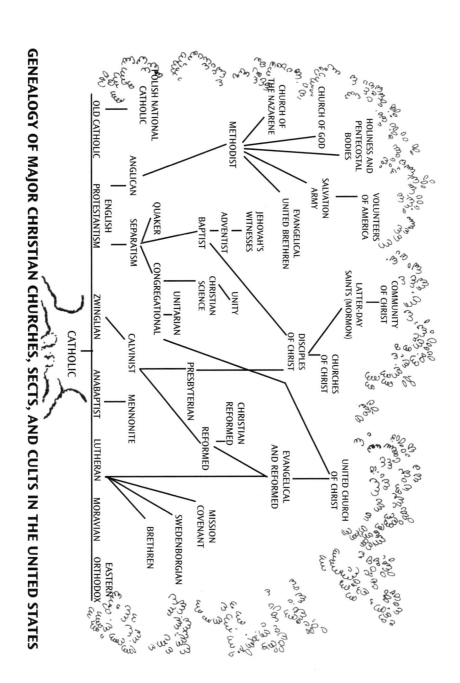

INDEX

NOTES

NOTES

NOTES

NOTES

ABOUT THE AUTHOR

AFTER FORTY-TWO YEARS AS DIRECTOR OF PUBLICATIONS AND A journalism professor, William J. Whalen retired from Purdue University. He has authored or co-authored fifteen books, mostly in the field of comparative religions, as well as more than two hundred fifty articles, pamphlets, and encyclopedia entries. Professor Whalen attended Notre Dame and received degrees from Marquette and Northwestern universities.

OUR SUNDAY VISITOR

*Your Source for Discovering
the Riches of the Catholic Faith*

Our Sunday Visitor has an extensive line of materials for young children,
teens, and adults. Our books, Bibles, booklets, CD-ROMs, audios, and videos
are available in bookstores worldwide.

To receive a FREE full-line catalog or for more information,
call **Our Sunday Visitor** at **1-800-348-2440**.
Or write **Our Sunday Visitor** / 200 Noll Plaza / Huntington, IN 46750.

Please send me: __A catalog

Please send me materials on:

__Apologetics and catechetics   __Reference works

__Prayer books   __Heritage and the saints

__The family   __The parish

Name_____

Address_____Apt._____

City_____State____Zip_____

Telephone (   ) _____

A29BBABP

Please send a friend: __A catalog

Please send a friend materials on:

__Apologetics and catechetics   __Reference works

__Prayer books   __Heritage and the saints

__The family   __The parish

Name_____

Address_____Apt._____

City_____State____Zip_____

Telephone (   ) _____

A29BBABP

Our Sunday Visitor
200 Noll Plaza
Huntington, IN 46750
Toll free: **1-800-348-2440**
E-mail: osvbooks@osv.com
Website: www.osv.com